FRAIL VESSELS

FRAIL VESSELS

*Woman's Role in Women's Novels
from Fanny Burney
to George Eliot*

by
HAZEL MEWS

UNIVERSITY OF LONDON
THE ATHLONE PRESS
1969

Published by
THE ATHLONE PRESS
UNIVERSITY OF LONDON
at 2 *Gower Street, London* WC1

Distributed by Tiptree Book Services Ltd
Tiptree, Essex

Australia and New Zealand
Melbourne University Press

U.S.A.
Oxford University Press Inc
New York

485 11105 5

Printed in Great Britain by
WESTERN PRINTING SERVICES LTD
BRISTOL

To
I.F.M.
my sister

PREFACE

THIS BOOK has been long in the making. It owes its title to
Henry James who, in his Preface to *The Portrait of a Lady*, pays
a graceful tribute to George Eliot's own portraits of Hetty
Sorrel, Maggie Tulliver, Rosamond Vincy and Gwendolen
Harleth, slightly misquoting her opinion that in such 'frail
vessels is borne onward through the ages the treasure of human
affection'; George Eliot's actual expression was 'delicate
vessels' but Henry James improved upon it by including those
overtones of human frailty of which she was so well aware. In
his explanation of his conception of *The Portrait of a Lady* as
the story of a 'certain young woman affronting her destiny'
James is sharing George Eliot's attitude to women and their lot,
but he reveals that he himself regarded it as a deep difficulty
for a novelist to make of these frail vessels 'the all-in-all for
our attention'. For women writers, however, what James
describes as small female fry possess quite naturally their own
importance at the centre of concern, and this importance would
be appreciated without conscious surprise by very many women
readers; it was certainly my own case in a girlhood in which the
novels of Jane Austen, George Eliot, the Brontës and smaller
female writing fry formed not so much a part of my reading as
of my life. An 'Eng. Lit.' training did not destroy this for me.
Then the chance purchase in Johannesburg of a secondhand
copy of the Everyman edition of Mary Wollstonecraft's *Vindication of the Rights of Woman*, which printed John Stuart Mill's
The Subjection of Women in the same volume, brought to my
attention one formative period in the social history of women
which threw light upon the work of the creative writers of the
same epoch, and which led me to make a detailed study of the
English women writers during those years, written in the form
of a doctoral dissertation for the University of Pretoria.

Returning to England after a long absence and with the
perspective of distance and of seven years spent in the study of

vii

the women writing before 1870, it was with something of the outlook of a Victorian Rip van Winkle that I saw the changes brought about in the position of women in this country since the last war. During a year spent at Girton College I viewed the higher education of women in Britain with a curious double vision: familiar with the aspirations of those who had been dedicated to the task of making university education available for women, I was confronted with a reality in which their battle was won and a tradition of feminine scholarship indubitably established, but the contemporary circumstances of the lives of women students were unbelievably changed. It was a change which the pioneers could not have foreseen, even if all their energies had not been absorbed in what needed to be done to make that education available. The welfare state, student grants, early marriage and the permissive society had altered the background so that it was no longer true that university women would always be a group of gifted and privileged scholars devoting their lives to the training of similar women. All connected with women's education and, beyond that, all connected with women's changing world, faced the need for a reassessment and an understanding of what was required of them for the future. Women had to work out a new constructive role for themselves, not emancipated from contemporary circumstances, but one which would enable them to play an adequate part in the environment in which they would affront their destinies day by day.

This realization, narrowly interpreted for my own work, threw into focus the fact that the authors in whose world I had lived for years had been doing precisely the same thing at an earlier stage in the social lives of Englishwomen, a stage that was complete in itself and which had led to a turn in the road which had now been reached. The eighty years formed indeed a contained period which could not be repeated. Seminal ideas of such importance to half England's population would not again have such immediate concern for those members of the half who were artists. The energies that went into the Regency and Victorian woman's novel today find their outlet in the newspaper article, the television interview, the social investigation; women's novels no longer differ greatly from those of men. This study,

Preface

therefore, seeks to analyse the effect the changes in the role of women had upon the work of the great women novelists in that earlier time. It is not a literary social study but an examination of the emotional and intellectual reaction to the new ideas transmuted into creative works, ideas reacted to from the inside.

During the various stages that have led up to the present work, I have incurred many debts, both in South Africa and in England, and to name all those who helped me, sometimes unconsciously, would not be possible. I must, however, mention the encouragement given to me in South Africa by Professor Titlestad and Professor Barbara Mackenzie, and in England by Margaret Ives, Fellow of Girton College, and by the necessarily anonymous Reader for the Athlone Press. My gratitude for moral support and much help with typing and checking from my sister is inadequately expressed by my dedication. Nor can I remain silent about an intellectual debt usually taken for granted, the pleasure of the company for many years of Fanny Burney and Maria Edgeworth, the Brontë sisters and Mrs Gaskell, Jane Austen and George Eliot.

Reading H.M.
August 1968

CONTENTS

1

Introduction

'SCIENCE HAS NO SEX' said George Eliot,[1] but she added that it is an immense mistake to maintain that there is no sex in literature. Writers are men and women living in a world in which the sexes play different parts and their experience of their own role must be deeper than their experience of the counter one, however penetrating their imaginative insight may be; this deeper experience will be reflected in the literature they create.

In a period when the tradition of the novel was largely masculine, women writers who tried their prentice hands at writing fiction had either to write as men wrote (if they could) or to write as women with a woman's different awareness of life; by doing the latter they gradually worked out their own tradition. This feminine tradition, if it may be so called, could not be separate and distinct, any more than the lives of men and women are separate and distinct, but it could, and did enlarge the novel's contribution to the understanding of the total human condition, rendering it at once more comprehensive and more sensitive. At the end of the eighteenth century in England there were several groups of women writers beginning to engage in just such pioneer activities and their efforts prepared the soil in which greater work could flourish and in which Jane Austen's and George Eliot's novels had their roots. These early women novelists worked against a background of political, economic and social upheaval and, most importantly for them, in times of far-reaching changes in the lives of women affected by the radical reconsideration of woman's long-accepted role in society. Two publications may be taken as milestones marking the beginning and end of the first phase of this still-continuing social movement—the earlier book was Mary Wollstonecraft's *Vindication of the Rights of Woman*, published in 1792, and the

1

Introduction

later John Stuart Mill's essay on *The Subjection of Women*, which appeared in 1869. Mary Wollstonecraft's seminal work was the most famous contribution by an Englishwoman to the revolutionary ideas about women's emancipation then in the air, while Mill's brief study was evidence of the support accorded to these ideas by one of the most influential masculine thinkers of mid-Victorian England and although his views were not widely shared by those in power, the course of the emancipation of women may be traced in an unbroken line from that date. The first phase occupied almost eighty years.

These eighty years began in a period of revolution when the discussion of the rights of women played a subordinate part in the general debate on the rights of Man, and both the American War of Independence and the French Revolution can be regarded as outward and visible signs of the power unleashed by the new doctrines and their implications. During our eighty years these revolutionary struggles were succeeded by the Napoleonic wars and then again by new political and social changes.

In England it was, additionally, a period of accelerated industrial revolution, when new inventions in machinery and new technological discoveries were applied to the manufacture of textiles in the north of England, and the consequent rise of the dark satanic mills gradually brought profound changes in the daily lives of ordinary people all over the country. This changed pattern affected women very closely: paradoxically it gave to some of them, the wives and daughters of the successful manufacturers, increased leisure, and to others, the working-class women, it brought hardship and suffering in long hours of labour in mines and unhealthy factories. Yet for the working woman it was, again paradoxically, a return to industrial importance. As in the lost days of the flourishing home industries, industrial opportunity was once more being offered to women, but this time it was opportunity for work outside the home instead of inside it. In Britain the phrase 'workers of the world' in strict truth no longer embraced men only, although there was no inclination amongst women workers to unite; for them the return to so changed a life of industrial production was very difficult and every step brought new problems which neither they nor, for that matter, most men were adequately equipped either to understand or to solve.

At a deeper level many men and women must have shared a feeling of bewilderment and alienation in their changed environment; the transition from the habit of accepting values and meanings imposed by authority and carrying with them long-accepted sanctions to the realization of the fact that the individual had gained more freedom to think out new values for himself—and even for *herself*—necessitated much heart-searching. Such a fundamental change in old habits of thought could not be accomplished painlessly. A new social conscience had to be forced into awareness by confrontation of the consequences of the industrial revolution visible in the social misery of the new towns, where men and women, uprooted from their past, worked as 'hands' in an impersonal industrial process that had no tradition of human concern for the welfare of its faceless workers. It was not possible for everyone to push these problems aside; some felt they must seek for remedies and take their share of responsibility for their neighbours' welfare in a way of life so different from any they had known, one in which the old signposts were inadequate guides to the new path.

Confusion was also created by the ebb and flow of event and counter-event and by conflicting emotional reactions to them. The bliss of the revolutionary dawn was succeeded by the dark night of the Terror in France and the anti-Jacobin reaction in England; exaggerated hopes after the great Reform Bill of 1832 faded in the stark reality of widespread poverty, hunger and overcrowding in the alleys of the great cities. When belief in the sufficiency of cool reason to solve all difficulties proved mistaken hope was invested in the sovereign power of pure and natural feeling—only to be dashed again by the event. All the political and social changes, all the fashions of thought and emotion interacted, and yet in the welter of bewilderment the individual had for his health of mind and his sanity to come to terms with his environment and to establish his own personal identity within this world of changing values and ill-defined roles.

These perplexities were common to men and women but for the latter the problem was more difficult; women shared men's

3

Introduction

general alienation in the post-Revolutionary years but they had
to experience an added alienation of their own. After living for
centuries a sheltered existence whose limits were defined by the
church and by widely accepted social convention, they were
suddenly confronted with new possibilities of freedom that cut
across the past. Vague vistas arose as the logical outcome of
reconsideration of the nature of man and woman in the abstract
and in an abstract society. In order to work out these ideas into
some practical way of life women had to contend not only with
the recalcitrance of the problems themselves but with the
emotional consequences of the general contempt and vilifi-
cation heaped upon those who supported the new doctrines in
any way. When Horace Walpole described Mary Wollstonecraft as a 'hyena in petticoats' he was merely feminizing a
familiar term of political abuse, but few women were con-
ditioned to such usage and it is not surprising that only the
bolder spirits took the road of defiance. Even as late as 1850
Mrs Gaskell confided to a friend that she was 'sometimes coward
enough to wish that we were back in the darkness where
obedience was the only seen duty of women'.[2] But the new ideas
pointed to the future and the clock could never be put back to
quite where it was before.

The seventeenth and eighteenth centuries had been well
aware of the psychological importance to the individual of a
clear and acceptable notion of the role in life he was expected to
play and guidance in book and sermon had been provided both
for men and for women in their various walks of life, including
even a handbook for what was styled 'the lady's calling'.
Similar instruction was no longer adequate, especially as it was
often given by clergymen of conservative views with no first-
hand experience of women's new difficulties, men moreover
who were filled with apprehension over any departure from the
tried and safe paths trodden by women in the past. Women
themselves, ill-educated as they almost invariably were, and
ill-equipped with any knowledge of matters outside the home to
give them breadth of outlook, still experienced the emotional
drive of their need for a restatement of their role in life; whether
they realized it or not, many of them were searching for a
clearer idea of their place in society and a new sense of social

4

Introduction

purpose. The new ideas had largely taken the form of a discussion of their 'rights' whereas they had been more accustomed to think along the lines of their 'duties'. What were their new duties? These needed to be investigated, and the investigation could not be left entirely to men.

A factor in their perplexity was the tension caused by society's two different images of woman, inherited from the long past. On the one hand a woman was viewed with suspicion as a temptress and a siren, on the other looked up to as a tender and holy virgin; the picture of the public beauty, the 'toast of the town', was contrasted with that of the obedient and submissive daughter and wife and the devoted mother; the admired and courted queen of society was yet a person treated as a minor in the eyes of the law. A woman was urged to be chaste and retiring and modest, yet the rewards she could most easily understand were frequently given in the form of admiration for beauty unaccompanied by such virtues. She was expected to be strong-minded enough to deny importunate pleas from a lover but submissive enough never to exert her personality against her husband And now, for the first time, the measure of emancipation they were beginning to visualize if not to enjoy was making women aware of themselves as human beings with interests, talents and capacities for intellectual development that, no less than those of men, demanded to be exercised and not left to rust away; biological and emotional fulfilment was not, even when it was attainable, enough.

That women were in their different ways aware of these changes, even if they themselves did not read the views of the Radical writers, cannot be doubted; the debate raged in certain areas but the still waters were also disturbed. That women writers should reflect these changes in their work was also inevitable. These eighty years saw the emergence of England's greatest women novelists. Whether the flowering of their genius during this particular period was fortuitous or not is difficult to decide until the hidden sources of literary power and inspiration are more fully understood; it seems at least probable that the upheaval in old ways of thought in the minds of women should provide some release of power for works of the imagination, the response of the women writers matching the dynamic of the transitional changes that confronted them. The fact remains that these women writers were of a number and calibre that have not been seen again. They included England's two pre-eminent women novelists, Jane Austen and George Eliot, and the lesser but still outstanding novelists Fanny Burney, Maria Edgeworth, the Brontë sisters and Mrs Gaskell, together with Susan Ferrier and Mrs Radcliffe, as well as the three women poets Elizabeth Barrett Browning, Emily Brontë and, at the very end, Christina Rossetti. This is still not to mention the clusters of names now forgotten except in literary histories but active in their time and contributing their own mite to the common stock. The novel was their supreme achievement and in the working out of their own changed position in society the novel was obviously the genre most suited to their needs.

How far these writers were consciously or unconsciously concerned about the new role of women, or with a re-examination of their old role, varied with the individual, but some such preoccupation can be uncovered in nearly all of them. It was not a theoretical or external matter to them although many indeed did consider it theoretically and took their stand for past or for new values, but their concern was woven into the very fabric of their attitude to life and art.

In their novels they had to depict their female characters in a certain role, whether true to contemporary conditions, in which case the mirror they held up was a plane one, or changed and idealized in some way, in which case the mirror exhibited a significant curve. What qualities were singled out for admiration and for censure, any special insight or any obtuseness of vision, all helped to reveal the viewpoint of the artist. Because of the changes in something so fundamental to themselves as the position of women, these writers were also in search of their own new identity; they took many different ways in their search, some seeking the shelter of old paths, some endeavouring boldly to change the views of society to match the deeper understanding they believed themselves to possess. Some looked for new causes with which to identify themselves or new responsibilities outside the narrow and circumscribed life of the past, responsibilities that would call forth new powers to meet new needs. Each made her own contribution, either by a deepened understanding of accepted ways, or by an extension of the field of vision. Inevitably, there came about an interaction between their views and those of their readers. The novels may indeed be seen as one method of communication between women who lacked the societies and clubs which served as the meeting-places of men. It was not a form of communication which needed special training or knowledge on the part of the intelligent reader to enable her to recognize the truth or falsehood of what was depicted or to arouse her sympathy or dislike for what she read. The often derided female propensity for reading novels ensured an audience far wider than that which read more formal works, and the circulating libraries in London and the provincial towns extended the sphere of influence to women all over England who could afford the library subscription. It was an audience whose attention would have a genuine personal interest and concern behind it. In this way the feminine novel may be seen as an instrument for changing opinion and moulding behaviour.

This known preoccupation of women writers with certain fundamental problems during a comparatively short period of time may also be used as a literary probe. By analysing their treatment of women and their role it is possible to examine the writers' transmutation of this part of their experience of life into creative literature, and such an analysis should have its own small beam of light to cast upon the work of art so examined. This study attempts such a probe into the works of the group of major women novelists from Fanny Burney to George Eliot. A woman's role is largely concerned with relationships—she is so often thought of as 'Sydney's sister, Pembroke's mother' rather than as an individual in her own right; our analysis therefore will deal at greatest length with the way these novelists saw women in relationships, first as young girls awaiting marriage (the traditional occupation of the heroines of fiction) and then as wives and mothers; this will be followed by some consideration of their treatment of the woman standing alone, either as spinster or as teacher or as artist.

As an indication of the background against which the major writers worked, the next chapter gives a brief sketch of the contemporary climate of opinion concerning women; this is followed by a glance at the lesser women writers of the time, those who provided the common stock from which greater minds could draw.

2

The Climate of Opinion

RECENT YEARS have produced many histories of the changing
status of women in England,[1] so that only a few brush strokes
are needed here to suggest the familiar picture and accentuate
some points of particular relevance to this study.

Women's blessings at the end of the eighteenth century are
not often counted but they did of course exist in the joys of love
and motherhood, of security and community of feeling within
the immediate family or the extended family and neighbourhood, and in the special rewards of a life devoted to the happiness of others. On another level there were the satisfactions of
good housekeeping, of the domestic arts of needlework and
embroidery, and, in some cases of music at home; and the
pleasures of clothes, fashion and graceful behaviour. Such of
these blessings as any individual woman found it her lot to
enjoy, alloyed or unalloyed according to circumstances, were
not however peculiar to our period. Most of them are the common joys of happy women at all times.

The balancing disadvantages were more closely linked to the
age. At that time women were without any direct power,
political or economic, and were virtually minors in the eyes of
the law. Any money they might inherit or earn by their labours
became part of a joint matrimonial or family estate, unless
specially secured to them by settlement or allowance. It was not
possible for a woman to obtain a divorce before 1857 except by
an Act of Parliament. Married women usually spent many years
in child-bearing and their expectation of life was not long; the
high rate of infant mortality added to their sorrows. Women's
education, when they had any, was of the flimsiest kind. Certainly the post-Renaissance 'new woman', as she has been
called, was learned by any standards but she was to be found
only in a few eminent families like that of Sir Thomas More.

9

The exclusive salons of the bluestockings had ceased to flourish by the latter end of the eighteenth century, their early excitement for Hannah More, the last survivor, having been absorbed into more serious evangelical studies. For the ordinary middle-class woman education was confined to the three r's and to lady-like accomplishments such as drawing-room music, sketching, flower-painting and embroidery. Religious and moral instruction was taken care of by attendance at church and family prayers, by parental guidance and by reading books of devotion. Closely related as many of their disabilities were to the time, they were not necessarily to endure for ever, but the ways to change them had still to be worked out both by women themselves and by those men who interested themselves in these matters.

Changes were gradually taking shape against the conservative background of long-accepted ideas about the position and correct behaviour of women. If Englishwomen up to the end of the eighteenth century did not know their place or understand their role it was not through want of sermon to point it out or conduct book to reiterate the instructions that were preached from the pulpit, and they had the important satisfaction of knowing exactly what was required of them. The path women were urged to tread was the accepted path of any contemporary Christian in a Christian country, but special guidance was added for their conduct as women as well as Christians—guidance based upon certain statements and implications of the books of Genesis and Proverbs and the Epistles of St Paul which were difficult to interpret in the very different circumstances of the end of the Age of Reason in Europe. To summarize very briefly, women were required to love and obey their parents, to love and obey their husbands, to love and care for their children and bring them up in the way they should go; they must exercise justice towards their servants, and, if they were themselves servants, they must obey their masters and mistresses. They were exhorted not to spend too much time in front of their mirrors, dressing their hair and painting their faces and not to spend too much money and thought on dress and fripperies. The example of Eve was constantly pointed to as a warning of their own weakness in the face of temptation and their own propensity to entice men. They were also advised to be on guard against their love of gossip and slander and their tendency towards jealousy, suspicion, affectation and frivolity and they were strongly warned not to nag their husbands. Such were the basic standards of female behaviour, but it is only fair to say that many writers wrote about them in the conduct books of the time with a considerable degree of understanding and concern. So widely were such conduct or courtesy books disseminated that the period 1760–1820 has been called by one scholar 'the age of courtesy books for women'.[2] Several of these books were written by clergymen and one of the most famous was the work from which Mr Collins read aloud to the ladies at Longbourne[3] one evening after dinner; this was James Fordyce's *Sermons to Young Women* (1765), a book that Fanny Burney also mentions in her early diary (1773). Its tone must surely have had a special appeal for Mr Collins, because its 'love-like phrases of pumped-up passion' formed one of the features to which Mary Wollstonecraft objected. The well-known Evangelical divine, Thomas Gisborne, to whom Hannah More dedicated her *Christian Morals*, also wrote *An Enquiry into the Duties of the Female Sex* (1797) which was popular enough to have reached its eleventh edition by 1816. Gisborne deals with female education, female conversation and epistolary correspondence and gives guidance on dress, on amusements, the employment of time, matrimonial and parental duties and the duties belonging to the middle and the decline of life; he also includes some perceptive warnings about the dangers of 'sensibility'. His tone is rational and dignified and Jane Austen thanked her sister Cassandra for recommending 'Gisborn' (presumably this book); she was pleased with it in spite of having once determined not to read it.[4]

Some contemporary advice and instruction was given in verse form, as in *Fables for the Female Sex* by Edward Moore, which Fanny Burney read in a circulating library at Bath in 1779. Directing his fables at 'the proud, the envious and the vain/The jilt, the prude' Moore asserted that

> Truth under fiction I impart
> To weed out folly from the heart,
> And show the paths that lead astray
> The walking nymph from wisdom's way.

The walking nymph could not always be certain however that wisdom was the most advantageous way for her feet to tread; it was certainly women's experience that men did not invariably accord their greatest admiration to those who cultivated their minds rather than their appearance. With refreshing honesty Dr Johnson had admitted as much when he wrote in *The Rambler*:

We recommend the care of their nobler part and tell them how little addition is made by all their arts to the graces of the mind. But when was it known that female goodness or knowledge was able to attract that officiousness, or inspire that ardour, which beauty produces whenever it appears?[5]

This ambivalence was a long-continuing perplexity for young women and the newly emerging views on the role of women which originated with the revolutionary thinkers of France and were transmitted by the Radical writers of America and England added to their perplexities. Tom Paine gave the matter sympathetic consideration when in the *Pennsylvania Magazine* for 1775 he summarized women's difficulties in the following terms:

. . . even in countries where they may be esteemed the most happy, constrained in their desires in the disposal of their goods, robbed of freedom and wills by the laws, the slaves of opinion, which rules them with absolute sway and construes the slightest appearances into guilt; surrounded on all sides by judges, who are at once tyrants and their seducers . . . Who does not feel for the tender sex?[6]

Already in 1790 the less influential voice of Judith Sargent Murray, writing on the subject of the disparity between the opportunities open to men and to women at the time of the American Revolutionary War, was expressing opinions similar to those to be restated later in *Shirley* when she said:

Should it still be vociferated 'Your domestic employments are sufficient'—I would calmly ask, is it reasonable that a candidate for immortality, for the joys of heaven, an intelligent being, who is to spend an eternity in contemplating the works of Deity, should at present be so degraded as to be allowed no other ideas, than those which are suggested by the mechanism of a pudding or the sewing the seams of a garment?[7]

But the traditional advice continued to be given and yet another way of conveying it was by publishing letters addressed to young relatives, real or supposed, after the example of the Marquis of Halifax's *The lady's new year's gift, or, advice to a daughter*. The eighteenth century's best-known handbook of advice in this form was Dr John Gregory's *A father's legacy to his daughters* (1774); this little volume was frequently reprinted in England, became a best-seller in the American colonies and was translated into French. Mary Wollstonecraft assumes that all her readers will be familiar with this 'celebrated legacy', of which she entirely disapproves. Her detailed and incensed analysis of the views expressed by Gregory and Fordyce and even Rousseau, in her section called 'Animadversions on some of the Writers who have rendered Women Objects of Pity, bordering on Contempt' in the *Vindication of the Rights of Woman* (1792), is an indication how widespread she believes the influence of these writers to be. She states:

I may be accused of arrogance; still I must declare what I firmly believe, that all the writers who have written on the subject of female education and manners, from Rousseau to Dr. Gregory, have contributed to render women more artificial, weak characters than they would otherwise have been; and consequently more useless members of society.[8]

She particularly dislikes Gregory's entangling 'the grand motives of action, which reason and religion equally combine to enforce, with pitiful worldly shifts and sleight-of-hand tricks' (such as being cautious in displaying good sense and keeping any learning a profound secret). 'It is this system of dissimulation, throughout the volume that I despise. Women are always to *seem* to be this and that.'[9] Her basic contention in the *Vindication* is that women should be treated first and foremost as human beings with their own inalienable right to develop their faculties and deepen their characters and to seek after virtue. She condemns all falsehood, sham and flattery in the treatment of women and deplores the low standards of conduct currently excused in them as members of the so-called weaker sex. Ignorance, false refinement, concentration on the superficial arts of pleasing, trivial employments have all made women

13

triflers; they need to acquire strength of body and mind and should abandon the artificial cultivation of physical delicacy and mental frivolity. To avoid exclusive economic dependence on men, women should be educated so that they can earn a living for themselves. It should be possible for them to become physicians as well as nurses, to study politics and the history of man, to enter business and to have an acknowledged civil existence of their own in the state. They should feel it more respectable to earn their own bread than to be admired as beauties. Mary Wollstonecraft roundly condemns in women their folly, their lack of character, their propensity for believing anything, however unreasonable, their addiction to sentimental novels, their concentration of thought and effort on dress, their false sensibility, and their ignorance of the right way to bring up children and to treat servants. Her final challenge, selected from the welter of text she had written in a hurried six weeks, may be quoted as: 'Let men make their choice. Men and women were made for each other, though not to become one being; and if they will not improve women, they will deprave them.'[10] She allows that women have different duties to fulfil from those of men, 'but they are *human* duties, and the principles that should regulate the discharge of them, I sturdily maintain, must be the same'.

The timing of the publication of the *Vindication* was unfortunate, so soon was it followed by the Terror in France, which cast suspicion on any views that could be called Jacobin. Mary Wollstonecraft left this country for some years and when she returned she did not renew her original intention of writing a second part to her book, dealing this time with woman's duties, as a counter-balance to her rights.[11] One authority has said of the *Vindication* that it is 'perhaps the most original book of its century, not because its daring ideas were altogether new, but because in its pages for the first time a woman was attempting to use her own mind'.[12] Possibly its outstanding characteristic is its honesty; it tries to face the truth about women without currying favour with anyone or blindly accepting the views of others, and it brings genuine personal experience to bear on the problems of woman's education and her need to be trained to earn her own living. As an ex-governess

14

and journalist working in the Radical circle of writers surrounding the bookseller Joseph Johnson, Mary had both the personal knowledge and the moral courage to express such views and to drive them home with vehemence.

Some serious-minded women were worried about the poor quality of the education available to young girls and they began to take a certain amount of the guidance of their sex into their own hands and to produce books to help improve their education. In this also Mary Wollstonecraft was a pioneer for she wrote her *Thoughts on the education of daughters: with reflections on female conduct in the more important duties of life* as early as 1787, before both her *Vindication of the Rights of Men* in 1790 and her *Vindication of the Rights of Woman* two years later. Although the style of the *Thoughts* is mannered the book is an unusually frank and courageous confrontation of the actual facts of ordinary women's lives; it reveals first-hand experience of the handicaps suffered by young women facing the world on their own and makes an honest attempt to tackle some of their difficulties with common sense. In contrast to Dr Gregory's young woman, Mary Wollstonecraft's is 'not solicitous to act a part, her endeavour is not to hide, but to correct her failings'. Many of the other conduct books written by women for women were also concerned with their education, which for them had so often to be self-education, at least after the most elementary stages. A very famous book in this genre was Hester Chapone's *Letters on the Improvement of the Mind, addressed to a Young Lady*. Mrs Chapone had written one of the *Rambler* essays and thus gained an unassailable reputation as a moral writer and it may be recalled that it was amongst the recommendations of Thackeray's Miss Barbara Pinkerton as an educator of young ladies that she had been the correspondent of Mrs Chapone herself. Fanny Burney recommended her own great-niece to read Mrs Chapone's book once a year. The first three letters in this revered collection deal with the study of the Scriptures and the remainder cover such subjects as politeness and accomplishments, the government of the temper and the regulation of the heart and affections; thus, the book treats of both moral and intellectual subjects. Similar guides for young women continue to be published throughout our period; they include the *Letters to a Young Lady* by Jane Austen's contemporary, Jane West, rise higher in the social scale to Elizabeth Hamilton's *Letters addressed to the daughter of a nobleman,* and even aspire to the highest level in Hannah More's *Hints towards forming the character of a Young Princess,* a volume making suggestions for the education of Princess Charlotte. Hannah More also wrote *Strictures on the Modern System of Female Education with a View to the Principles and Conduct of Women of Rank and Fortune* and in her Introduction she makes the unusually forthright declaration that:

It is a singular injustice which is often exercised towards women, first to give them a very defective education, and then to expect from them the most undeviating purity of conduct;—to train them in such a manner as shall lay them open to the most dangerous faults, and then to censure them for not proving faultless.

Mrs More, to give her her courtesy title, always believed that woman's destiny was to be a daughter, wife and mother and that her entire duty lay in these spheres; any responsibility woman had for influencing society could only be fulfilled through her own religious conduct, by which she could help to raise the depressed tone of public morals. Educated women, provided they were educated wisely and modestly, could however exert more influence than their uneducated sisters and Hannah More believed that 'the regeneration of society on a christian basis could be achieved by the moral excellence of educated women'.[13]

Obviously much faith was placed in the good that would follow from the improved education of women, even by women as different as the Evangelical Hannah More and the Radical Mary Wollstonecraft, and out of this faith there grew the long campaign for the higher education of women in this country which, beginning as a movement for the better training of the governesses who were themselves to be the educators of so many young women, culminated in the establishment of Bedford College in the University of London, Girton College in Cambridge, and later the other Oxford and Cambridge women's colleges. This story has been retold in recent years but it is mentioned here as one of the active forces helping to expand the role of women. Tennyson's treatment of the movement in *The*

Princess was topical, even if his handling of it renders the subject slightly ridiculous. His poem was published in 1847 but ten years later a more whole-hearted examination of the fuller implications of the higher education of women appeared in Elizabeth Barrett Browning's *Aurora Leigh.* The contemporary impact of this verse-novel advocating the training of women to take a place equal with men in the creative work of the mind was forceful. Ruskin considered the poem as unsurpassed by anything but Shakespeare; George Eliot and G. H. Lewes were reading it for the third time in 1857; Swinburne wrote that its advent 'could never be forgotten by any lover of poetry who was old enough at the time to read it'.[14]

It was possible also to look to the lives of famous women for guidance in exploring woman's role. Some religious writers examined the lives of women in the Bible and drew the lessons to be learned from these exemplars. Mrs Frances Elizabeth King's *Female Scripture Characters; exemplifying female virtues* was one of the most popular of such works. The conduct of Eve naturally receives very close examination from many authors, and Eve had a great attraction as a subject even as late as Elizabeth Barrett Browning and Christina Rossetti. Mid-nineteenth-century writers who were worried about current wrangling over women's rights often went back to Eve to support the conservative case, but other authors managed, with considerable ingenuity, to reverse the charges against her. Mrs Hale, an American writer, was so bold in 1853 as to remark bluntly:

Most commentators, *men*, of course, represent woman as the *inferior*, and yet the most *blamable*. She could not have been both. If man, who had the greatest strength of body, had also the greatest wisdom of mind, and knew, as he did, that the serpent was a deceiver, then surely man was the most criminal. He should have restrained or at least have warned his wife.[15]

Collections like Mary Hays's *Female Biography* and Matilda Betham's *Biographical dictionary of the celebrated women of every age and country* also gave material to those who sought to find out what the great women of the past had done, to assist in the re-exploration of their role for the guidance of contemporary womanhood. There was, naturally enough, a market for a more sensational kind of female memoir but the experiences of of the courtesan Harriette Wilson could scarcely be regarded as providing a desirable example for contemporary youth to emulate. The genre also provided an irresistible temptation to a man like Thomas Amory, who made use of it in his first book, *Memoirs of Several Ladies* and its sequel *The Life of John Buncle*, wherein he described the rapid courtship of eight wives in quick succession. In an adaptation of the more serious tradition however Mrs Jameson published her *Characteristics of women, moral, political and historical*, in which, by analysing the characters of Shakespeare's women, she 'endeavoured to illustrate the various modifications of which the female character is susceptible, with their causes and results'; she did this because it appeared to her that 'the condition of women in society, as at present constituted, is false in itself, and injurious to them', therefore, instead of 'flinging her opinions in the face of the world in the form of essays on morality and treatises on education' she had rather chosen to illustrate certain positions by examples and left her readers to 'deduce the morals themselves, and draw their own inferences'.

Later French thought also had an important contribution to make to the continuing reassessment, in particular, the ideas of Auguste Comte and the Positivists. Harriet Martineau considered Comte's works of such wide-reaching importance that she undertook the considerable labour of translating and condensing them for the benefit of her younger and less privileged contemporaries. George Eliot also shared some of his views. Comte had no doubt about women's necessarily inferior position but he granted them superiority in sympathy and affection and he believed that in the family the spiritual power, which he considered the nobler power, belonged to them. It was their function in life to feed the flames of pure feelings. To a certain extent this view fitted in with the generally high valuation placed on what was termed 'woman's influence', a rather nebulous quality obviously meant to denote something that ennobled those with whom women came into contact. A very popular book published a few years after Queen Victoria came to the throne was *Woman's Mission*, adapted by an anonymous writer from the French work of L. Aimé-Martin called *Education des mères de famille ou de la civilisation du genre humain par les femmes*. It bases its claim for the importance of woman's role upon the influence she is able to exert, particularly on her sons, and it deprecates the view that woman is only an ornament of society. George Eliot admired this book and read both the abridgement and the original, while Charlotte Brontë's attention was attracted to it through a review which suggested that the profession of a dissenting clergyman might be open to any individual woman 'strong in purpose'.

Widely read by the simpler early Victorian woman was the series of volumes written by Mrs Sarah Stockney Ellis with the titles *The Women of England* (1839), *The Daughters of England* and *The Wives of England*; these ran into tens of editions in a few years and received approving reviews in the *Court Journal* and the *Evangelical Magazine*. Mrs Ellis stresses the importance of the influence of women but she has no doubts about the superiority of men. She is not above recommending the practice of a little deception, however: in a passage of mild humour describing a husband tying up a parcel with, she ventures to say, 'often a great deal of unnecessary bustle and importance', she recommends that:

A respectful deportment, and a complying disposition, evinced in these and similar cases, with a general willingness to accommodate all household arrangements to a husband's wishes, making every other consideration subservient to his convenience, will ensure for the wife who consistently does this, a large portion of that confidence upon which her influence and her happiness so much depend.[16]

The ferment of idea and discussion continued amongst those most deeply concerned, and Mrs Hale, the American writer quoted above, claimed that the 'Destiny of Woman' should be cited as the dominant subject of thought in the nineteenth century. Changes in outlook progressed more rapidly once they were worked out in so many ways by women themselves. The extent of the advance from the timid conformity of earlier views may be judged by Mrs Craik's statement in *A Woman's Thoughts about Women* (1850), a best-seller in America, that she considered the great mistake at the root of most women's education to be that the law of their existence was held to be not right, but propriety, a

certain received notion of womanhood, which has descended from certain excellent great grandmothers, admirably suited for some sorts of their descendants, but totally ignoring the fact that each sex is composed of individuals, differing in character almost as much from one another as from the opposite sex.[17]

She suggests that self-dependence is one of women's first duties and that they should not hand their consciences, duties, actions and opinions over to someone else, although she admits that such abdication of responsibility is the easier way to take.

Even in matters outside their own family many women declined to take the easiest way of sitting back and leaving the responsibility to the men. Care for the welfare of the poor on the estate or in the village had been enjoined on women in the conduct books of previous centuries but the accelerated tempo of industrial development in the new towns caused suffering beyond the power of the local lady bountiful to ameliorate. Signs of this suffering in the homes and streets around them were often more clearly visible to women than to men, although they could do little to change the situation by attempting alleviation on a small scale. Their concern in the face of these intractable problems reinforced their desire for better education for themselves to enable them to understand more clearly the causes of the problems and to see possible solutions. It also made them impatient with the limitation of their own much-lauded 'influence', an influence on legislation only at one remove, and strengthened the energies they put into the fight for the franchise.

That some women had influence, even direct and open influence, was undeniable, as in the case of Harriet Martineau and the Leaders she wrote for the newspapers, but hers was an exceptional case. Even the great Whig hostesses provided only the social milieu in which masculine liberal thinkers could gather and feel at home. It might be supposed that the campaign for votes for women would have formed part of the battle for the extension of the franchise to working men but although the first draft of the 'People's Charter' had made provision for the suffrage of women the clause was later omitted since (according to William Lovett) 'several members thought its adoption in the Bill might retard the suffrage of men'.[18] Subsequently all resources were absorbed in securing the removal of the subjection of labour by capital, and women's franchise was left aside.

John Stuart Mill did range himself beside the women. How much his views on the subject owed to another example of 'woman's influence', that of Mrs Harriet Taylor, it is difficult to assess, but he certainly believed that 'women cannot be expected to devote themselves to the emancipation of women, until men in considerable number are prepared to join with them in the undertaking'.[19] The end of our eighty years sees only the beginning of this phase of the campaign.

3

The Lesser Women Novelists

THE CLIMATE OF OPINION was created not only by formal writings in works of political and social theory, in conduct books, periodical essays, and serious examinations of the lives of women of the past, but also by informal comment and discussion, by the voluminous letters of the time and through the increasingly important medium of the novel. As has been mentioned, the circulating libraries made novels available to an ever-widening circle of readers and although Clara Reeve inveighed against these libraries as 'one source of the vices and follies of our present time',[1] their popularity carried its own challenge; Hannah More's expressed intention in writing her one novel was to benefit the subscribers to the circulating library, 'a little to raise the tone of that mart of mischief and to counteract its corruption'.[2] This story, *Coelebs in Search of a Wife* (1809), was really a conduct book in disguise and the fact that such a dull work had already reached its fourteenth edition by 1813 can only be interpreted as an indication of the contemporary eagerness to read about this topical subject in a novel written by a lady whose respectability and sound judgement were above reproach. Coelebs, the hero at whose name Jane Austen cavilled,[3] undertakes a journey in search of an ideally suitable young woman to be his wife; after meeting many disappointing candidates he finally discovers a quiet, modest, good-tempered, compliant and religious female who, he feels sure, will make him happy. She is obviously the model to be imitated by Miss More's readers, for whose guidance the faults of the unsuccessful candidates are carefully exposed.

The taste for novels had developed from the French romances to which women as different as Mrs Pepys and Dorothy Osborne were addicted. Two of the most popular of these huge and rambling tales were themselves the work of a woman, Madeleine de Scudéry, author of *Le Grand Cyrus* and *Clélie*. What was gained from such reading was not merely entertainment: Dorothy Osborne discussed seriously with Sir William Temple the views of Mlle de Scudéry on the character of 'l'honneste homme'. Such serious attention was widespread and is attested by the fact that the long conversations of *Clélie* were separately published in a small format so that readers could study the discussions on the passions and the virtues without being forced to page through the formidable tomes of the original romance in search of them.

The kind of women who in an earlier age might have read the French romances avidly may not have found the more masculine eighteenth-century works of Fielding and Smollett so much to their taste, but in the leisurely epistolary novels of Samuel Richardson they discerned a genuine sympathy with the concerns of women and an obvious willingness to devote a great deal of attention to the problems of their daily lives. The novelist's sympathetic interest provided his readers with an emotional outlet into a world of literature which they could understand. Richardson's considerable European reputation was equalled by the devoted admiration of comparatively simple women; the Scots poetess, Jean Adam, walked from Scotland to London just to see the revered creator of Clarissa.

Rousseau shared with Richardson the admiration of the female novel-reading public, possibly because in contrast to the general eighteenth-century material attitude to love, he 'threw enchantment over passion', as Byron expressed it, and avoided the familiar tendency to reduce women to mere instruments of pleasure. Rousseau was read so eagerly that many of the conduct books uttered warnings against what they considered to be his too-heady influence; even Mrs Barbauld's ill-starred marriage was ascribed by her brother to 'the baleful influence of the *Nouvelle Héloïse*'.

Both Richardson and Rousseau wrote novels in the epistolary form and this technique recommended itself readily to many eighteenth-century women who were themselves dedicated letter writers. Here was a method that seemed to be within their own capacities: the progress from writing the chatty, circumstantial letters that leisured women penned for relatives

23

and friends to welding such letters into a story appeared a comparatively easy one, and it opened up the way into the novel for many women writers. Before the latter part of the eighteenth century women novelists had been rare, Eliza Heywood, Sarah Fielding and Charlotte Lennox being the only names mentioned in most histories of the novel; but Oliver Elton sees the year 1780 as marking the abolition of the Salic law of the novel and women's admission to their rightful inheritance.[4] Of 190 English epistolary novels written between 1780 and 1790, 48 were by known women writers, others were written 'by a lady' and still others, to judge by their titles, must have been the work of women.[5]

Women liked to read what other women had written, to enter a new world where, for the first time, it was the men who were 'the others', considered only in their relationships as father or husband or son, instead of holding the centre of the stage. Avid readers of women's novels were not confined to Britain; in America even as early as the decade 1790–9 three novels by women[6] became best-sellers, while Rousseau's 'The New Eloisa' was only a runner-up; significantly enough, Richardson's *Clarissa* had reached the same level of popularity in the previous decade.

Why did women turn to novel-writing? Some of them of course wrote from economic necessity, to provide for fatherless children or ailing parents or a sick husband. Some wrote from vanity, fancying themselves as 'authoresses'—every conduct book censures presumption of this kind. Yet others wrote as a pastime for elegant young ladies or almost as a fashionable parlour game. The slightly improved education of some middle-class women would stimulate them to use their increased leisure in this way; it was an outlet for the imagination demanding a different talent from the writing of verses and it had the added attraction of novelty. Emulation doubtless entered into it: a book 'by a lady' could arouse the spirit of competition in another lady. Many wrote for moral and instructive ends, using the novel as a means to those ends. For others it was an escape from humdrum circumstances into fantasy and extravagant daydreams. A few must have found that the exercise of the creative imagination provided both stimulation and liberation.

Underneath it all was women's growing need to explore their own new position in society. Since the novel renders the role of the individual more clear cut and powerful than in real life, it must have brought to both writers and readers an increased clarity of vision. In 1776 the *Critical Review* observed that the women writers 'seem to be animated with an emulation for vindicating the honour of women in general rather than for acquiring to themselves the invidious reputation of great accomplishments';[7] they were indeed beginning to write as women and in the process adding a new dimension to the novel by illuminating aspects of women's lives unknown to the on-looker, and exploring the details of their own psychology and their own changing role.

The most picturesque of the groups of women novelists writing towards the end of the eighteenth century were the writers of Gothic novels, comprising Ann Radcliffe, Charlotte Smith, Regina Maria Roche and, more historical and less Gothic, the two Porter sisters. The story of the Gothic novel has been often told and here need only be mentioned the seemingly surprising fact that this should be a genre in which 'the gentle sex' was so successful. It is arguable, however, that adventures and horrors viewed from a safe distance in the pages of the novel may have contained an element of compensation for lives lived in circumstances too sheltered and confined. The events described in the Gothic novels are such as would shake the bravest of men, yet they are endured by delicate young women. The Gothic heroines themselves seem to have been wishful portraits of women as their authors would like them to be, possessed of the qualities of person and mind most admired by society, endowed with beauty, grace, intelligence, taste, sensitivity, sympathy and 'softness'. These young ladies were princesses in all but name, living lives of high adventure far away from cramping limitations and everyday shifts and compromises. The happenings in these novels are seen through the eyes of the heroines and, with an intensity of reaction equal to their own, we are caught up in the mounting wave of sensibility which swept so many feminine hearts along with it. Indeed it is sometimes difficult to draw a definite line between the Gothic novels and those novels of feeling, sentiment or sensibility whose excesses were satirized in *Sense and Sensibility* as the Gothic novels themselves were mocked in *Northanger Abbey*.

The popular writers of the sentimental school had a precursor in Sheridan's mother, of whose *Memoirs of Miss Sidney Bidulph* Dr Johnson remarked that he did not know whether she had a right, on moral principles, to make her readers suffer so much. An Irish approach seemed to occasion even greater excesses in this genre, for the limits reached by the idealization of the heroine may be seen in Lady Morgan's popular *The Wild Irish Girl*, where Glorvina is described thus:

Her form was so almost impalpably delicate, that as it floated on the gaze, it seemed like the incarnation of some pure ethereal spirit, which a sigh too roughly breathed might dissolve into its kindred air; yet to this sylphide elegance of spheral beauty was united all that symmetrical *contour* which constituted the luxury of human loveliness.

Although not all heroines reached such exquisite standards, they were in fact the superhuman heroines of the Gothic novels without their backgrounds of mystery and horror, that is, they were still ideal, escapist, daydream pictures of women of beauty and enchanting sensibility and softness, but placed in circumstances more familiar to their readers than the remote and embattled haunted castles of the Gothic landscape. To that extent the identification of the reader with such heroines would be easier and the escape from humdrum daily life would appear less of a fairy story.

Such novels invited parody. The fact that William Beckford's half-sister wrote fashionable effusions of this kind gave him the opportunity of scoring hits against her and her fellows when he produced *Modern Novel Writing, or the Elegant Enthusiast; and Interesting Emotions of Arabella Bloomville. A Rhapsodical Romance, interspersed with Poetry*, purporting to be by Lady Harriet Marlow, and followed it with *Azemia, a descriptive and sentimental novel interspersed with pieces of poetry*, which its 'author', Miss Jacquetta Agneta Mariana Jenks, dedicated to Lady Marlow. Both books are tissues of improbability and inconsequence, filled with ghosts, grottoes, suffering maidens, picturesqueness and sentimentality.

Fashion in escape changes with the changes in society and the

Victorian daydreams took form in the materialistic and snob-bish 'silver fork school' of novels, pictures of fashionable ladies in well-upholstered high life, not maidens of ethereal sensibility in uncomfortable surroundings.

Very far removed from fashionable escape, however, was the group of women novelists connected with Radical intellectual circles in the revolutionary years at the end of the eighteenth century. That arch-baiter of Radicals, the *Anti-Jacobin Review*, referred to them as 'philosophesses'. Mary Wollstonecraft was the most famous of the group, the others were Mary Hays, Mrs Inchbald and Mrs Opie. The extent of their commitment to political Radicalism varied considerably and the perspective of history has brought them more closely together than they were during their lifetime, when their varying religious views divided them. In their books they all however pay serious attention to the new ideas about the rights of women and give them fair consideration instead of condemning them out of hand. Mrs Opie's *Adeline Mowbray, or, the Mother and Daughter* (1804) is one of the clearest expositions of the views of the Radical women on marriage, divorce, and the education (in the wider sense of upbringing) of daughters. The heroine, Adeline, is an ideal female character with advanced views inherited partly from her mother. But the mother had lost herself in an ideal world of 'fatal and unproductive studies' and 'while professing her unbounded love for the great family of the world, she suffered her own family to pine under the consciousness of her neglect'. She had withheld the warning voice of experience and good judgment when Adeline most needed it but Adeline, through her own suffering, is gradually led to see the wisdom of some of the rules of society which she had formerly condemned and is finally convinced of their value as a means of disciplining wayward human nature.

The main tradition of women novelists comprised those who concerned themselves with contemporary manners described without conscious or intentional distortion and often in the familiar epistolary form, or a method growing out of that form. These women brought to their work a close observation of the social scene, clear-sightedness for the minutiae that reveal character, and a developed moral sense; they often wrote too with definitely didactic and moral intentions. Such writers included the Scottish trio Elizabeth Hamilton, Mrs Brunton and Susan Ferrier, who contributed a Scottish vigour and vitality to some of their portraits of women of strong character. However, although Mrs Brunton's novel *Self-control* (1811) whose title sufficiently reveals its purpose was popular enough to be sold out within a month of publication, Jane Austen said of it that, in spite of the fact of its being an 'excellently-meant, elegantly-written Work', it was 'without anything of Nature or Probability in it'.[8]

Jane West may be taken as a fair representative of the women who used the novel as a definite channel of instruction. She was the author of one of the epistolary conduct books called *Letters to a Young Lady, in which the Duties and Characters of Women are considered*, in which she advocated the accepted code of behaviour, and she had begun to write moral tales a little earlier than Maria Edgeworth, her first being *The Advantages of Education; or the History of Maria Williams* (1792). Her *Gossip's Story* was an anti-sensibility novel which contrasted the fates of two sisters, one of them named Marianne and one Louisa; Marianne destroys her own happiness through excessive emotionalism but Louisa's good sense enables her to face her difficulties and to overcome them. This novel has naturally received some critical attention because of the similarity of its basic theme to that of *Sense and Sensibility*. In the Introduction to her later novel, *The Infidel Father* (1802), Mrs West notes that 'the rage for novels' does not decrease and states that although she considers them by no means

the best vehicles for 'the words of sound doctrine'; yet, while the enemies of our church and state continue to pour their poison into unwary ears through this channel, it behoves the friends of our establishments to convey an antidote by the same course, especially as those who are most likely to be infected by false principles, will not search for a refutation to them in profound and scientific compositions.

She goes on to explain that the particular design of *The Infidel Father* is to show the 'superiority which religious principle possesses when compared with a sense of honour, moral fitness,

28

or a love of general applause', and to declare that her book is directed at 'the middle classes of society' and their faults. She is open-minded enough to explore the implications of some of the accepted codes of women's behaviour for herself; after admitting that she is 'not an entire convert to the utility of the doctrine of conjugal non-resistance' and giving an example of its inefficacy, she asks the more penetrating question whether husbands who are never contradicted are in truth happier than those with less compliant wives. She doubts whether the description 'unreproving', which she says 'in the estimation of the *superior* sex is the best epithet that can be bestowed on a wife', is in truth a pointer to the best way towards family happiness.

As women's interests widened these were explored in the novels that women wrote. The most appealing of contemporary causes was that of anti-slavery. Mrs Trollope published her anti-slavery novel, *The Life and Adventures of Jonathan Jefferson Whitlaw* in 1836, Harriet Martineau's *The Hour and the Man* followed a few years later, and the most famous emancipation novel of them all, *Uncle Tom's Cabin*, written by an American woman, appeared in 1852; it is possible to consider that year, during which one million copies of Harriet Beecher Stowe's book were sold in England, as the year in which women's new concern for their more distant neighbours was indubitably established; the former total limitation of their interest to the moral improvement of the individual woman or her immediate family was now removed and seen to be removed. Nearer home, child labour in the factories was also a subject likely to engage women's sympathies and it was dealt with by Mrs Trollope in her *Life and Adventures of Michael Armstrong, the Factory Boy* (1840). The poor law was her topic in *Jessie Phillips: a tale of of the present day* and Charlotte Elizabeth Tonna depicted the sufferings of factory women in *Helen Fleetwood* (1841). Moral purpose and the dissemination of information about economic and social conditions mingled in all these tales, as they did in Mrs Gaskell's more distinguished contributions to the industrial and social novel.

But not all Victorian women novelists were crusaders for causes outside the home: the average writer like Mrs S. C. Hall, Charlotte Mary Yonge, Mrs Craik and Mrs Oliphant, made a narrower but very solid contribution to the novel by using it to paint a picture of home and neighbourhood life from the accepted Evangelical or the High Church view of woman's role. The good sense of the Evangelical novelists formed part of the most solid strata in the foundation on which George Eliot built, just as the tradition of Mrs Brunton and Mrs West led to Jane Austen, and certain features of the Gothic novel are found even in *Wuthering Heights*.

The greater novelists realized the limitations within which it was possible for them to exercise their art: Jane Austen eschewed the Napoleonic wars for the few neighbourhood families that she could understand in total depth and George Eliot's broad intellect was used to enrich understanding of provincial society rather than stretched in an attempt to paint a huge canvas of dynastic struggles. It was the lesser artists who undertook too much in their efforts to encompass a wider view. Sweeping economic surveys were better left to other minds than the women novelists', but domestic and social conditions near at hand could find no better pens. The very exercise of the craft of the novelist, which places the limitation of artistic discipline upon poetic flights of the mind, brought its own increased skill and its own satisfaction. The mutual interaction and interdependence of literature and life increased both writer's and reader's understanding of themselves and of their place in society. This increased understanding, the achievement of so many differing talents, provided the common stock out of which more enduring literary masterpieces were produced; it also prepared a sound basis from which they could be appreciated.

4

Women Awaiting Marriage (1)

Fanny Burney, Maria Edgeworth, Jane Austen

TURNING from the lesser women novelists of our period to the greater our analysis must be a closer one. In order to facilitate a comparison between the authors' differing viewpoints, it is proposed to examine first their views on women awaiting marriage, next their views on women as wives and mothers, and finally, on women as individuals. By far the greatest amount of attention in the novels under discussion is paid to the heroines awaiting marriage, that is to young women on the point of forming the most important relationship of their lives before disappearing from the scene to live happily ever after. This emphasis was due partly to the tradition of the novel and the romance and partly to contemporary convention. Long fidelity to the principle of the marriage vow of obedience to husbands caused public discussion of marital problems from the woman's point of view to be seen as a form of disloyalty and betrayal. Outspokenness on any intimate details of the marriage relationship would have been a breach of contemporary good taste which most upper and middle class women authors would naturally wish to avoid. As far as the maternal relationship was concerned it was not at that time the subject of such heart-searching reappraisal as the theoretical position of women in society and therefore attracted less of the attention of our novelists. What they had to say about women was focused mainly on their young lady characters and most of the evidence for their attitude towards women's problems has to be uncovered from their treatment of their heroines. This chapter and its successor should therefore provide the richest quarry for our enquiries.

31

Women Awaiting Marriage (1)

Fanny Burney

In Fanny Burney's novels the young women awaiting their fate
are ideal young ladies, judged by the standards of the John-
sonian age. No bold and original thinker, least of all on the role
of women in her own society, Miss Burney adheres to the
standards laid down for her, showing her approval of the
retired virtues of modesty, reserve, delicacy, propriety, prudence, sweetness and softness. Her novels are staunch suppor-
ters of accepted standards of behaviour, they are, indeed,
'courtesy novels'. Her first novel *Evelina* (1778) shows the
world as it appears to a girl of seventeen, 'a young woman of
obscure birth, but conspicuous beauty', who has 'a virtuous
mind, a cultivated understanding, and a feeling heart', and in
the background there is a kind mentor in the shape of the Rev.
Mr Villars,[1] her guardian, to whom she turns for advice and
sympathy in all her difficulties. Although Fanny says that her
heroine is 'no faultless Monster, that the world ne'er saw', this
is only true if Evelina is compared with the heroines of the early
Romances and Gothic novels who were not only beautiful (and
Evelina is this) but also endowed with knowledge of several
languages, faultless musicianship, artistic taste and extensive
acquaintance with poetry, together with supreme physical and
moral courage in situations which would cause the stoutest
heart to falter. By less exalted standards it is very difficult to
find any faults in Evelina, except for her unconscious snobbery
and a certain impulsiveness of action and judgment in times of
crisis. Her conduct meets with the approval of all the virtuous
elders in her circle: she is exceedingly submissive to her guardian
and addresses him in terms that sound fulsome in twentieth-
century ears but are in fact no more fulsome than the terms in
which Miss Burney addressed her own father in the poem dedi-
cating this book to him. In addition to filial piety Evelina
possesses the other virtues required of a young Christian
gentlewoman—innocence, kindness, courtesy and humility
within the confines of her social position. She does however
commit the perilous imprudence of falling in love with Lord
Orville before he has declared himself and her guardian warns
her strongly of this danger to her peace, urging her to exert

herself to avoid the evils with which it threatens her, 'evils which, to a mind like yours, are most to be dreaded, secret repining, and concealed, yet consuming regret'; he beseeches her to make an effort which may be painful but which he assures her is requisite. This advice may be compared with the long discourse written to Camilla by her father in Fanny Burney's third novel: in the eyes of the eighteenth century such premature forming of an attachment was a most dangerous folly against which women should constantly be on guard. On the whole however Evelina's difficulties are social embarrassments rather than real calamities or dangers and her conduct during them all is impeccable, until she is finally united with 'the object of her dearest, her eternal affection', although this cannot, of course, take place until 'the willing yet aweful consent' of her guardian has been obtained. She is the very model of a late eighteenth-century middle-class girl, possessed too of a talent for fresh observation on her surroundings and a delectable amount of vivacity.

The tone of Fanny Burney's second novel, *Cecilia, or Memoirs of an Heiress* (1782), was more obviously didactic than that of *Evelina.* She was now an accepted and respected author with the power to induce Edward Gibbon to read through the five volumes of *Cecilia* in one day, thereby spoiling Edmund Burke's record of three days. Cecilia herself, rich, sought-after and beautiful, lives in a milieu of fashion and frivolity in the house of the Harrels in Portman Square. Although considered an object of envy by others, she is uneasy and discontented; having no mentor to whom she can turn for advice she has to work out for herself 'a scheme of happiness at once rational and refined'. The basis of her plan is to become mistress of her own time and to drop all idle and uninteresting acquaintance; she resolves to choose only such friends as 'by their piety could elevate her mind, by their knowledge improve her understanding, or by their accomplishments and manners delight her affections'. She realizes that this decision, if strictly adhered to, will soon relieve her from the fatigue of receiving many visitors and she can therefore have all the leisure she could desire for the pursuit of her favourite studies, music and reading.

Although this plan will enable her to regulate her personal

life, she must as an heiress consider her special obligations to the community—'her affluence she . . . considered as a debt contracted with the poor: and her independence as a tie upon her liberality to pay it with interest', so 'not without trembling' she begins to look forward to the claims which the income she will soon possess will call upon her to discharge, and

Many and various, then, soothing to her spirit and grateful to her sensibility, were the scenes which her fancy delineated; now she supported an orphan, now softened the sorrows of a widow, now snatched from iniquity the feeble trembler at poverty, and now rescued from shame the proud struggler with disgrace. (Vol. 1, Ch. 7)

Such daydreams carry their own danger for an inexperienced girl and the novel goes on to show the mistakes Cecilia makes by indiscriminate gifts; her payments of the Harrels' debts, for instance, proves to be ill-judged. The sage and experienced Mr Albany is however able to assist her to be more prudent and presumably after marriage and after the end of the novel her husband will be the source of similar advice.

Incidentally, one of Cecilia's better-judged acts of liberality is to the deserving family of Mr Hills, a carpenter who has been ruined by the Harrels. More than once in her novels Fanny Burney makes clear the hardships caused by thoughtless and heartless rich women who do not pay for the luxuries they order.

In addition to the implied admiration for feminine softness (of which Cecilia possesses an engaging amount), fortitude in a crisis is also accorded high praise. In the dreadful scene of the suicide of Mr Harrel at Vauxhall Cecilia plays a very brave part and she is commended for it by Delvile's mother the next morning; the actual words of praise reveal the reason for the commendation for Mrs Delvile points out that 'a heart, less under the dominion of well-regulated principles, would have sought only its own relief by flying from distress and confusion', whereas Cecilia's conduct showed such 'propriety of mind as can only result from the union of good sense with virtue'.

As well as exercising fortitude on public occasions, it was also necessary for a woman to cultivate it in bearing her own personal disappointments. Reflecting on the course of her connection with Delvile, Cecilia has not a doubt remaining but that some fatal obstacle prevents their union, and 'to collect fortitude to bear it with composure was now her only study'. In order to summon this fortitude she allows herself no time for dangerous recollection, she makes sure that the subject should not be mentioned in conversation, she goes for her old walks and renews her old acquaintance, and by resolution and 'a vigorous exertion of active wisdom' she finds that her task is not as difficult as she had feared. These were obviously the expedients that Marianne Dashwood *ought* to have resorted to after her disappointment over Willoughby instead of doing all she could to feed her own suffering.

Comparable with fortitude in disappointment is the self-control required of a woman who finds herself falling in love before the young man has declared himself. As already mentioned, the importance of this is pointed out to Evelina by Mr Villars but Cecilia has to take herself to task when, after her first meeting with Delvile, she finds she has been 'struck with an involuntary admiration of his manners and conversation'. She soon perceives her danger and instantly determines to give 'no weak encouragement to a prepossession which neither time nor intimacy had justified'. She therefore denies herself the deluding satisfaction of dwelling on his good points and is unusually assiduous in occupying all her time so that she has no leisure for day-dreaming.

Secret marriages, that is, marriages without the knowledge and full consent of the families concerned, are by implication very strongly censured in *Cecilia*. The heroine is horrified at her own impulsive consent to a secret marriage which 'terrified her as undutiful and shocked her as clandestine', and she immediately regrets it. She considers it to be a judgment from heaven when the ceremony is tragically interrupted.

Contrasted with Cecilia herself are two other young women, Lady Honoria Pemberton and Henrietta Belfield, who fall short of the standards required of a heroine. Lady Honoria is censured as a 'rattle'. She has received a fashionable education, which means she sings a little, plays the harpsichord after a fashion, does a little needlework and dances a great deal; she has 'quick parts and high spirits' but alas her mind is uncultivated and she has no judgment or discretion; she is careless of giving offence and indifferent to all that is thought of her; she has much levity but little heart. Thus, although Lady Honoria's sprightliness can be amusing, Cecilia cannot esteem her.

Henrietta Belfield is more like Cecilia in character and indeed Cecilia is at one time convinced that Mortimer Delvile is in love with Henrietta. But he sets her mind at rest by pointing out that, although Miss Belfield's heart is 'all purity', her temper all softness and her manners charmingly simple, yet when the novelty of such uninformed simplicity is over it becomes wearisome and softness without dignity is too indiscriminate to give delight, for 'heavily drags on the load of life when the companion of our social hours wants spirit, intelligence, and cultivation'.

The standards of good manners required both of men and of women in this book are in essentials the same: good principles and thoughtfulness for others are the basis for both. Fanny Burney implies however that the bad manners of men have a disproportionate effect upon women; she is particularly concerned with the perplexity caused in the minds of young girls when their admirers seem to blow hot and cold. Prevented by convention from confronting the man concerned and asking for a clarification of his feelings, the young women have to make their own adjustments and to be on guard against interpretations which might not subsequently be confirmed by an actual 'declaration'; this provides another reason for women to be cautious.

By the time she wrote *Camilla* (1796), dedicated to the Queen herself, Fanny Burney (now Madame d'Arblay) was taking her moral purpose as a writer very seriously indeed. In letters of 1795 to her family she insisted that *Camilla* was not a novel but a 'work'. Her father praised her because 'your book, my dear Fanny, seems the best system of *Education* I ever saw, particularly for females,' and she was greatly gratified when the Duchess of Portland approved it as a 'study for youth';[2] during the increasingly tedious delay of the happy ending through five volumes there is ample time for the young reader to be instructed. The copy of the novel used for the present investigation included the list of original subscribers; amongst the names of many of the nobility and the famous were Edmund Burke, who subscribed for five sets, and David Hume, who bought one. Very fittingly Dr Gisborne also bought a copy, as did Mrs Piozzi, Mrs Radcliffe, Miss Hannah More, Miss Edgeworth and 'Miss J. Austen of Steventon'. Jane Austen not only read her copy appreciatively but assumed that her personal correspondents had also read it with similar pleasure.

The heroine herself, Camilla Tyrold, is beautiful, good and spirited, but impulsive and apt to be led astray by too much sensibility; the 'reigning and radical defect of her character' was 'an imagination that submitted to no control'. Camilla is contrasted with two close female connections; one of these is her quieter sister, Lavinia, who lives at home in the vicarage and is virtuous in a more submissive way than Camilla, and the other is their cousin, the beautiful but selfish Indiana Lynmere. There is a third sister, Eugenia, who had been a beautiful child but was crippled in an accident and scarred by smallpox. To make amends for his own carelessness in the accident that crippled her Sir Hugh Tyrold, her uncle, makes Eugenia his heiress and by so doing exposes her to the unscrupulous attentions of fortune hunters.

This novel has a good deal to say about feminine beauty and its dangers, and it also includes philosophic considerations designed to help young women who are plain. Those who have both beauty and virtue, like Camilla and Lavinia, triumph and find happiness, even if only after considerable delay; the possessors of beauty without feminine virtues, like Indiana and Mrs Berlinton, find only a fleeting or a flawed happiness, while Eugenia, who has no beauty save that of the intellect and spirit, suffers grievously but finds peace in the end. A considerable section of the book, after Eugenia has overheard some very unkind remarks about her own ugliness and deformity from some passing countrywomen, is devoted to the arguments used by her father to comfort her and reason her out of her determination to flee the world.

Fanny Burney's belief in the necessity for women to conceal their tenderness for any man who has not yet declared himself is again illustrated in *Camilla*. Mrs Tyrold glories in 'the virtuous delicacy of her daughter', Camilla, because she so properly conceals her tenderness for Edgar, while her father writes her a discourse running to some fourteen pages, admonishing her that she should 'beyond all other care,—shut up every avenue by which a secret which should die untold should further escape you'. A corollary to the delicacy that forbids a young woman to give a young man the slightest hint that she loves him is the necessity to keep silent about any rejected suitors; Eugenia believes it to be a high point of female propriety never to publish an unsuccessful conquest.

The undesirability of popularity and public notice for a young lady is stressed on several occasions. Mrs Arlbery, discussing Lady Isabella Irby with Lord O'Lerney in Tunbridge Wells, asks: 'Why is she not surrounded by volunteer admirers? Why, with a person and manner so formed to charm, joined to such a character, and such rank, has she not her train?' Lord O'Lerney replies that the reason is, Lady Isabella must be sought and the world, always lazy, will not pursue the most perfect if trouble is required to do it. At this Edgar, ever ready to underline any lessons in female virtue, thinks: 'Admirable Lord O'Lerney . . . what a lesson is this to youthful females against the glare of public homage, the false brilliancy of unfeminine popularity'. And Lord O'Lerney, always solicitous, speaking of Camilla herself, tells Lady Isabella and Edgar that he would be glad to hear that she were either well established, or returned to her friends without becoming an object of public notice, since a young woman 'is nowhere so rarely respectable, or respected, as at these water-drinking places, if seen at them either long or often'.

Although so much stress is laid on the virtues of self-control and modesty, more positive acts of virtue are also enjoined upon young women of means. When the servant, Jacob, learns that Camilla is to marry Edgar, he rejoices because of the good she will do when she is mistress of Beech Park, visiting the poor, making them 'clothes, and broths, and wine possets, and baby-linen, all day long'.

It was not until she was over sixty that Fanny Burney published her last novel, *The Wanderer, or Female Difficulties* (1814), which appeared in the same year as *Waverley* and *Mansfield Park*, and although it is the least successful of her books as a work of art it is interesting as an indication of a half-realized feeling of frustration in her consideration of the role of women; even the title she chose reveals this. As woman is traditionally the homemaker, it is contrary to her nature to be a wanderer: in Goethe's *Hermann and Dorothea* (1798) it is the young woman whose unhappy lot has made her an exile, in a reversal of the usual roles. Madame d'Arblay's heroine, Incognita, 'Miss Ellis', or Juliet Granville as she finally turns out to be, is indeed a wanderer in this sense; she lacks identity, even to the extent of suffering a frequent change of name and for the period of the book she has no acceptable place in society. Significantly she is a member of the French aristocracy who has been brought up in the old tradition and has fled to England in disguise 'during the dire reign of the terrific Robespierre'; she has no money and is unable to meet her friends or to tell anyone what her name is for fear of pursuit. She tries various methods of earning her living, teaching the harp, doing embroidery, working in a milliner's shop, and at a mantua maker's and acting as companion to a very unpleasant lady, Mrs Ireton. In each of these occupations she is subjected to ill treatment of various kinds and each position she occupies is shown to have its particular drawbacks and difficulties. From time to time Juliet laments 'the severe DIFFICULTIES of a FEMALE, who, without fortune or protection, had her way to make in the world', the capitals being Miss Burney's.

Juliet is completely conventional and may even be said to make a god of propriety. She has great beauty and all the accomplishments of an aristocratic young lady: she plays the harp and sings divinely, she is skilled in 'the useful and appropriate female accomplishment of needlework', she has 'beautiful handwriting, and correct punctuation and orthography', and she can sketch well, dance a French cotillion and read aloud pleasingly in both English and French. Her conduct is always exemplary and her language that of 'polished life' in spite of all her distresses. But none of these accomplishments really enables her to earn her living nor to find happiness in any way of life open to her. She is contrasted with Elinor Joddrell, a believer in the rights of women, who has absorbed her ideas from Revolutionary France, and who acts in exactly the opposite manner to that of convention and the Wanderer, even to the extent of herself declaring her love to Albert Harleigh, its object. Elinor does not receive the prize of happy love; Juliet however finally does. Fanny Burney's only solution for Juliet's plight is to bring about the acknowledgement of her family and rank, enabling her thus to regain her name and identity; a suitor for whom the old criteria remain all important is also provided for her. But the eighteenth-century tradition of the lady does not really provide the solution for less-privileged young women who find themselves in situations removed from the sheltered comfort necessary to maintain the old standards. Madame d'Arblay can only offer the empty abstract phrases and capital letters with which she ends the book:

How mighty, thus circumstanced, are the DIFFICULTIES with which a female has to struggle! Her honour always in danger of being assailed, her delicacy of being offended, her strength of being exhausted, and her virtue of being calumniated!

Yet even DIFFICULTIES such as these are not insurmountable, where mental courage, operating through patience, prudence, and principle, supply physical force, combat disappointment, and keep the untamed spirits superior to failure, and ever alive to hope.

Fanny Burney was obviously concerned throughout her life with the difficulties faced by different types of young women, as the very titles of her novels show—*Evelina, or a Young Lady's Entrance into the World*; *Cecilia, or Memoirs of an Heiress*; *Camilla, or a Picture of Youth*; *The Wanderer, or Female Difficulties*, and she explored these difficulties in her books, from the point of view of the young women themselves. Evelina, Cecilia, Camilla and even Juliet are not just beautiful heroines, they are girls faced with the special problems and doubts and embarrassments that did face young women in eighteenth-century society, they are all uncertain of their own behaviour, alternately impulsive and then frightened to take the slightest step forward, too easily moved by the entreaties of feckless brothers and sponging friends, forced to be passive before the puzzle of men's fluctuating attentions, and, underneath it all, absolutely dependent upon a secure social background and the guidance provided by older people and by accepted rules of conduct. These young women show more clearly than any direct pleas could do the need for a reconsideration of the role of women in a rapidly changing society. Hazlitt accused Fanny Burney of having formed for herself an abstract idea of perfection in common behaviour which is quite as romantic and impracticable as any other idea of the sort,[3] but this idea was not in fact one that Miss Burney had formed for herself. She was only faithful to the accepted code for young women belonging to the leisured and cultivated classes of her time; within a sheltered and happy environment it could be observed and its practice would add to the graces of life and to a young woman's quiet contentment with her lot, but outside such an environment it was totally inadequate. As Fanny Burney was content not to penetrate into the deeper layers of their personalities, her characters were imperfectly realized as human beings, although fascinating as figures in a period picture of eighteenth-century social life and manners. It may be claimed however that she played a more important literary part than she knew by providing material and incentive to one admiring Steventon subscriber and reader who had the creative power necessary to transform such young women into some of the most vividly realized female characters of English literature.

Maria Edgeworth

The novels of Maria Edgeworth that concern this study are not, unfortunately for the reader, her light-hearted pictures of the Irish gentry in *Castle Rackrent* and *The Absentee* but the more serious-minded novels she wrote under the guidance of her father.

Miss Edgeworth saw the world largely through her father's eyes; indeed she had little option in the matter so carefully did he guide her life and her work and so devoted were father and daughter to each other. Encouraged by him it was Maria's accepted task in her writings to help people to come as near to moral perfection in their appointed place in life as they could. She began with educational works and with tales for children and young people and then turned to stories set in the circles of fashion, to point out, as her father states in his preface to her *Tales of Fashionable Life*, 'some of those errors to which the higher classes of society are disposed'. It was a purpose of which she was fully conscious, not over-rating its literary value but believing in its social usefulness and enjoying the approval of it by those whose opinions she respected. Writing to Mrs Stark in 1834 she explains that few readers can put themselves in the place of great criminals. They know they cannot fall to the depth of evil at once so they have no fear; but show them their little faults which may lead to the greatest and they shudder, that is, if it is done with truth enough to bring it home to their consciousness: 'This is all, which by reflection on my own mind and comparison with others, and with records in books full as much as observations on living subjects, I feel or fancy I have sometimes done or can do'.[4] In her efforts to bring home these matters to the consciousness of her readers Maria was well served by the great zest she had for the realistic details of domestic life as lived in her own schoolroom world and by her very delicate appreciation of its small flaws.

She herself was able, with a great measure of family encouragement, to go beyond the limits of this world and to attain wide fame: she was even the lion of the London season of 1813 (her predecessor in 1812 having been Byron!). But she held the rather circumscribed views on the role of women that were the standards of her immediate environment. The examples of women held up in her novels for emulation were virtuous in the accepted sense and charitable; they did all they could to promote domestic happiness and to bring up children with care. Perfection of the individual woman's character, within conventional limits, was believed to be attainable, just as perfection in many other human spheres was believed possible after the Enlightenment. Like Jane Austen Miss Edgeworth was more concerned with the steps women should take along the road to this individual perfection or improvement than she was with any consideration of the new ideas about women's rights. Her young women were expected to keep watch on their own faults by self-examination although not of a deeply penetrating kind; they were to avoid the dangers of affectation and the fashionable indulgence of their sensibility which would be easier if they refrained from dangerously enervating reading. They possessed knowledge of a practical sort but they never paraded any learning they might have acquired. Maria Edgeworth

considered that women were only too prone to seek after petty
power and that in their hands it was dangerous. It was a pity
that her intention to write a *Coelebina in search of a Husband*[5]
as a companion to Hannah More's *Coelebs in search of a Wife*
came to nothing because this might have led to a franker, less
unexceptionable statement of her views on women.

In her earliest work *Letters for Literary Ladies, to which is
added an Essay on the Noble Science of Self Justification* (1795),
she sets out opinions that are in essence the same as Dr Gregory's
but which are more open and honest in intention and in their
common-sense approach to women's problems. The cause of
education was the one closest to her heart and on this topic she
does express herself freely. She felt it desirable to educate
women in order to cure them of their tendency to frivolity; true
ideas should be instilled into their minds instead of 'preposterous notions'. Married women would be able to 'embellish
domestic life' if educated in the right way and unmarried
women who had stored their minds with knowledge could
amuse themselves without the danger of becoming burden-
some to their friends or society:

... though they may not be seen haunting every place of amusement
or of public resort, they are not isolated or forlorn; by a variety of
associations they are connected with the world, and their sympathy
is expanded and supported by the cultivation of their understandings:
nor can it sink, settle, and concentrate upon cats, parrots, and
monkeys.

She is just as sensible about the desirability of allowing a young
woman to read widely. In a letter on this topic purporting to be
written by 'a father' he says that he has no fear that the truth
upon any subject should injure his daughter's mind, rather, it is
falsehood that he dreads:

I dread that she should acquire preposterous notions of love, of
happiness, from the furtive perusal of vulgar novels, or from the
clandestine conversation of ignorant waiting maids—I dread that
she should acquire, even from the enchanting eloquence of Rousseau,
the fatal idea, that cunning and address are the natural resources of
her sex, that coquetry is necessary to attract, and dissimulation to
preserve the heart of man.

43

Miss Edgeworth even went so far as to let the same father state
that he would not proscribe an author because he believed some
of his opinions to be false, preferring to have his daughter read
and compare various books and correct her judgment by listen-
ing to persons of sense and experience. He refutes the charge
that he is a champion of the rights of women, since he is too
much their friend to be their partisan and is more anxious for
their happiness than intent upon a metaphysical discussion of
their rights; he declares that

their happiness is so nearly connected with ours, that it seems to me
absurd to manage any argument to set the two sexes at variance by
vain contentions for superiority. It ought not to be our object to
make an invidious division of privileges, or an ostentatious declaration of rights, but to determine what is most for our general advantage.

Miss Edgeworth does refer to Dr Gregory's mention of the
pleasures men of science and literature enjoy when married to
women who can converse with them as equals but her own
viewpoint is much less clouded with condescension. She puts
forward sound reasons for distrusting the artificial cultivation of
sensibility:

You ask, why exercise does not increase sensibility, and why sympathy with imaginary distress will not also increase the disposition to
sympathize with what is real?—Because pity should, I think, always
be associated with the active desire to relieve. If it be suffered to
become a *passive sensation,* it is a *useless weakness,* not a virtue. The
species of reading you speak of must be hurtful, even in this respect,
to the mind, as it indulges all the luxury of woe in sympathy with
fictitious distress, without requiring the exertion which reality
demands: besides, universal experience proves to us that habit, so
far from increasing sensibility, absolutely destroys it, by familiarizing
it with objects of compassion.

The kind of education for women that the Edgeworths, both
father and daughter, advocated was one likely to lead to
women's happiness in society as then constituted, not in an
ideal society not yet found on earth. In considering the literary
side of women's education they stated that 'her imagination

44

must not be raised above the taste for necessary occupations, or the numerous small, but not trifling pleasures of domestic life'. They also felt that since so much depended upon the temper of women this ought to be most carefully cultivated in early life and to this end 'girls should be more inured to restraint than boys, because they are likely to meet with more restraint in society. Girls should learn the habit of bearing slight reproofs'. These beliefs are discernible in the women Miss Edgeworth created in her novels. In *Belinda* (1801), which Jane Austen admired, the heroine has 'early been inspired with a taste for domestic pleasures', she is fond of reading, and is 'disposed to conduct herself with prudence and integrity'. She does indeed conduct herself with prudence and integrity throughout the whole novel which never for one moment forgets its moral intentions. Even the revelation by Lady Delacour, a brilliant leader of London society, that she is dying of cancer of the breast is used mainly as a moral lesson to point out this lady's remorse for a life of folly. The whole story of Lady Delacour's life is inserted so that the heroine can extract from it a lesson of the emptiness of worldly pleasures and Belinda duly concludes that 'if Lady Delacour, with all the advantages of wealth, rank, beauty and wit, has not been able to make herself happy in this life of fashionable dissipation . . . why should I follow the same course and expect to be more fortunate?'

Maria Edgeworth in common with other mentors of young women of that time stresses the need to be on guard lest an ill-placed attachment creep into the heart. Belinda feels that it is 'peculiarly incumbent on her to guard, not only her conduct from reproach, but her heart from the hopeless misery of an ill-placed attachment'; she therefore examines her own feelings with firm impartiality and by so doing she gives evidence of her practised skill in this form of self-examination. Recollecting the excessive pain she endured when she first heard Clarence Harvey say that Belinda Portman was a compound of art and affectation, she dismisses this as evidence of emotional danger, deciding it was only 'the pain of offended pride of proper pride'.

The results of faulty education were naturally excellent

45

material for Miss Edgeworth, and in *Angelina, or l'Amie In-connue* (*Moral Tales,* 1801) she shows the effect on the heroine Angelina Warwick, of 'certain mistakes in her education' committed by her father and mother 'who cultivated her literary taste but who neglected to cultivate her judgment: her reading was confined to works of imagination; and the conversation which she heard was not calculated to give her any knowledge of realities'. At a circulating library Angelina finds a new novel called *The Woman of Genius* whose heroine charms her beyond measure. She seeks out the author but is bitterly disillusioned. Eventually under the friendly and judicious care of Lady Frances Somerset, one of the sensible titled ladies who were anxious to provide guidance for Miss Edgeworth's heroines, Angelina acquired 'that which is more useful to the possessor than genius—good sense'. The story ends with the comforting statement that 'we have now, in the name of Angelina Warwick, the pleasure to assure all those whom it may concern, that it is possible for a young lady of sixteen years to cure herself of the affectation of sensibility, and the folly of romance'.

Maria Edgeworth's young ladies moved in more sophisticated circles than those of Jane Austen but they were expected to see fashionable follies for what they were and to avoid them. They were assisted either by examples of what not to do, or by good advice, but the effort after improvement had to be made by themselves. If they lived good and useful lives their own happiness would inevitably follow. Miss Edgeworth's experience of emotion was very limited but she did feel deeply about the importance of the education of women and the value of the work of governesses to the welfare of the community. Her type of superior girl, 'so rational, so prudent, so well-behaved, so free from silly romantic notions, so replete with solid information',[6] was the ideal towards which very many English educators worked. No longer can Ruskin's pronouncement that 'all Miss Edgeworth has ever written is eternal and classic literature—of the eternal as much as Carlyle—as much as Homer'[7] be read without amazement, but that it could be said at all is a measure of the great influence she had on those who were interested in the education of women.

Jane Austen

Jane Austen's view of the role of women was, like Fanny Burney's and Maria Edgeworth's, far from revolutionary but she looked beyond the code of behaviour into the values upon which that code had been based and which gave it deeper meaning. It was by these more searching standards that she judged the women in her novels, that is, by the genuine ideals of the eighteenth-century Christian gentlewoman. Although these ideals were widely accepted and lip service was constantly paid to them, to live by them without compromise and hypocrisy was difficult indeed; it was a life lived under the guidance of strict principles. These included the principle of self-discipline and, as an aid to this and to self-knowledge, the practice of self-examination as set out, for example, in the widely-read handbook on *Self-Knowledge* by John Mason and in Mrs Chapone's instructions on 'the regulation of the heart and affections' and 'the government of the temper'. Such disciplines were required of all men and women of Christian integrity living in a Christian society but Jane Austen explored their application in depth chiefly in her women characters whose ways of life were so familiar to her. That she herself practised daily self-examination may be deduced from her evening prayers, in which she says: 'May we now, and on each return of night, consider how the past day has been spent by us, what have been our prevailing thoughts, words and actions during it, and how far we can acquit ourselves of evil.'[8] Certainly those of Jane Austen's characters who meet with her own approval aimed at these ideals even if their performances faltered from time to time. They graced all their sensitive goodness, however, with wit and elegance of mind. Jane Austen vitalized, refined and enchantingly embodied these high standards in the characters of Elizabeth Bennet, Elinor Dashwood, Fanny Price, Emma Woodhouse, Anne Elliot. They possessed the endowments which, according to Gisborne, formed 'the glory of the female sex' and which he describes as follows:

Were we called upon to produce examples of the most amiable tendencies and affections implanted in human nature, of modesty, of delicacy, of sympathizing sensibility, of prompt and active

47

benevolence, of warmth and tenderness of attachments; whither should we at once turn our eyes? To the sister, to the daughter, to the wife. These endowments form the glory of the female sex. They shine amidst the darkness of uncultivated barbarism; they give to civilized society its brightest and most attractive lustre.[9]

It was Gisborne also who drew attention to the dangers of sensibility, including its nurturing of unmerited attachments, its inclination to look for a degree of affection, perhaps of sudden affection, from friends and acquaintances, which could not reasonably be expected, its tendency, under the impulse of groundless disappointments, to resent rather than cordially to accept the manifestations of sincere and rational regard, and, again, its inability in some instances of maternal fondness to discern the faults of children. Some of these excesses are, of course, worked out in *Sense and Sensibility* (1811), where Marianne Dashwood's sensibility is contrasted with Elinor's strength of understanding, coolness of judgment, and knowledge of how to govern her own strong feelings.

When Elinor is surprised at Marianne's giving to Willoughby, although not engaged to him, 'the most pointed assurance of her affections', she ventures, following the code so often stressed by Fanny Burney, to suggest the propriety of self-command. Marianne's opposite point of view is however fairly and persuasively put, although its inherent dangers are meant to be recognized by the reader: 'she abhorred all concealment where no real disgrace could attend unreserve; and to aim at the restraint of sentiments which were not in themselves illaudable, appeared to her not merely an unnecessary effort, but a disgraceful subjection of reason to commonplace and mistaken notions' (Ch. 11). Gradually the wisdom of the more conventional conduct is pointed out by her sister. Another example of Marianne's imprudence is her visit to Allenham, which leads very soon to impertinent remarks from Mrs Jennings; it is not however such remarks that cause her to see her action as imprudent; only through the sympathetic understanding by Elinor of her sister's temperament is the latter induced to realize her own indiscretion. After Willoughby's unexplained departure Elinor thinks 'with the tenderest compassion of that violent sorrow which Marianne was in all probability not merely giving way to as a relief, but feeding and encouraging as a duty'. Marianne is 'without any power, because she was without any desire of command over herself'; 'she would have thought herself very inexcusable had she been able to sleep at all the first night after parting from Willoughby, and she would have been ashamed to look her family in the face the next morning, had she not risen from her bed more in need of repose than when she lay down on it'. The gentle humour is more telling than any precepts. This 'indulgence of feeling' and 'nourishment of grief' is practised every day, nor will Mrs Dashwood help the situation by asking Marianne whether she is or is not engaged to Willoughby, for 'common-sense, common care, common prudence', are all sunk in 'Mrs Dashwood's romantic delicacy'.

Another weakness of Marianne's character is censured directly, her tendency, characteristic of excessive sensibility, to judge others by the effect of their actions upon herself; the incident used to show this fault is the one where Mrs Jennings, governed by an impulse of the utmost goodwill, hands Marianne a letter from her mother with a remark which leads Marianne to expect it to be an apology from Willoughby; this action sinks Mrs Jennings still lower in Marianne's estimation because 'through her own weakness, it chanced to prove a source of fresh pain to herself'. There is a parallel letter-incident for Elinor when Lucy Steele takes Edward's letter out of her pocket——Elinor 'was almost overcome—her heart sunk within her, and she could hardly stand; but exertion was indispensably necessary, and she struggled so resolutely against the oppression of her feelings that her success was speedy, and for the time complete'. The reference to the ring is greeted with 'a composure of voice under which was concealed an emotion and distress beyond anything she had ever felt before. She was mortified, shocked, confounded', but fortunately the visit is not long, the Miss Steeles return to the Park and Elinor is then 'at liberty to think and be wretched'. From her nearest and dearest she knows she will receive no assistance; she must be her own comforter, she must have higher standards and greater inner strength than those around her. 'She was stronger alone, and her own good sense so well supported her, that her firmness was unshaken, her appearance of cheerfulness as invariable, as, with regrets so poignant and so fresh, it was possible for them to be.'

Elinor also possesses an 'address', tact and imagination in dealing with other people which 'Marianne would never condescend to practise' and by its exercise she is able to gain her own end and to please Lady Middleton at the same time, an achievement that Marianne could certainly not equal in her dealings with Mrs Jennings.

But self-command is no easy virtue and Elinor has had to pay a price for hers in personal suffering and effort; the sources of her strength must be explained. In reply to Marianne's question as to how she has been supported during the four months after hearing of Edward's engagement to Lucy, Elinor says:

By feeling that I was doing my duty. My promise to Lucy obliged me to be secret. I owed it to her, therefore, to avoid giving any hint of the truth; and I owed it to my family and friends not to create in them a solicitude about me, which it could not be in my power to satisfy. . . .

'Four months! and yet you loved him!'

'Yes, but I did not love only him; and while the comfort of others was dear to me, I was glad to spare them from knowing how much I felt.' (Ch. 37)

And she continues, pointing out to Marianne that the composure of mind she now has and the consolation she has been willing to admit, 'did not spring up of themselves' but have been 'the effect of constant and painful exertion'.

A further source of Elinor's strength lies in the self-discipline of facing facts with all their implications, of examining steadily all that her lot in life seems to demand of her. 'When I see him again', she says to herself, as the door shuts Edward out, 'I shall see him the husband of Lucy.' And with this anticipation she sits down to reconsider the past, recall the words and endeavour to comprehend all the feelings of Edward, and, of course, to reflect on her own way of adjustment to the future. With an even more probing understanding of the task before the woman of integrity in such a situation, Jane Austen says:

Elinor now found the difference between the expectation of an unpleasant event, however certain the mind may be told to consider it, and certainty itself. She now found, that in spite of herself, she had always admitted a hope, while Edward remained single, that something would occur to prevent his marrying Lucy; that some resolution of his own, some mediation of friends, or some eligible opportunity of establishment for the lady, would arise to assist the happiness of all. But he was now married, and she condemned her heart for the lurking flattery which so much heightened the pain of the intelligence. (Ch. 48)

This moral power reverberates in an eighteenth-century harmony to the similar notes in Christina Rossetti's rigorous facing of hopeless love.

The habit of serious reflection and consideration for others in place of concentration upon the self alone can be learnt and practised. Marianne seems calmer when she returns home after her illness, and Elinor

who had seen her, week after week, so constantly suffering, oppressed by anguish of heart which she had neither courage to speak of, nor fortitude to conceal, now saw, with a joy which no other could equally share, an apparent composure of mind, which in being the result as she trusted of serious reflection, must eventually lead her to contentment and cheerfulness. (Ch. 46)

Yet Marianne's generosity of feeling has its virtues as well as its excesses and her exposition of her change of heart is repentance and confession on an ample scale. Her illness has given her leisure to see her conduct as it really was, the pain it caused her mother and her sister and the ingratitude it had shown for the unceasing kindness of Mrs Jennings. The account is added up item by item and the indication it gives of the deep trust and friendship between the two sisters sounds a strong overtone in its effect.

Self-command is necessary even in times of joy and composure must be preserved even when the agitation is caused by happiness. When Elinor learns that Edward is free, Lucy having married another,

she was oppressed, she was overcome by her own felicity; and happily disposed as is the human mind to be easily familiarized with any change for the better, it required several hours to give sedateness to her spirits, or any degree of tranquillity to her heart. (Ch. 49)

On a different level, Jane Austen leaves no doubt about the equally high standards a lady should require of herself for 'real elegance and artlessness'. Lucy Steele exemplifies the opposite, the false standard that *seems* rather than *is*, 'the thorough want of delicacy, of rectitude and integrity of mind' when insincerity is joined with ignorance. The shortcomings of the more fashionable ladies, Lady Middleton and Mrs John Dashwood, are also analysed: 'there was a kind of coldhearted selfishness on both sides, which mutually attracted them; and they sympathized with each other in an insipid propriety of demeanour, and a general want of understanding' (Ch. 34). The disqualifications for being socially agreeable are specifically set out as 'want of sense, either natural or improved—want of elegance—want of spirits—or want of temper'.

In *Sense and Sensibility* the faults and virtues of two women are contrasted; in *Pride and Prejudice* (1813) the faults of pride in a man and prejudice in a woman are both examined. The possibility that the title was suggested by a passage in *Cecilia* and that Mr Darcy's excessive pride of birth echoes that of the Delvile family is only important here as another example of the indebtedness of Jane Austen to her contemporary women writers, her 'book-built' approach to her early novels, but Elizabeth Bennet is much more than an anti-Cecilia heroine.

The different attitudes to marriage adopted by the chief female characters in *Pride and Prejudice* reflect the shallowness or depth of the whole woman. The lowest is exemplified in Lydia, the flirt, and the highest in Elizabeth, who will only marry where she both loves and esteems; the attitudes of Charlotte Lucas with her clear-sighted opportunism, and Jane Bennet, affectionate but not too percipient nor critical, lie between these extremes. Describing these views of marriage in another way, one may say that they stand at varying distances from the despicable baseness of 'acting by design' in such matters, that is, the unworthy determination to get a husband, any husband, and to get him by any means.

Charlotte Lucas's engagement to Mr Collins is closely examined. Elizabeth's and Charlotte's differing viewpoints on all aspects of courtship and marriage begin to manifest themselves when Elizabeth notices that Bingley admires Jane: it is evident to her sister that Jane is in a way to be very much in love but Elizabeth draws pleasure from the fact that it was not likely to be discovered by others, since Jane's composure will guard her from the 'suspicions of the impertinent'. Charlotte on the contrary reveals that she considers it a disadvantage for a woman to conceal too closely her affection from the object of it; she also feels that Elizabeth's insistence on Jane's learning to understand Bingley's character is mistaken, since she believes that 'happiness in marriage is entirely a matter of chance'. To this Elizabeth replies: 'You make me laugh, Charlotte, but it is not sound.' Lack of the highest standards of taste and moral judgment is a flaw in Charlotte's character contrasted with the superior excellence of Elizabeth's. It is of course a bitter blow to Elizabeth's respect for her friend to learn of her engagement to Mr Collins and, in reply to Jane's affectionate but not very penetrating defence of Charlotte, Elizabeth puts into words the basic reason for her condemnation:

You shall not defend her, though it is Charlotte Lucas. You shall not, for the sake of one individual, change the meaning of principle and integrity, nor endeavour to persuade yourself or me, that selfishness is prudence, and insensibility of danger security for happiness. (Ch. 24)

But when Elizabeth visits Charlotte, now married to Mr Collins, she reflects in the solitude of her chamber on Charlotte's degree of contentment and her composure in bearing with and guiding her egregious husband and she is forced to acknowledge that it is all done very well. The distance between the friends however cannot but be widened by this indication of the lack of comparable fineness in Charlotte's judgment and taste. Charlotte has made the best of a situation which to Elizabeth would have been intolerable. Charlotte had decided that the position of unmarried women without fortune was sufficiently unpleasant for her to prefer to accept Mr Collins 'solely from the pure and disinterested desire' of an establishment—the ironic use of the two adjectives accentuates the implied censure. Realizing that Mr Collins is neither sensible nor agreeable, that his society is irksome and his attachment to her must be imaginary, she is yet able to put these difficulties aside in order to be preserved from want in the pleasantest way open to her. Another side-light is thrown upon the author's view of Charlotte's 'prudent' behaviour when, in reply to her aunt's statement that she would be sorry to think Wickham mercenary, Elizabeth asks what is the difference in matrimonial affairs between the mercenary and the prudent motive? Where does discretion end and avarice begin?

The case of Jane Bennet is different but her view of marriage and her attitude to her lover do not reach the higher excellence of her sister's. An acknowledged beauty, with an affectionate nature and not too much discernment, she can expect, and she finally does make a happy and advantageous marriage. But Mr Bingley has 'that easiness of temper and want of proper resolution' which Elizabeth cannot think about 'without anger, hardly without contempt'. He allows himself to be diverted from his attachment to Jane without showing any real resistance. Although Jane behaves in an exemplary way under the scurvy treatment she receives from the Bingley family, Elizabeth's slight annoyance at Jane's determination to think ill of nobody in the face of the clearest evidence of the contrary is a lesser degree of the contempt the younger sister is tempted to feel for Bingley himself. Jane's part is largely a passive one; she is an example of the kind of woman who is almost bound to make a good marriage in the world's valuation of a good marriage but who is too negative to arouse very much interest in her future.

Elizabeth Bennet, of course, has chosen the more difficult path of refusing to accept a second best. Mr Darcy has solid virtues and principles and a basic strength of character which make it possible for Elizabeth to respect her marriage partner, while, by contrast, in her father's disastrous marriage no respect can dwell. The difference is poignantly expressed in Mr Bennet's advice to her when he feels she does not truly esteem Mr Darcy and cannot look up to him as a superior; he shrinks from the grief of seeing his daughter unable to esteem *her* partner in life. The reader may be permitted to feel however that Elizabeth really has more to give than Darcy to the marriage relationship just as she has in her family relationships, even with her beloved father and elder sister. Elizabeth's lively talents are part of her inheritance, she is indeed her father's daughter; but she, largely through her own energy and self-discipline, will be able to make more of her life than her father has of his. She is honest and straightforward, disclaiming emphatically the fashionable practice of 'increasing love by suspense' which Mr Collins imputes to her—'Do not consider me now as an elegant female, intending to plague you, but as a rational creature speaking the truth from her heart.' One of the sources of her strength is her practice of self-examination, an equal help to her as to Elinor Dashwood. Realizing the truth about Wickham and Darcy, she comes to her crisis of self-knowledge as do Marianne Dashwood and Emma Woodhouse, and, seeing her former pride in her own discernment as the poor self-deceiving thing it is, she exclaims 'Till this moment I never knew myself'. It is necessary for her to be alone to reconsider events in the light of this flash of self-revelation and it takes her two hours of wandering along the lane alone before she can feel able to appear as usual and repress such reflections as must make her unfit for conversation. Elizabeth uses the solitary walk to help her in her smaller social trials and to get perspective and a little healthy humour into her judgments; under the stress of conversation with Lady Catherine de Bourgh not a day went by without a solitary walk in which she might 'indulge in all the delight of unpleasant recollections'. And like Elinor Dashwood Elizabeth also needs a period of quiet even in her joy; when she has persuaded her father that she really wishes to marry Mr Darcy it is only after half-an hour's quiet reflection in her own room that she is able to join the others with tolerable composure.

In *Pride and Prejudice* the pleasure, help and consolation offered by friendship between women is again made evident in the relationship between Elizabeth and Mrs Gardner, the aunt who takes the place of the unsatisfactory mother and, of course, in the relationship between Elizabeth and Jane. But in the latter Elizabeth is the stronger of the two and she must give more comfort than she receives.

The function of Catherine Morland as an anti-heroine of the Gothic novel has often been stressed and certainly *Northanger Abbey* (published 1818 but written earlier) on its very first page

lists all the characteristics that made her as unlike as possible
to the super-human Gothic heroines. Catherine is an ordinary
young woman with a 'mind about as ignorant and uninformed
as the female mind at seventeen usually is'. When she realizes
how little she knows, as when she learns to look at the countryside through the trained eyes of the Tilneys, she is heartily
ashamed of herself. Jane Austen, referring obliquely to the
doctrines of Dr Gregory and other conservative conduct-book
writers, calls this an advantage, for 'where people wish to attach,
they should always be ignorant'; 'to come with a well-informed
mind is to come with the inability of ministering to the vanity
of others, which a sensible person would always wish to avoid',
and a woman 'especially if she have the misfortune of knowing
anything' should do her best to conceal it. She notes that the
advantages of natural folly in a beautiful girl have already been
set forth 'by the capital pen of a sister author', presumably a
reference to Indiana in Fanny Burney's *Camilla*. This touch of
asperity sets off the basically tolerant attitude to Catherine of
her creator. Catherine is an unsophisticated young woman with
insufficient knowledge of the world to recognize false friends
when she meets them and insufficient common sense to keep
Gothic horrors out of her expectations during a stay in an
eighteenth-century English country household. But she has
qualities in a young girl which are held up for genuine admiration, characteristics more important than the exaggerated
delicacy of the Gothic heroine, virtues which justify her winning,
after a necessary period of education by life itself and of increased self-knowledge (including the tears of shame she sheds
when she admits the folly of her suspicions), the love of such a
pleasant man as Henry Tilney. Her good points are an affectionate heart and a 'disposition cheerful and open, without conceit
or affectation of any kind'. These qualities are appreciated by
Henry Tilney when, after he has teased her about losing
Isabella as a friend, she shames him a little by taking his
questions at their face value and he replies, with a sudden rush
of sincere admiration: 'You feel, as you always do, what is most
to the credit of human nature. Such feelings ought to be investigated, that they may know themselves' (Ch. 25). The
suggestion that Catherine has not investigated her own feelings

is an indication of her youth and guilelessness, she is indeed 'open, candid, artless, guileless, with affections strong but simple, forming no pretensions, and knowing no disguise'. Isabella Thorpe, the young woman to whom this last description is ostensibly and ironically applied, is in truth the reverse of guileless. She is Catherine's opposite—beautiful, fashionable, informed about the ways of a certain section of the world –but she is insincere, and her shallow artifices and husband-hunting scheming are contrasted throughout the book with Catherine's honesty. Catherine cannot tell a falsehood, 'even to please Isabella', and in her candour she is triumphant, whereas Isabella's schemes are all defeated.

Eleanor Tilney, with wealth, position, good looks, taste and a good education on her side, has principles sufficiently firmly based to recognize and welcome in Catherine the natural and simple good qualities that, as her brother knows, will give her pleasure. Contrasted with Isabella, the selfish friend, Eleanor is the good woman friend. She does not even scheme, as she might well have done, to keep Catherine and her brother apart. She is a more privileged, finished and reserved Catherine and she receives the same kind of quiet approval.

The young people in this book get very little help from the older generation but those who are honest manage well and the author applauds those who are willing to learn from their mistakes and to advance in self-knowledge and self-improvement. This is a work in which sincerity and the absence of self-seeking are taken seriously enough to constitute the grounds on which ordinary young women may be considered worthy of being heroines of a novel of good manners, using that expression in its best and widest sense.

After a gap of eight years and an increase of seriousness in Jane Austen's art, whether purely personal in origin or a reflection of the more generalized evangelical seriousness already making itself felt in English society, *Mansfield Park* (1814) sounds a note with deeper harmonics than the three early novels. Lionel Trilling summarizes the essential moral judgment of the novel when he says that 'it takes full notice of spiritedness, vivacity, celerity, and lightness, but only to reject them as having nothing to do with virtue and happiness, as being, indeed, deterrents to the good life'.[10] Fanny Price lacks the attractiveness of Jane Austen's other heroines, indeed, the balance is deliberately tilted against her—she is not very pretty, her health is poor, she comes from a sordid home, she is often terrified and her spirits frequently droop, so that she gives the impression of creeping about, weeping. She is however one of those 'poor in spirit' who is enabled to see clearly both good and evil round her and she has the moral strength to act upon her own sound principles in a lax environment which is calculated to make acceptance of lowered standards almost inevitable. Fanny's standards remain high; her eye is keen and she continually passes judgment on the behaviour of those around her, acting as the conscience of the book. After watching the behaviour of Miss Bertram and Mr Crawford on their visit to Sotherton Fanny is 'again left to her solitude, and with no increase of pleasant feelings, for she was sorry for almost all that she had seen and heard, astonished at Miss Bertram, and angry with Mr Crawford' (Ch. 10), and when Henry Crawford says he was never happier than during the times they were practising theatricals Fanny repeats to herself with silent indignation, 'Never happier!—never happier than when doing what you must know was not justifiable!—never happier than when having behaved so dishonourably and unfeelingly! Oh, what a corrupted mind.'

Fanny's basic strength of character is tested to the utmost when Henry Crawford wishes to marry her and Sir Thomas Bertram endeavours to persuade her to accept him. The basic requirement for a husband by Fanny's standards is lacking. Sir Thomas asks her in a voice of authority 'Have you any reason, child, to think ill of Mr Crawford's temper?'. 'No, sir', she says, though she longs to add, 'but of his principles I have', but her heart sinks under 'the appalling prospect of discussion, explanation, and probably non-conviction'. To displease Sir Thomas seems base ingratitude for his kindness in taking her into his home, yet to marry a man without principles is against Fanny's deepest convictions and she has to stand out against it. The actual incident of Henry Crawford's falling in love with Fanny may not carry complete conviction but it gives her an unmatched opportunity to show her strength of charac-

ter in continuing to refuse a match so advantageous from the
worldly point of view, so much in accordance with the wishes
of those whom she respects and to whom she owes a debt of
gratitude and, indeed, by contemporary standards, obedience.
Her principles and steadfastness could face no harder test.

Mary Crawford has all the advantages that Fanny lacks—
good looks, cultivated taste, wit, style, vivacity, grace, warmth
—but she lacks the essential foundation of good principles. Her
conversation is fascinating and Edmund, duly bewitched,
defends her against Fanny when the latter asks him what right
Miss Crawford has to suppose he will not write long letters when
he is absent:

The right of a lively mind, Fanny, seizing whatever may contribute
to its own amusement or that of others; perfectly allowable, when
untinctured by ill humour or roughness; and there is not a shadow of
either in the countenance or manner of Miss Crawford; nothing sharp,
or loud, or coarse. (Ch. 7)

And so Fanny has to watch Edmund fall in love with Mary. The
pain this causes her is not only on account of her own feeling
for Edmund but because she feels Mary does not deserve
Edmund. Fanny's penetrating analysis of those around her has
realized the hidden weakness of Mary's character: Fanny sees in
her, in spite of some amiable sensations, and much personal
kindness, a mind 'led astray and bewildered, and without any
suspicion of being so, darkened, yet fancying itself light'. She
believes there is scarcely a feeling in common between Mary and
Edmund and, if Edmund's influence in this season has done so
little in clearing Mary's judgment and 'regulating her notions,
his worth would be finally wasted on her even in years of
matrimony'. To the reader Mary Crawford's conversation is
fascinating and only a close study of the text reveals the insincerity, selfishness and levity behind it, yet these are clearly
evident from the first to the eyes of Fanny.

After emotional tumult, Fanny, like Miss Austen's other
heroines, needs to be alone to reflect and to re-establish her
peace of mind. After Henry Crawford's farewell visit, for instance, when he has touched her hand for the last time and made
his parting bow, 'she might seek directly all that solitude could

do for her'. Fanny's fortitude is all the more surprising because her upbringing was not one which would be likely to provide wise guidance for life. Possibly the very fact that she has been forced, although naturally timid, to find her own way in life, without comfort except for the affection of her brother, has brought out in her a hidden independence of judgment and will, uncorrupted by any compromise with the ways of the fashionable world. Although she is unused to the conventions of society, Fanny's consideration for others, based on deeper principles than mere good manners, does not allow her to let her own moods and emotions upset those who are around her. In contrast, the Misses Bertram, fashionable young ladies though they are, have no such thoughtfulness; when Miss Bertram is omitted from an invitation to the Parsonage so as to leave her free to entertain Mr Rushworth, she is vexed, and as Mr Rushworth does not come, the injury is increased: 'she had not even the relief of showing her power over him; she could only be sullen to her mother, aunt, and cousin, and throw as great a gloom as possible over their dinner and dessert'.

Concerning the double moral standard for men and women, Jane Austen permits herself in this novel an expression of opinion in the following comment on Henry Crawford's intrigue with Mrs Rushworth:

That punishment, the public punishment of disgrace, should in a just measure attend *his* share of the offence is, we know, not one of the barriers which society gives to virtue. In this world the penalty is less equal than could be wished; but without presuming to look forward to a juster appointment hereafter, we may fairly consider a man of sense, like Henry Crawford, to be providing for himself no small portion of vexation and regret. . . . (Ch. 48)

The criticism, so indirectly implied, is based upon the effect of the misdeed itself upon two human souls, not specifically upon the difference between the punishment meted out to women and to men. This is, of course, characteristic of Jane Austen's whole approach: there is no special pleading for women in her novels, her women are expected to accept their difficulties and to turn them into sources of moral strength. Fanny Price does this in full measure and her achievement is, in its own small domestic setting, a great moral triumph.

Women Awaiting Marriage (1)

In *Emma* (1816) the heroine's successes can scarcely be claimed as great moral triumphs. It is only through the humble Miss Bates that Emma is led to experience that moment of truth which brings to her the needful amount of painful and salutary but indispensable self-knowledge. The great Miss Woodhouse, handsome, clever, rich and admired, stoops to be rude to the bustling little woman and Miss Bates, although pained, exhibits no resentment; it is Mr Knightley's rebuke that causes Emma to see her rudeness in its true light. After the incident she

> was vexed beyond what could have been expressed—almost beyond what she could conceal. Never had she felt so agitated, mortified, grieved, at any circumstance in her life. She was most forcibly struck. The truth of his representation there was no denying. She felt it at her heart. How could she have been so brutal, so cruel, to Miss Bates! How could she have exposed herself to such ill opinions in any one she valued! And how suffer him to leave her without saying one word of gratitude, of concurrence, of common kindness! (Ch. 43)

Emma makes an amending call on Miss Bates at the earliest possible opportunity, following the dictates of her stricken conscience and her basically kind heart. As her reflections on this incident have helped her to greater self-knowledge, so later in the novel another disturbing reflection, the almost unbearable possibility of Harriet's becoming the wife of Mr Knightley, is faced in a similar way and used for self-discipline:

> the only source whence anything like consolation or composure could be drawn, was in the resolution of her own better conduct, and the hope that, however inferior in spirit and gaiety might be the following and every future winter of her life to the past, it would yet find her more rational, more acquainted with herself, and leave her less to regret when it were gone. (Ch. 48)

To strive always to be more rational, more acquainted with oneself, was the eighteenth-century ideal. How much her creator's expressed liking for Emma owes to the latter's willingness to be checked and to learn, to accept from life its lessons of 'profitable humiliation to her own mind' can only be a matter of speculation, but in this endearing willingness Emma is like a more mature Catherine Morland.

Emma shows, of course, a pleasing filial affection for her fond but most trying father. Also, as becomes a Christian gentle-woman, she relieves the distresses of the poor with genuine concern and kindness, deceived by no romantic expectations of extraordinary virtue in those for whom education has done so little and realizing that the sights she sees in the poor cottages she visits are good for her, making everything else appear trifling, and restoring her own balance of judgment.

The triumphs of Jane Fairfax were more admirable than Emma's, if less endearing. Jane has the same personal endowments as Emma—beauty, refinement and musical talent, but she has none of Emma's advantages of family and fortune. Although she makes the most of her own opportunities and shows certain excellencies of taste and behaviour that Miss Woodhouse does not approach, she lacks the important virtues of openness and candour and she even consents to a secret engagement, a most reprehensible step. In these respects she cannot receive her creator's fullest approval as an excellent woman, although a rather subdued sympathy for Jane's difficult lot can be detected.

The theme of the difference in women's destiny runs through Miss Austen's last novel and the sadness of this difference adds to the general autumnal melancholy pervading the book. *Persuasion* (1818) takes note of the factitious importance given to some women by the status accorded them by the men in their lives, either fathers or husbands: the handsome but unfeeling Elizabeth Elliot is mistress of Kellynch Hall, her sister Mary has 'acquired a little artificial importance by becoming Mrs Charles Musgrove', while Anne, whose 'elegance of mind and sweetness of character . . . must have placed her high with any people of real understanding' is 'nobody with either father or sister; her word had no weight, her convenience was always to give way—she was only Anne'. Still unmarried at twenty-seven and living with a family both vain and unfeeling, she must submit to the constant opportunities for self-discipline on a small scale that are provided by her normal social life, as when, during her visit to Uppercross, her sister and brother-in-law show their basic lack of interest in affairs at Kellynch and, although Anne already knows this from past experience, 'she believed she must now submit to feel that another lesson, in the art of knowing our own nothingness beyond our own circle, was become necessary for her' (Ch. 6). Such a woman is also handicapped by the restricted life she has to lead and the effect of such restriction on her emotional state. The conversation in which Anne discusses women's constancy with Captain Harville underlines this point: she considers it women's fate rather than their merit that they do not forget men as rapidly as men forget women they have loved: 'We cannot help ourselves. We live at home, quiet, confined, and our feelings prey upon us'; she points in contrast to the professions and business which take men back into the world and help them to forget. Yet she is fair enough to allow that with all the labour and toil to which men are exposed it would perhaps be too hard if women's feelings were added to all this: 'All the privilege I claim for my own sex (it is not a very enviable one; you need not covet it), is that of loving longest, when existence or when hope is gone'.

Some years before, Anne's reliance on the judgment of an older woman had caused her to break off an engagement with Frederick Wentworth but she had not, she could not have, forgotten him. 'She had been forced into prudence in her youth, she learned romance as she grew older—the natural sequel of an unnatural beginning.' Because of this unnatural beginning the now faded young woman has a doubly difficult battle for command when the same man comes back into her life and seems to find her sadly changed. Jane Austen describes in detail the efforts which a woman of Anne's integrity *must* make in such circumstances.

Many a stroll and many a sigh were, of course, necessary to dispel the agitation of the very idea that Captain Wentworth's sister was likely to come to live at Kellynch but it is in connection with Captain Wentworth's own visit that the greatest demands on Anne's self-control are made, commencing with the necessity to inure herself to hear people talking so much about him. The ordeal is worse when they actually meet. After the first time they have been together in the same room she begins to reason with herself and to try to feel less; she regards the passage of eight years as rationally as she can, working out how much change it must bring, measuring the fact that it has included nearly a third part of her own life:

Alas! with all her reasonings she found that to retentive feelings eight years may be little more than nothing. Now, how were his sentiments to be read? Was this like wishing to avoid her? And the next moment she was hating herself for the folly which asked the question. (Ch. 7)

The knife is turned in the wound when Mary tells her that Frederick has found her greatly altered, but she uses even this adversity to brace her spirits:

So altered that he should not have known her again! These were words which could not but dwell with her. Yet she soon began to rejoice that she had heard them. They were of sobering tendency. They allayed agitation; they composed, and consequently must make her happier. (Ch. 7)

The efforts have to continue, the battle has to be refought after every fresh incident. She is quite ashamed of herself for being overcome by agitation when Captain Wentworth thoughtfully removes a troublesome child who is teasing her, 'but so it was, and it required a long application of solitude and reflection to recover her'.

The walk with Captain Wentworth and the Miss Musgroves calls for heroic efforts at self-command without the help of solitude; Anne's object is not to be in the way of anybody and to keep with her brother and sister:

Her *pleasure* in the walk must arise from the exercise and the day, from the view of the last smiles of the year upon the tawny leaves and withered hedges, and from repeating to herself some few of the thousand poetical descriptions extant of autumn, that season of peculiar and inexhaustible influence on the mind of taste and tenderness. . . . She occupied her mind as much as possible in such like musings and quotations; but it was not possible that, when within reach of Captain Wentworth's conversation with either of the Miss Musgroves, she should not try to hear it. . . . (Ch. 10)

The literary medicine for a broken heart which she prescribes for Captain Bentwich was doubtless the same as she had found to be efficacious for herself: she hopes he did not only read poetry, since it could seldom be safely enjoyed by those with strong feelings, and she recommends rather such 'works of our best moralists, such memoirs of characters of worth and suffering as occurred to her . . . as calculated to rouse and fortify the mind by the highest precepts'. If there is irony in the stilted words it is surely brought about by the difficulty of the cure to which such medicine should contribute, not by any flippancy about the sickness.

Even after Captain Bentwich's engagement to Louisa Musgrove is known and Frederick Wentworth is thus left free, Anne is on guard against the temptation of hope:

It was not regret which made Anne's heart beat in spite of herself, and brought the colour into her cheeks when she thought of Captain Wentworth unshackled and free. She had some feelings which she was ashamed to investigate. They were too much like joy, senseless joy! (Ch. 18)

And when she meets Frederick in Bath she is still battling for wisdom; 'she hoped to be wise and reasonable in time; but alas! she must confess to herself that she was not wise yet'. The uncertainties and the subsequent renewed efforts at self-discipline continue after hope has begun to dawn; even over the invitation to the party when others were reckoning his coming as certain, 'with her it was a gnawing solicitude never appeased for five minutes together'. When all is explained and happiness is to be hers she re-enters the house feeling obliged to find an alloy to her joy in some momentary apprehension of its being impossible to last: 'an interval of meditation, serious and grateful, was the best corrective of everything dangerous in such high-wrought felicity; and she went to her room and grew steadfast and fearless in the thankfulness of her enjoyment' (Ch. 23). The composure attained by such courageous facing of the inner truth of any situation and by the exercise of such self-command in every adjustment to that truth was not only to be used by a woman for her own benefit but also for the happiness of those around her. After reading the details of Anne's struggles no one could imagine that the prize of inner poise was easily attained, or that Miss Austen's ideal woman possessed no deeper qualities than vivacity, affection, a playful sense of the foibles of society, and an ironic intelligence.

As Jane Austen's heroines lived in novels they had their rewards within the pages of the books and fate brought them for their life companions such men as Mr Knightley, Edmund Bertram, Captain Wentworth, Henry Tilney, Mr Darcy. In the estimation of the eighteenth-century upper-middle-class circles in which the girls moved, which placed much emphasis on suitable family alliances and on settlements counted in tens of thousands of pounds, these were good matches—one at least was a great match. It was more important to Jane Austen however that these men had characters worthy of such wives, that they were gentlemen of principle and integrity. Money and family status are never ignored in Miss Austen's novels but are tacitly accepted in the background as facts of social life which it is not her concern to criticize. Such facts are used to throw light on the central preoccupation of the books, the characters of the parties concerned. Mr Darcy, in spite of his wealth and exalted connections, wins a wife whose personal worth equals if not exceeds his own; Willoughby, for whom Marianne's portion was too small, makes a worse bargain with his £50,000 heiress, and only John Dashwood could be so obtuse as to say to Elinor that for Miss Morton there could be no difference between marrying Edward or marrying Robert, once Robert is considered as the eldest son. Irony comes into play whenever money is mentioned and alerts the reader to look for future enlightenment. When *Mansfield Park* opens with the statement that 'Miss Maria Ward of Huntingdon, with only seven thousand pounds, had the good luck to captivate Sir Thomas Bertram', it is an indication that the captivation *was* more lucky for Miss Ward than for Sir Thomas, and the novel goes on to prove this by revealing Lady Bertram's shortcomings as a mother who totally neglects the moral training of her daughters.

The differences in her heroines illustrate how Jane Austen high-lighted certain of the qualities in a woman which she deemed admirable and such as would enable their possessor to fulfil the role of a lady with both taste and tenderness. It was evidently to her a most excellent thing in woman to have wit and character and style, but these should be rooted and grounded in firm principles of moral conduct. Where charm and personal discipline are combined, though not without the dust and heat of adjustment to difficult circumstances, we have the most successful of her heroines, Elizabeth Bennet and Emma Woodhouse, 'the best of womanhood, as endearing to women as to men'.[11] The graces are less brilliantly embodied in Anne Elliot, with her resignation so hardly won, and in Catherine Morland, guileless and fresh but as yet unformed in character. The least successful is possibly the apparently priggish Fanny Price, contrasted with the fascinating Mary Crawford. Mary on close examination is an example of the type of woman who cultivates the outward style of sensitivity, vivacity and intelligence without the firmly based principles needed to support the structure under stress, without the inner discipline, clear moral judgment and continual exertion required to make the heroine the guardian of her own repose. As well as lacking principle Mary lacked tenderness of heart, and it will be recalled that Emma considered there was no charm equal to that; Fanny, wanting the vitality and health of Elizabeth and Emma, yet has abundant tenderness.

As Jane Austen saw women their role required of them that they should learn to govern themselves, control their tempers, master their feelings, exercise fortitude, cultivate sound understanding, be realistic, clear-sighted and considerate in personal and social relationships, avoid excesses of sensibility for sensibility's sake, cultivate taste and elegance of mind and manners, and, with all this, have tenderness of heart. For most of them it could not be a life that was a 'model of right feminine happiness' such as was the lot of Isabella Knightley, who 'passed her life with those she doted on, full of their merits, blind to their faults, and always innocently busy'; this was not to be a woman of full stature. A more admirable way was one more closely in touch with reality which must be faced and accepted. A danger to be avoided was any descent to the level of the second-rate and the goal to be attained was to maintain high standards within a milieu composed of very ordinary companions

The values that Jane Austen upheld and the guidelines for

behaviour that she so subtly laid down are fundamentally the same as we have found in her contemporaries, although she penetrates more deeply into their meaning and potentialities. The wonder of her achievement lies in her full realization and embodiment of these qualities in young women of such enchantment and grace.

To some it is a matter for regret that Jane Austen did not range a little more widely in her novels: the road of evil is never explored, although Sylvia Townsend Warner[12] suggests that 'in controlled grimness' *Lady Susan* looks forward to 'a masterpiece never written', yet the nineteen-sixties may regret this omission more than an age less accustomed to horror in literature. And not only did Miss Austen never go outside her class, she did not include a place for the many servants who must have formed part of the life of those large country houses. Even within the limits of her own class, the story of an unmarried woman, unrewarded by a Captain Wentworth as husband, might have been considered well within her scope and her personal experience, but Miss Bates, although a kindly portrait, is not a major one, Jane Fairfax has Frank Churchill in the background, and even Miss Taylor is married off to Mr Weston before the novel begins. One is forced to the conclusion that the social environment of the Austen novels could make no place for a 'new woman'. As Fanny Burney's *Wanderer* so clearly shows, the perfect eighteenth-century lady was lost if her sheltered background was shattered by change. The exquisite picture on the famous piece of ivory could not be transferred to a wider canvas or painted in new pigments. The perfection of the Austen novels as they stand allowed no further advance, they were not just a reflection of an age but a crystallization of one part of it, complete and unalterable.

5

Women Awaiting Marriage (2)

The Brontë sisters, Elizabeth Gaskell, George Eliot

THE YEARS following Jane Austen's early death were a time of social readjustment after the Napoleonic wars and of preparation for the age of reform that was to come, and the 1820s and 1830s afforded a breathing space in women's contribution to the strongest tradition of the English novel. The women who wrote during these years were not powerful novelists but pleasant poetesses engaging in the unquestionably lady-like occupation of writing verse or producing graceful sketches such as Mary Russell Mitford's vignettes of village life. The decade of the 'thirties offered a rich market for verse in the popular keepsakes and annuals then appearing on the market; they had the double attraction of paying high fees for the effusions they published and of being edited by ladies of title in some cases. Mrs Hemans and L.E.L., 'the English Sappho', were particularly successful in this kind of exercise and they were held in esteem both for the graceful sentiments they expressed and the technical skill of their presentation; at the same time a more truly poetic talent, that of Elizabeth Barrett Browning, was beginning to earn more solid respect for poetry written by women. Following current fashion even the Brontës' first published volume was the *Poems* of Currer, Ellis and Acton Bell, but they had served an apprenticeship in Angria and Gondal that was to lead them to make the most startling of the Victorian contributions to novels written by women. In conflict with the eighteenth-century belief that it was dangerous for women to dwell upon their powerful feelings and that reputable novels should help women to control their passions, the Brontë sisters gave

69

intense expression to these emotions, the intensity rising steeply from Anne through Charlotte to Emily.

Anne Brontë

Anne Brontë's spiritual distance from the eighteenth-century tradition of women's novels was the shortest; her work belonged to those novels of manners with serious moral intentions behind them, but her milieu was that of a new age and her experience that of a working governess fighting her battles outside the shelter of her own home, facing the problems of the early Victorian young lady grappling with the world in its harsh reality. In her first novel *Agnes Grey* (1847), which her sister Charlotte stated was 'the mirror of the mind of the writer',[1] the professional and social difficulties of a young governess in two successive posts in contrasted households are fully explored. Her social difficulties are caused by the snobbery, stupidity and unkindness of her employers and their unpleasant children and by her own feelings of disappointment, loneliness and isolation, and her sense of physical inferiority. The Brontës gave much agonized thought to the difficulties of plain women and the occasion when Agnes spends some time before her mirror is the opportunity for a long soliloquy on the difficulty of adjusting to plainness; it is worked out in a manner that has considerable poignancy and suggests that the writer had fully explored this topic:

They that have beauty, let them be thankful for it, and make a good use of it, like any other talent: they that have it not, let them console themselves, and do the best they can without it—certainly, though liable to be overestimated, it is a gift of God, and not to be despised. Many will feel this, who have felt that they could love, and whose hearts tell them they are worthy to be loved again, while yet they are debarred, by the lack of this, or some such seeming trifle from giving and receiving that happiness they seem almost made to feel and to impart. As well might the humble glow-worm despise the power of giving light, without which, the roving fly might pass her and repass her a thousand times, and never light beside her; she might hear her winged darling buzzing over and around her; he vainly seeking her, she longing to be found, but with no power to

make her presence known, no voice to call him, no wings to follow
his flight . . . the fly must seek another mate, the worm must live
and die alone. (Ch. 17)

After this it is only fair to point out that Agnes's second post at
Horton Lodge does give her the opportunity of meeting her
future husband, the local curate.

In contrast with the hard life facing the young Agnes at the
Lodge we are shown the advantages enjoyed by the Murray
daughters. Of the two girls, Rosalie and Matilda, the first is a
flirt—at seventeen everything else began to give way to the
ruling passion, the all absorbing ambition to attract and dazzle
the other sex—the second is a hoyden who, following her
father's example, has learnt to swear like a trooper. The
dialogues between Agnes and these girls provide opportunities
for demure amusement and irony while Anne Brontë's impatience with affectation and her moral judgment on the
frivolity of these teenagers are obvious but not overstressed;
the dialogue allows them to be condemned out of their own
mouths.

A greater measure of courage to write with realism was
demonstrated in Anne Brontë's picture of marriage to a dipso-
maniac in her *succès de scandale*, *The Tenant of Wildfell Hall*
(1848). Helen is an ideal womanly woman, beautiful, loving,
fervent, intelligent and earnest. Although her aunt warns her
against Arthur, she falls a comparatively easy prey to his
charming manners and dashing courtship, saying that 'there
was a certain graceful ease and freedom about all he said and
did, that gave a sense of repose and expansion to the mind, after
so much constraint and formality as I have been doomed to
suffer'. She does have some moments of doubt, wishing that
Arthur could be serious sometimes: 'I don't mind it *now*, but
if it should always be so, what shall I do with the serious part
of myself?', but she also holds the dangerous belief that she can
reform Arthur, an error of judgment about that 'woman's
influence' in which so many Victorian women put their faith.
Her disillusion in her marriage must wait for a later chapter of
this study.

Charlotte Brontë

Of all the Brontës, Charlotte made the strongest impact on her contemporaries, and here indeed was a writer to startle the early Victorians. *Jane Eyre* (1847) was published in the same year as Tennyson's *Princess* and the climate was favourable for theoretical discussions of the higher education of women, but Charlotte Brontë's revelation was of the frustrations and rebellions and terrible strength of women's passions. George Sand's early novels had described such passions, but the fact that she was a Frenchwoman distanced the uncomfortable disclosures. Lady Eastlake's famous review of *Jane Eyre* in which she declares that the book, if it be written by a woman, must be by one who for some sufficient reason had long forfeited the society of her own sex, is not, except for the ferocity of its expression, very remote from the reaction of large numbers of Charlotte's fellow-countrywomen. Harriet Martineau's view of Charlotte Brontë may be quoted as more level-headed, when, in her review of *Villette*,[2] she says that 'all the female characters, in all their thoughts and lives, are full of one thing, or are regarded by the reader in the light of that one thought—love' and she goes on to point out that the reader is under the uncomfortable impression that the heroine has either entertained a double love, or allowed one to supersede another without notification of the transition. Charlotte Brontë herself believed that, since such deep and powerful feelings as she described were of paramount importance to her, they were of equal importance to all women, and she clung tenaciously to her conviction that her own standards in these matters were absolute ones. In a letter to Miss Martineau she said:

I *know* what love is as I understand it; and if man or woman should be ashamed of feeling such love, then is there nothing right, noble, faithful, truthful, unselfish in this earth, as I comprehend rectitude, nobleness, fidelity, truth and disinterestedness.[3]

It was the singular intensity of her feelings which imparted to her novels their power, undimmed after a hundred years and, since such states of feeling were indeed true in the experience of many women, if not all, and since they had not been expressed until then, they needed to be described in art in its function of exploring the nature of human beings. Certain passages in a few earlier novels, including Harriet Martineau's own *Deerbrook* (1839), had given a suggestion of burning coals of feeling but only the transmuting power of Charlotte Brontë made them fire an entire novel. The hostile reception given to *Jane Eyre* strengthened her determination to 'bend as my powers tend— I must have my own way in the matter of writing—I am thankful to God, who gave me the faculty; and it is for me part of my religion to defend this gift, and to profit by its possession'.[4] It was by this intensity and dedication that she effected what has been called a 'displacement' of the English novel, raising it to a new power.

The fervent romanticism of *Jane Eyre* had not yet fully blossomed in the novel written earlier, *The Professor* (published 1857), whose subdued tone is more reminiscent of *Agnes Grey* than any other of Charlotte's works. It depicts however a type of woman that was to be Charlotte's special contribution to the heroine of the English novel—intelligent, independent, ardent but controlled, conscious of her own individuality, one to whom Charlotte gives her just deserts in the form of a suitable lover, in spite of her lack of beauty in the accepted sense of the term and in spite of her dynamic qualities in an age that admired female passivity. Crimsworth finds such a woman in his pupil Frances. He hates 'that boldness which is of the brassy brow and insensate nerves', but he loves 'the courage of the strong heart, the fervour of the generous blood'. Although such statements may carry little conviction as likely to come from a young man they obviously express the views of the novelist herself. The description goes on for some time, ending in appreciation of Frances as the 'silent possessor of a well of tenderness, of a flame, as genial as still, as pure as quenchless, of natural feeling, natural passion —those sources of refreshment and comfort to the sanctuary of home.'

The setting of *The Professor* was foreign and the heroine herself only half English but in *Jane Eyre* Miss Brontë created an Englishwoman with similar views, presenting new ideas about woman's position in the English social fabric. Jane, poor but independent, convinces Rochester that she has as much mind and soul as he has, with considerably more heart, and that she need not sell her soul to buy happiness—she can earn her own living and her inner strength will sustain her so that she need not sink below her own standards of behaviour. The book is a plea for a more vivid and satisfying life for women; Jane expresses this with fervour when she says:

It is in vain to say human beings ought to be satisfied with tranquillity: they must have action; and they will make it if they cannot find it. Millions are condemned to a stiller doom than mine, and millions are in silent revolt against their lot. Nobody knows how many rebellions besides political rebellions ferment in the masses of life which people earth. Women are supposed to be very calm generally: but women feel just as men feel; they need exercise for their faculties, and a field for their efforts as much as their brothers do; they suffer from too rigid a restraint, too absolute a stagnation, precisely as men would suffer; and it is too narrow-minded in their privileged fellow-creatures to say that they ought to confine themselves to making puddings and knitting stockings, to playing on the piano and embroidering bags. It is thoughtless to condemn them, or laugh at them if they seek to do more or learn more than custom has pronounced necessary for their sex. (Ch. 12)

She even welcomed for its activity the seemingly small incident of helping Rochester when his horse slipped on the ice: 'trivial, transitory though the deed was, it was yet an active thing, and I was weary of an existence all passive.' This resembles the rebellion against a life of sheltered triviality, although on a different social level, which in Florence Nightingale's active and practical personality found expression in organizing the nursing services for the Crimean War.

Just as women need exercise for their faculties and a field for their efforts as much as their brothers do, so in the relationship of love two human souls are also equal, in spite of custom and convention: Jane passionately proclaims this to Rochester in the well-known passage which ends: 'I am not talking to you now through the medium of custom, conventionalities, nor even of mortal flesh:—it is my spirit that addresses your spirit; just as if both had passed through the grave, and we stood at God's feet, equal—as we are!' (Ch. 23).

The kind of relentless self-examination to which Charlotte

Brontë's heroines subject themselves differs from that practised by Jane Austen's. The stress is on putting a stop to
indulgence in foolish hopes and exalted expectations rather than
on achieving a reasonable equanimity. It is self-chastisement
rather than an ordering of the mind by calm consideration.
When Jane Eyre finds herself day-dreaming about Rochester's
liking for her, she arraigns herself at her own bar in harsh terms:
'Blind puppy!—Go! your folly sickens me.—Poor stupid dupe!'
She forces herself to make two drawings, one in chalk of her own
plain face and one, on smooth ivory, of the beautiful Blanche
Ingram, and to compare them so that she can weigh the
probability of Rochester's taking any notice of a governess,
'disconnected, poor and plain' when he could win the noble
lady's love. She says that she had reason to congratulate herself 'on the course of wholesome discipline to which I had thus
forced my feelings to submit'; but the method carries within it
elements of excess.

Shirley (1849) can almost be regarded as an artificially contrived vehicle for the expression of Charlotte Brontë's views on
the intellectual and emotional privations of women. Dr J. M. S.
Tompkins has suggested that Charlotte changed her intentions
about Caroline Helstone at a certain stage in this novel.[5]
Caroline seems originally to have been designed for the single
life but, because of the death of Anne Brontë with whom
Caroline has been identified, her sister felt she could not treat
her less lovingly than she had treated Emily in the guise of
Shirley Keeldar and she allotted to both of them the happy
marriages that life had denied their models. Certainly such an
hypothesis explains why the elaborate preparation for Caroline
to live out her life as an old maid is largely wasted by Robert
Moore's change of mind; it might also explain the unexpected
introduction of Robert's brother, Louis, to be paired off rather
unevenly with Shirley. The old maid theme is definitely stressed
in the early part of the book. When Caroline Helstone is facing
the possibility of old maidhood she discusses with Shirley the
wish that they could have a profession, something absorbing and
compulsory to fill their heads and hands and to occupy their
thoughts: they go on to the question of whether 'hard labour
and learned professions' make women 'masculine, coarse,

unwomanly'. The solution does not lie, either, in becoming a governess: Mrs Pryor explains to Caroline the humiliations of a governess's life with all the bitterness of personal experience. Caroline is able to find some help and relief in her appreciation of poetry and in discussing Cowper's *Castaway* with Shirley she states her belief that the gift of poetry, the 'most divine bestowed on man' was granted 'to allay emotions when their strength threatens harm'. But her efforts to achieve contentment with her lot are unsuccessful and she grows more joyless and wan. Her emotional longings are stronger than the methods she uses to still and sublimate them.

It is however not so much the loss of Robert Moore that makes life so difficult for Caroline as the lack of *any* kind of love in her life, and it is the discovery of her mother that really restores her to health and quiet happiness. She would have had to face the rigours of old maidhood without either the possibility of sublimation in work or the comfort and strength of family affection and the feeling of being needed by somebody. Mrs Pryor cannot supply the work but she supplies the affection and the purpose.

Another familiar perplexity for women is touched on in *Shirley*, the difficulty of deciding a man's 'intentions' when his moods change and there is no real understanding between the lovers. On the morning after the evening when Caroline and Robert had seemed so close to each other she finds his manner has altered:

A lover masculine so disappointed can speak and urge explanation; a lover feminine can say nothing: if she did, the result would be shame and anguish, inward remorse for self-treachery. Nature would brand such demonstration as a rebellion against her instincts, and would vindictively repay it afterwards by the thunderbolts of self-contempt smiting suddenly in secret. Take the matter as you find it: ask no questions; utter no remonstrance; it is your best wisdom. (Ch. 7)

The strength of the emotions of Charlotte's heroines throws light on what may have been the intention behind the eighteenth-century warnings examined above, for instance, in the Burney novels, that no young woman should allow herself to fall in love with a young man until she is sure of his love in return; the apparently cold hearted prudence may have shown a deeper insight into the difficulties to be encountered in lives without much occupation to channel away their emotions.

In Shirley herself, beautiful, rich and free, we may allow ourselves to see Charlotte Brontë's ideal of what a young woman of spirit should be. Shirley is the 'sister of the spotted, bright, quick, fiery leopard'. Her views on most matters are given out to be advanced, but they are vague. Although she inveighs against Milton's Eve, saying that she was the image of his cook rather than the first woman on earth, Shirley's idea of the first woman is only that she was 'heaven-born: vast was the heart whence gushed the well-spring of the blood of nations', and so on, all rather nebulous. She has the courage to condemn Mr Sympson's attitude to marriage as that of a fish-tailed Dagon but such titanic words browbeat rather than inform. It is understandable that she does not wish for a husband who can lead and teach her but a master, a man 'I shall feel it is impossible not to love, and very possible to fear'. She is compounded of certain idealized qualities of passionate womanhood above and beyond ordinary experience.

In her last novel Charlotte Brontë shows no disposition to be bemused with admiration for her heroine and in *Villette* (1853) she returns to the kind of woman she could visualize with complete authenticity, a young woman, quiet and subdued, but longing for love, capable of terrible emotional intensity, fighting to maintain her integrity against the world. Lucy Snowe has a harder life than Jane Eyre because she lacks Jane's resilience: she expects the worst and it comes—after all she has gone through, M. Paul is still snatched from her by a doom she darkly foresees.

Miss Brontë concentrates on the means such a woman as Lucy has to take to maintain her integrity, even her sanity, in the face of such a destiny, and *Villette* is in this sense a small-scale epic, a woman's epic of stoicism, of the struggle for strength and fortitude, the effort to grasp meaning from a life lived under dire frustrations. The way, according to Charlotte Brontë, does not lie in escape or self-deception; it is the accepted despair of a proud woman that is depicted in *Villette*. Lucy insists on the necessity to confront suffering on the grand scale (grand, that is, for one with her personality and her restricted social opportunities), without trying to soften its gaunt outline and without flinching. From the beginning of her story, she feels her own dark destiny: 'I had wanted to compromise with Fate: to escape occasional great agonies by submitting to a whole life of privation and small pains. Fate would not so be pacified; nor would Providence sanction this shrinking sloth and cowardly indolence' (Ch. 4). Time after time she forces herself to stand up to the worst potentialities of any situation, for instance, she fights her feeling for Graham Bretton by asserting the fact that happiness of that kind is not for her, and, 'by degrees, a composite feeling of blended strength and pain wound itself wirily round my heart, sustained, or at least restrained, its throbbings, and made me fit for the day's work'. She does this again when she must face the possibility that M. Emanuel is destined to marry Justine Marie. The device by which she writes two letters to Graham each time, one for her own relief and the other for his perusal, is her safety valve. These methods of self-discipline do indeed bring a measure of relief but when she faces a long period of waiting and when the response she longs for depends on other people and is beyond her own command, they are less effective, inadequate for dealing with so powerful a flood of emotion. Thus, during the seven weeks when she received no letter from the Brettons:

I tried different expedients to sustain and fill existence: I commenced an elaborate piece of lacework, I studied German pretty hard, I undertook a course of regular reading of the driest and thickest books in the library; in all my efforts I was as orthodox as I knew how to be. Was there an error somewhere? Very likely. I only knew the result was as if I had gnawed a file to satisfy hunger, or drank brine to quench thirst. (Ch. 24)

The conflict lies in the fact that such a woman, filled with nervous and emotional energy and power, has no real outlet for her energies or her feelings. Dependent upon the affection of others, she exists in an environment where no affection can be shown. Governed equally by social convention and deeply accepted personal conviction, she disciplines herself in two ways, first in order to appear outwardly quite cool and independent of those who form the most important emotional element in her life, and secondly in order to kill in herself any false expectations that her needs will really be met.

Lucy's code of silence is also shared by Paulina, though a happy fate awaits the latter. Paulina tells Lucy that if she liked Dr John till she was 'fit to die' for liking him she could not be otherwise than dumb, as dumb as Lucy herself, who would, she knew, despise her if she failed in self-control and whined about some 'ricketty liking' that was all on her side. The strong feelings of Paulina are rewarded by the love of Dr John—she has both beauty and position, which make the match a suitable one—but the possibility of suffering is there, both in the days of her worship of John when she was a child and in her continuing capacity for experiencing emotional pain in after years. She may perhaps be considered a beautiful, sheltered counterpart to Lucy, equally vulnerable but more fortunate.

Paulina's emotional depth and her sensitivity are contrasted with Ginevra Fanshawe's shallowness and levity. Ginevra has no notion of meeting distress single-handed, she 'fights the battle of life by proxy' and suffers as little as any human being Lucy has known. Ginevra is beautiful and her beauty causes the author to exclaim again on the mystery of its power. When Lucy finds out that the despised Isidore is none other than Dr John, she upbraids Ginevra for scorning and torturing him and asks:

Have you the power to do this? Who gave you that power? Where is it? Does it all lie in your beauty—your pink and white complexion, and your yellow hair? Does this bind his soul at your feet, and bend his neck under your yoke? (Ch. 14)

In *Adam Bede* George Eliot also considers the power inherent in physical beauty, offering a philosophical explanation, but Charlotte Brontë leaves it as an enigma. Lucy is again faced with the problem when she watches M. Emanuel with Justine Marie, and finally there is the pathetic confession to the man himself: 'Ah! I am not pleasant to look at—' and the reassurance of his answer which, on this score at least, brings her peace.

Charlotte Brontë's view of a woman's life in *Villette* would seem to be that there is little hope of happy love for a woman of deep feelings unless she is beautiful or the fates are kind. But in her deprivation, a woman worthy the name must not seek escape in triviality or self-deception, she must accept her tragic destiny and wrest from it with courage the dignity of an uncomplaining spirit. The battle will be mighty.

Emily Brontë

Life as it is depicted in *Wuthering Heights* (1847) is not given to most women to know; it is poetic and melodramatic, not so much set against the background of the Yorkshire moors as itself part of that background along with the wind and the snow and the supernatural voices and the elemental powers. It has been remarked that there are few more impersonal novels in English than *Wuthering Heights* and we can find no trace of its author exploring her characters amid their social scene—there is no social scene that corresponds to anything known before, not even in the Gothic novel where at least moral judgment was implied. In *Wuthering Heights* there is no right or wrong, such terms have no relevance in this vision of a life created with its own integrity but only seemingly connected with contemporary England. Even if the portrait of Heathcliffe be considered as a study of the effect of social humiliation, this cannot adequately explain a character of such demoniac quality. The young women in the novel are less young women than young creatures, immature, cruel, impersonal, and neither love nor marriage soften them; indeed the powerful passions stated to be love in this book are not love as that word is used in other novels, even those of Charlotte Brontë. We have Charlotte's word that her sister believed that man and woman should not be considered separately and that nothing moved her more than any insinuation that 'the faithfulness and clemency, the long-suffering and loving kindness which are esteemed virtues in the daughters of Eve, become foibles in the sons of Adam'; such a mind would rise above the more transient considerations of sex and see only a larger unity of humanity.

Wuthering Heights must be counted as part of the total achievement of English women writers but it is not the work of a woman writing as a woman: it is rather the work of a spirit of imagination and power in whose eyes sex has been transmuted into something transcending human limits and ignoring moral values. *Wuthering Heights* is the only novel in our survey which could be quoted in support of a contention that art has no sex.

Elizabeth Gaskell

By contrast, Mrs Gaskell's novels show an art that was unmistakably feminine. Lord David Cecil has called her 'the typical Victorian woman'[6] and her books are an attractive expression of the thought of an average woman of her time, not fully conservative and yet not radically advanced. Henry James said she was a writer whose genius was 'so little of an intellectual matter' and 'so obviously the offspring of her affections, her feelings, her associations', that it was 'little else than a peculiar play of her personal character'; he adds however that he wishes to be understood as 'valuing not her intellect the less, but her character the more'.[7] She began writing when she held the views that a handsome middle-class Victorian lady might be expected to hold, looking 'up to man as her sex's rightful and benevolent master'[8] and accepting the contemporary ideal of the submissive woman. As the wife of a Unitarian Minister in Manchester she had the opportunity of seeing the misery and suffering brought about by the conditions of the factory-workers and she was moved by her concern for the troubles of others and her reverence for average human nature to write about this suffering and to appeal to the sympathy of her readers by bringing it to their attention. Her work gradually grew in depth and boldness of approach but even an early story like *Libbie Marsh's Three Eras*, which she contributed to *Howitt's Journal* in 1847, deals with the lot of a humble young seamstress, poor and plain, not at all the typical heroine of fiction. Libbie lodges with the Dixon family, all fine spinners earning good wages; they are away from home all day in the factory and Libbie is left alone. Watching from her window she sees a cripple child for whom she buys a canary and arranges an outing. After the death of the little boy Libbie goes to live with his termagant mother, whom she has softened by her kindness to the child. It is a simple tale with some of the sentiments of the Sunday School but its sympathy with the life of a struggling young working-class woman, battling against poverty and (again) plainness in the new environment of the factory town, adds a new dimension to the description of women's life in the Victorian novel.

Mary Barton: a tale of Manchester Life (1848), Mrs Gaskell's first full-length novel, is acknowledged as a noteworthy contribution to the understanding of conditions in the cotton towns. The story is factually more correct and specific in detail than, for example, Mrs Trollope's earlier *Life and Adventures of Michael Armstrong, the Factory Boy* (1840), for unlike Mrs Trollope Elizabeth Gaskell had first-hand knowledge of the circumstances in which many of the factory hands lived. When she mentions John Barton's habit of chewing opium to forget his troubles and exclaims, 'Oh, how Mary loathed that smell', the detail indicates how familiar that smell must have been, while the mention of the wooden mockery of a handsome tombstone which, having served its purpose for John Davenport's grave, went on to do temporary duty over another, brings a precise revelation of the pity of it.

The characters of the three young women in the story are contrasted with the evident intention of letting them serve as examples and lessons for young women readers. Margaret Jennings, who goes blind, is the most noble in her unselfishness; she is gentle and humble, loving and beloved. The heroine, Mary Barton, is beautiful and wilful, and might have gone astray like her aunt Esther, had she not been saved in time. Sally Leadbetter is a common and malicious gossip. The work that these young women do to earn their living offers an opportunity for comment on the difficulties facing working women. The stress is laid on the moral dangers encountered in their lives and not on any lack of satisfaction in the work as such to the individual who performs it. The false values that lead the sixteen-year-old Mary to become a dressmaker's apprentice are described at some length. Her father dislikes the idea of factory life for a girl so that there are only two possibilities left, going out to service and the dressmaking business; Mr Barton's radical views consider domestic service as a form of slavery, a 'pampering of artificial wants on the one side, a giving up of every right of leisure by

day and quiet rest by night on the other' (a view very different
from Alice Wilson's), but

Mary's determination not to go to service arose from far less sensible
thoughts on the subject than her father's . . . she knew she was very
pretty . . . with this consciousness she had early determined that her
beauty should make her a lady; the rank she coveted the more for
her father's abuse; the rank to which she firmly believed her lost
aunt Esther had arrived. Now, while a servant must often drudge
and be dirty, a dressmaker's apprentice must (or so Mary thought)
be always dressed with a certain regard to appearances; must never
soil her hands, and need never redden or dirty her face with hard
labour. (Ch. 3)

Aunt Esther's view on the other hand is that dressmaking is a
bad life for girls as they have 'to be out late at night in the
streets, and after many an hour of weary work, they're ready to
follow after any novelty that makes a little change'. This danger
is proved to be a real one in Mary's case because young Carson
waits for her as she comes out of Miss Simmonds's dressmaking
establishment in the evenings.

The novel's ideals of modesty in the behaviour of young
women towards young men are those acceptable in contemporary society and the language used to describe them has a truly
Victorian coyness. When Mary has dismissed Jem and is
beginning to repent she learns from Margaret that he is in
Halifax: this makes her sad, 'for Halifax was all the same to her
heart as the Antipodes; equally inaccessible by humble, penitent
looks and maidenly tokens of love', and at Jem's trial, when a
barrister asks Mary which of the two young men, Henry Carson
or Jem Wilson, is the favoured lover, her reaction is:

And who was he, the questioner, that he should dare so lightly to
ask of her heart's secrets? That he should dare to ask her to tell,
before that multitude assembled there, what woman usually whispers
with blushes and tears, and many hesitations to one ear alone.
(Ch. 32)

But the interest of Mrs Gaskell's views on women in *Mary
Barton* lies largely in the fact that, alongside her acceptance of
contemporary standards and her use of the language in which
those standards were usually expressed, she also tries honestly

to face the difficulties confronting girls working amongst the temptations of the new industrial cities and endeavours to work out an acceptable code of behaviour in these novel conditions. She goes even further and implies that women's influence may help in the solution of many of the fresh problems of over-crowding and poverty and that the bitter feeling of the poor towards the rich can be dissolved by human sympathy. Women should show sympathy, understanding and neighbourliness to those outside their own circle of family and friends of the same class which previously formed the boundaries of their interests. No longer is care for personal and household servants and for the poor of the village enough, there are wider areas about which women especially should be concerned, because women can best see the price of human misery paid in the daily life of families down the street. It is the function of the good women in *Mary Barton* to bridge with love and tenderness the gulfs existing between human beings.

Mrs Gaskell's view of 'fallen women' changed with the years. In *Mary Barton* there is no hope of Aunt Esther's ever returning to respectability but in *Lizzie Leigh*, the story written for *Household Words* in 1850, some return to normal life is made possible. In this tale Lizzie goes into service in Manchester and is seduced. Her employers cast her into the street and her father will have nothing to do with her, although he later forgives her on his deathbed. After Mr Leigh's death Lizzie's mother and her two sons move to Manchester in order to find Lizzie. Will, one of the sons, meets Susan Palmer, the daughter of a drunkard, and falls in love with her, but is afraid to tell her so because of the shame Lizzie has brought on the family. His mother goes to Susan however and tells her everything. It is then discovered that Nancy, Susan's 'niece', is really a child left in Susan's arms by an unknown woman and, of course, the unknown woman turns out to be Lizzie. Lizzie finally finds a home with her mother again and devotes the rest of her life to doing good to others.

Susan's attitude to Lizzie may safely be taken as the one which Mrs Gaskell felt to be right. Susan was a pleasant young woman, full of kindness to her neighbours—'she'll bring her thimble wi' her, and mend up after the childer o'nights; and she writes all Betty Harker's letters to her grandchild out at service; and she's in nobody's way', is how she is praised. Her attitude to Lizzie is indicated in a conversation with Will, when she says:

'Your sister was near the house. She came in on hearing my words to the doctor. She is asleep now, and your mother is watching her. I wanted to tell you all myself. Would you like to see your mother?'

'No!' said he, 'I would rather see none but thee. Mother told me thou knew'st all.' His eyes were downcast in their shame.

But the holy and pure did not lower or veil her eyes. She said, 'Yes, I know all—all but her sufferings. Think what they must have been. . .!'

He made answer, low and stern. 'She deserved them all; every jot.'

'In the eye of God, perhaps she does. He is the Judge; we are not.' (Ch. 4)

Although the condemnatory attitude of the brother is displeasing to the modern mind and the use of the adjectives 'holy and pure' to describe a pleasant young woman, however good, in contrast to one who has been seduced, is of course offensive to the modern ear, the very fact that Mrs Gaskell, the wife of a minister of religion, did write this story in which sympathy is expressed and the erring one is finally received back by certain members of her family, reveals an effort of understanding and sympathy in advance of the accepted standards of the mid-nineteenth century.

Three years later Elizabeth Gaskell was writing *Ruth* (1853) and by so doing became the first among the Victorians who actually made the fall and redemption of a seduced woman the main theme of a full-length novel. She set out to secure sympathy for Ruth by making her, except for her 'fall', the ideal Victorian heroine, beautiful, ignorant and innocent, gentle, submissive and loving. Ruth is alone in a hostile world, cast out by her employer, and she loves Mr Bellingham, her seducer, and cannot bear to cause him the pain of thinking she does not trust him. Whether Mrs Gaskell's portrayal of Ruth was completely successful in the eyes of her contemporaries, or those of her contemporaries who could bring themselves to read anything so shocking, it is difficult to judge in a post-Second World War study. The natural questions arise now, and may have arisen then, about the absence of even any mention of marriage. And even if ignorance is conceded, would not the shock of discovery of what was involved in cohabitation have had a greater effect upon a young girl's mind than is portrayed in the book, especially upon the mind of a girl so 'pensive and tender'? In the handling of this part of the story there may perhaps be detected a 'touch of false refinement' and, although in this case the fault must be considered characteristic of the author's age rather than a purely personal and artistic one, yet it makes the situation in the novel difficult to accept at the level obviously intended. Mrs Gaskell sidled past the main incident in order to concentrate on the situation afterwards and it is this which receives her brave and undivided attention and which gives her the opportunity of inducing her readers to reconsider the whole question, discarding the stock Victorian response to the situation expressed by Mr Bradshaw—'when such a woman came into my family there is no wonder at any corruption—any evil—any defilement'. Through the words of Mr Benson, the Nonconformist minister, a plea is made that the innocent victim of seduction should at least be given a chance to redeem herself: 'I state my firm belief . . . that it is God's will that the women who have fallen should be numbered among those who have broken hearts to be bound up, not cast aside as lost beyond recall' (Vol. 3, Ch. 3). Elizabeth Gaskell does not go so far as to expect normal happiness for Ruth but she pleads for her at least to be given the chance to expiate her sin. Jemima Bradshaw has the courage to consider the special responsibility which other women bear in their attitude to young women in Ruth's predicament: 'If [Ruth's] present goodness was real—if, after having striven back thus far on the heights, a fellow-woman was to throw her down into some terrible depth with her unkind, incontinent tongue, that would be too cruel!' (Vol. 3, Ch. 1). By her devotion to nursing the sick during an epidemic, including her betrayer himself, Ruth wins the admiration of all who know her. She also regains her own self-respect and has the strength of mind to refuse Bellingham's offer of marriage because she feels that he would exert an evil influence on the child. She contracts the fever from her former lover and dies, mourned and respected. Some readers, including Charlotte Brontë, rebelled at the necessity for Ruth's death, but Mrs Gaskell doubtless felt she had gone far enough in enabling Ruth to regain her self-respect and the respect of her neighbours.

The contrast between Ruth and Jemima is much more subtle than the contrast between Lizzie and Susan in *Lizzie Leigh*. Ruth as we have seen is, apart from her 'fall', the typical Victorian heroine, beautiful, gentle and rather dull. 'She knew that she was beautiful; but that seemed abstract, and removed from herself. Her existence was in feeling, and thinking, and loving.' She is also very dependent upon the love of others for herself. Jemima is more intelligent than Ruth; she is not beautiful, but she has a warm, affectionate, ardent nature, 'free from all envy or carking care of self'. Her attitude to her admirer, Mr Farquhar, has greater interest and vitality than Ruth's passive relationship with those who admire her beauty. Jemima has a hasty temper and has displeased Mr Farquhar, who has left without more leave-taking than a distant bow; the shock makes her realize his importance in her life:

For an instant she planned to become and to be all that he could wish her; to change her very nature for him And then a great rush of pride came over her, and she set her teeth tight together, and determined that he should either love her as she was, or not at all. Unless he could take her with all her faults, she would not care for his regard; 'love' was too noble a word to call such a cold calculating feeling as his must be, who went about with a pattern idea in his mind, trying to find a wife to match. Besides, there was something degrading, Jemima thought, in trying to alter herself to gain the love of any human creature. And yet, if he did not care for her, if this late indifference were to last, what a great shroud was drawn over life. Could she bear it? (Vol. 2, Ch. 7)

Such views show how far the exploration and discussion of relationships between the sexes have advanced since *Coelebs in in search of a Wife*. Ruth's gentleness and tact, contrasted with Jemima's uncurbed temper, almost make Mr Farquhar turn from the one to the other, and Jemima sees this and has the additional struggle with herself against incipient jealousy of Ruth. In these struggles she is sister to Jane Eyre, to Anne Elliot, to Lucy Snowe, but she has the added bitterness of knowing her unhappiness to be due to her own hasty temper and lack of self-control, not to fate, insignificance, plainness, or any other handicaps not of her own making. The struggle of a young woman against envy of another is made very real; although the temptation and the necessity for the battle against it are not doubted, the bitterness of the fight is not minimized. In a world of women who always keep the peace and express no views at all Jemima's honesty and intellectual vivacity stand out very attractively: at the dinner party for Mr Hickson she has been chafing under all that he has been saying

perhaps the more for one or two attempts on his part at a flirtation with the daughter of his wealthy host, which she resented with all the loathing of a pre-occupied heart; and she longed to be a man, to speak out her wrath at this paltering with right and wrong. (Vol. 2, Ch. 9)

She tries to see everything as clearly as she can and not merely to have views that will please the gentlemen. She struggles with herself over her hasty judgment of Ruth when she hears the story of Ruth's past and, although her father forbids her to have any connection with the Benson household, when she meets Mr Benson in the street she generously tells him that under different circumstances she herself might have been tempted as Ruth was—she thanks him for his kindness to Ruth and asks sincerely whether she herself can do anything for her. And all these qualities are displayed in a young heiress with a typical sheltered background and education and, even more important, with parents holding very conservative views.

In Mrs Gaskell's *North and South* (1855) the heroine provides an interesting further development in her exploration of the role of the Victorian woman. Margaret Hale has beauty but she has no submission to men of her own age; she thinks for herself and in this respect she may be seen as a development of Jemima Bradshaw, with the additional advantages of a more cultured family background and better breeding. Margaret is physically a fine creature, possessing 'muted physical splendour' and 'nerve and poise'; she has 'superb ways of moving and looking' and her movements, 'full of a soft feminine defiance, always gave strangers the impression of haughtiness'. She is instinctively brave, to the extent of physically shielding John Thornton from attack during the stone-throwing incident with his workmen. She is stronger in character than either her father or her mother, taking over from her father the duty of telling her mother that he has decided to resign his living and to leave the pleasant New Forest village for the smoke of the northern city. Margaret has a fierce hatred of all falsehood, although for the sake of Frederick, her brother, she has herself to tell a lie. The growth and expansion of her character through handling difficulties too great for the failing powers of her parents is interesting. When, early in the novel, she is living at the vicarage at Helstone she exhibits the familiar virtues of a parson's daughter, including dutifulness towards her parents (which she retains to the end) and interest in the welfare of the people of the parish:

She took pride in her forest. Its people were her people. She made hearty friends with them; learned and delighted in using their peculiar words; took up her freedom amongst them; nursed their babies; talked or read with slow distinctness to their old people; carried dainty messes to their sick; resolved before long to teach at the school, where her father went every day as to an appointed task . . . (Ch. 2)

At first, after leaving the security and beauty of Helstone for the discomfort and ugliness of Milton, she reacts by withdrawing into her pride as a lady. But the meeting with the Higgins family and the first-hand knowledge she gains of their struggles and sufferings, her growing realization of the wretched conditions of the workers, her incipient, though reluctant admiration for the virtues of men like John Thornton—all these new experiences deepen her and give her something more satisfying than the usual occupations of the women of her own class, ladies like her cousin Edith. She counters her mother's complaints about her having to do housework by saying 'I don't mind ironing, or any kind of work, for you and papa. I am myself a born and bred lady through it all, even though it comes to scouring a floor, or washing dishes'. She has always had intellectual interests, including a love for Dante (mentioned also in Mrs Gaskell's description of Cousin Phillis). She responds to the stimulation of the expanding development of the north and its plans for a great future with new delight. She is, for this reason, more interested in the conversation of men of affairs than in that of her own sex and when she goes out to dinner with her father she is glad when the gentlemen come into the drawing-room

because she could listen to something larger and grander than the petty interests which the ladies had been talking about. She liked the exultation in the sense of power which these Milton men had. It might be rather rampant in its display, and savour of boasting; but still they seemed to defy the old limits of possibility, in a kind of fine intoxication, caused by the recollection of what had been achieved, and what yet should be. If, in her cooler moments, she might not approve of their spirit in all things, still there was much to admire in their forgetfulness of themselves and the present, in the anticipated triumphs over all inanimate matter at some future time, which none of them should live to see. (Ch. 20)

This intoxication with the possibilities of the expanding industrial development of Britain does not find any echo in the wives and daughters of the Milton manufacturers themselves. Their conversation reminds Margaret of an old game of nouns she used to play as a child: these women took 'nouns that were signs of things that gave evidence of wealth—housekeepers, under-gardeners, extent of glass, valuable lace, diamonds' and formed their speech so as to bring them 'all in, in the prettiest accidental manner possible'. To offset such artificial contacts with the Milton women there are Margaret's contacts with Bessy: the sufferings of the Boucher family made it impossible for her to go away into comparative comfort and forget. All these influences help to enlarge her appreciation of true values.

After her Milton experience and her meeting with Thornton and the gradual growth of her knowledge of his character Margaret can never again be happy in a life of eventless ease. When she returns to the south and is staying in Harley Street after the death of her parents she first finds the comfort and luxury of the house soothing to her, but she is soon surfeited and is afraid 'lest she should even become sleepily deadened into forgetfulness of anything beyond the life which was lapping her round with luxury'. She is surrounded with kindness but the men she meets are either dull, or, if witty, they 'lashed themselves up into enthusiasm about light subjects in company, and

never thought about them when they were alone'. After Mr
Bell's death she feels alone and in despair but the fact that he
left her his fortune enables her to make plans for a different
future. She spends a good deal of time during a holiday in
Cromer thinking what she should do with her life, and

she learnt, in those solemn hours of thought, that she herself must
one day answer for her own life, and what she had done with it;
and she tried to settle that most difficult problem for a woman, how
much was to be utterly merged in obedience to authority, and how
much might be set apart for freedom in working. (Ch. 49)

This recognition that 'freedom in working' is necessary if the
best use is to be made by a woman of her life is new, as is the
recognition that there is any problem in balancing the claims of
the old conceptions of women's duties with changed conditions.
It is also a recognition of women's new dual role. In the past
there had been no question, woman's duty was clear, it was held
to be self-evident that she was to be 'utterly merged in obedience to authority'; but now there is the duty of exercising her
own talents, as much a gift of God as her attributes as a woman
The balancing of the two claims is already seen to be a difficult
feat.

For Margaret there is the additional problem of the best use
she can make of the wealth now entrusted to her. Hearing of
John Thornton's business difficulties, she decides to make an
offer to lend him some of her money so that he can carry on the
mill. But her work for the welfare of the mill is not confined to
lending money. More important to Mrs Gaskell is Margaret's
influence on John Thornton's attitude to his employees,
evidenced in his wish to cultivate some relationship with the
mill hands beyond the mere 'cash nexus'. He explains to Mr
Colthurst that he has arrived at the conviction that

no mere institutions, however wise, and however much thought may
have been required to organize and arrange them, can attach class
to class as they should be attached, unless the working out of such
institutions bring the individuals of the different classes into actual
personal contact. Such intercourse is the very breath of life. (Ch. 51)

Although Margaret is a pioneer in her acceptance of the
responsibilities of her class and sex to render industrial relations

more human, Mrs Gaskell never allows her to neglect the gentle, unobtrusive, long-accepted feminine duties such as the necessity to show unselfish consideration for the moods of those who are dear to her. She also suffers suitable agonies of maiden shame over the recollection of her impulsive act in defending Mr Thornton at the riot.

The contrast between two generations of 'north' and 'south' women is interesting. Mrs Thornton's daughter, Fanny, takes over the weaknesses of the south, imitating its airs and graces, and abandoning the north's uprightness and strength of character, while Mrs Hale's daughter makes the adjustment her mother is unable to make and combines the best of the north and the south—that is, to her own culture and gentle consideration for others, she adds the vigour and energy of the expanding and forward-looking north. Her intellectual and moral sympathies expand so that she feels she can bring something unique to the solution of the problems of life in the new areas.

Although *North and South* is usually classified as one of the Victorian social novels, the social scene in itself is not, as it was with some of the other social novelists, the author's chief preoccupation but is used to show the reaction of one young woman to the demands life makes upon her as she progresses from aloofness and pride into warmth and sympathy and is able to apply her own standards of truthfulness and love to the demanding problems of a new milieu. It is the tale of a girl's response to the challenge of an industrial civilization for which her upbringing has not specifically prepared her but to which, at its deeper levels, her own qualities enable her to make a real contribution.

Margaret Hale reaches the furthest point of development of of any of Mrs Gaskell's heroines. In *My Lady Ludlow* (1858), in interesting contrast, the author looked back to the standards of female behaviour of a previous age. Lady Ludlow had been maid of honour to Queen Charlotte; she is a gentlewoman of rank and honour, with very strict rules governing the obligations incurred by aristocratic birth. At Hanbury Court she 'entertains' six young gentlewomen who are her companions and to whom she gives the kind of training she considers suitable for young women placed as they are in the social scale.

Women Awaiting Marriage (2)

Their curriculum is simple: they learn to sew and do all manner of fine needlework to the most exacting standards, to make preserves and medicaments, and to read aloud. Their library for week-day reading includes the *Spectator*, *Mrs Chapone's Letters*, *Dr Gregory's Advice to young ladies*, and *Sturm's Reflections*, the last a book which Queen Charlotte had liked and which told the reader 'what to think about for every day in the year'. These ways of thought obviously belong to the accepted conservatism of the time of the French Revolution and the tale sets out to show both the virtues and the prejudices of an English lady of rank at that time. Lady Ludlow is always guided in her conduct by 'honour', which is, to her, second nature, although she never tries to find out on what principle its laws are based. Although My Lady sets herself against all kinds of change—she will not allow the vicar to conduct a Sunday School in the village and she is 'extremely against women usurping men's employments'—it is through her agency that Miss Galindo becomes a 'lady clerk'. Miss Galindo is a gentlewoman in reduced circumstances who makes a small income by sewing dainty night-caps for the 'repository' in the nearest assize town, a repository set up by the wealthy ladies of the county for the sale of the 'small manufactures of ladies of little or no fortune, whose names, if they chose it, were only signified by initials'. As Miss Galindo's patterns for night-caps are old-fashioned, her income from such work is growing smaller. With the dual purpose of helping her and avoiding training one of the village lads to assist her own steward in his work, Lady Ludlow asks Miss Galindo to act as clerk to the steward for a few hours a day. Her conduct and wit in the post are enchanting. It is not Miss Galindo's considerable efficiency as a temporary clerk, however, that converts Lady Ludlow to modern ideas, it is the vicar's noble conduct at the time of her son's death that brings My Lady round to his way of thinking about schools for the poor. Some delicately spun yarn and a capital pair of knitted stockings, the first fruits of the school, continue the process of reconciling Lady Ludlow to new-fangled ways. Eventually she even acknowledges the existence of the schoolmistress, the illegitimate daughter of a former lover of Miss Galindo's, and accepts her as the wife of the curate. She

93

also countenances the marriage of Captain James, a gentleman appointed to get her lands into order, to a Dissenting baker's daughter. This is a story of changing female social standards but the changes are accepted by the women most closely concerned, Lady Ludlow and Miss Galindo, for fundamentally human reasons, which finally overcome their long-cherished prejudices.

Mrs Gaskell considers in *Cousin Phillis* (1864) some of the new problems that arise when a country girl *is* given an education. Phillis, beautiful and innocent, is educated beyond the custom of the times by her stern, Puritanical father. She falls in love with a fascinating and worldly engineer who comes to recuperate from an illness on the farm in which this unusual family lives. The engineer goes to Canada and there marries; Phillis droops, and her father rebukes her for her unmaidenly conduct in allowing herself to love a man who does not love her, the old familiar theme. Phillis collapses and almost dies of a 'brain-fever'. The love of her parents and her father's regret for his harshness bring Phillis to a certain stage of recovery but she is only induced to make a final effort to regain her health by the reproaches of Betty, one of Mrs Gaskell's sensible servant-characters, who recalls Phillis to a sense of the duty she owes her family and herself.

Obviously the story is a further study of the mingling of the old and the new in the position of women, of a girl brought up with all the strict requirements of the old propriety but with an education which separates her from those who would be her normal companions and which can only find appreciation in wider circles than those in which she is confined. Mrs Gaskell, with all her sympathy for Phillis's difficulties, yet puts back upon the girl herself the final responsibility for regaining her old peace and self-respect within an accepted and familiar environment of inadequate opportunity but strong family affection and family duty.

Wives and Daughters (1866), the last and unfinished novel, introduces differing portraits of young Victorian womanhood in Molly Gibson and her stepsister Cynthia Kirkpatrick. Cynthia is beautiful and detached, conscious of her power to enslave and thoroughly enjoying the evidence of it, although this enjoyment is attributable, partly at least, to wounded vanity after her childhood experience of social slights. Her redeeming feature is her own honesty with herself most of the time: she does not see herself as better than she is. Molly, the heroine, is comparatively plain and makes heroic efforts to govern her instinctive feelings of jealousy towards Cynthia. She is shy and quietly affectionate. Considered as an artistic achievement, Cynthia is the more vital portrait, but the author's higher valuation of Molly is obvious. Indeed, the fascination that Cynthia exerts on the reader is, as Lord David Cecil points out, a tribute to the portrayal of a character who attracts in spite of her creator's condemnation.

Although Mrs Gaskell was a handsome woman herself and was not troubled with the feeling of deprivation that seems to reveal itself in the Brontës' obsession with the power of beauty, she does appear to have been puzzled by an indefinable attraction which some women exercised and to which she gave the description 'charm'. In her discussion of this quality in connection with Cynthia she decides that 'perhaps it is incompatible with very high principle'. Certainly the glamour that surrounds Cynthia prevents most people from judging her real, not very admirable character; Mr Gibson, her stepfather, puts his finger on her major weakness, defining it as a 'certain obtuseness of feeling', and this basic heartlessness and insensitivity is brought out well in the interview he has with her about her flirtations and her unfeeling encouragement of Mr Coxe.

There is no trace of heartlessness about Molly. She is the simple, good, loving, Victorian girl, dull and unexciting compared with Cynthia, but with a sterling character built on good principles, one which proves its worth in times of crisis. The inadequacy of her education is pathetic. Her father engages a Miss Eyre, daughter of a local shopkeeper, to help with his young apprentices and to keep Molly company and teach her a little; his attitude to women's education and character is well shown when he says to Miss Eyre:

Don't teach Molly too much; she must sew, and read, and write, and do her sums; but I want to keep her a child, and if I find more learning desirable for her, I'll see about giving it to her myself. After all, I'm not sure that reading or writing is necessary. Many a good woman gets married with only a cross instead of her name; it's rather a diluting of mother-wit, to my fancy; but, however, we must yield to the prejudices of society, Miss Eyre, and so you may teach the child to read. (Ch. 3)

It is only by 'fighting and struggling hard' that, bit by bit, Molly persuades her father to let her have French and drawing lessons, and to attend a dancing-class in the assembly-room of the principal inn of Hollingford. Although discouraged by her father in her intellectual efforts, she reads every book that comes her way, 'almost with as much delight as if it had been for-bidden'. Mr Gibson has an unusually good library and Molly has read, or tried to read, every book in its non-medical section. Thus, in her own gentle and persistent way, she overcomes the opposition of her father to giving her any education beyond the minimum and, in spite of being surrounded by lesser characters in her stepmother and her stepsister, her superior qualities of mind and heart will not be stifled.

The Squire and Mrs Hamley have a truer appreciation of Molly's worth than her own father and stepmother, and in the crisis when her father, not knowing she has been acting for Cynthia, accuses Molly of meeting Mr Preston in out-of-the-way places and exchanging letters with him in a clandestine fashion, she comports herself with a dignity and integrity greater than his own. She remains true to her promise and does not betray Cynthia in spite of her desire to please her father, but there is no real struggle in her mind because she has the knowledge of her own innocence and her pledged word is her sacred trust. What is more, she rises above the petty and passing considerations that are worrying her father and her insight is more penetrating than his. But it is, of course, true that 'for all Molly's bravery at the time of this conversation, it was she that suffered more than her father. He kept out of the way of hearing gossip; but she was perpetually thrown into the small society of the place.' It is another person outside her own family, Lady Harriet, who understands what Molly is really suffering, and who extracts the truth from Mr Preston and, by deliberately contriving to be seen with Molly and by calling upon her detractors, rehabilitates Molly's reputation in the eyes of the people of Hollingford. This grasp of the real significance of a situation by another woman's mind, followed by the taking of the necessary decisive action, can be paralleled by the action taken by the maid in *Cousin Phillis*. Thus, in a society in which most women smooth over difficulties with soothing conversation, Molly tries to see the truth as clearly as she can, even though to follow where it leads makes her life more difficult. Her virtues are thrown into relief by the less excellent women (apart from Mrs Hamley) who closely surround her.

To summarize very briefly, Mrs Gaskell's contribution to the analysis of the role of the Victorian woman was to extend the sympathy of her readers to the problems of working-class women and of 'fallen' women, and to interpret the challenge of the industrial development in the north, pointing out the significance it held for the women whose lives were affected by it, closely or remotely. She was also the first to recognize the problems confronting the working educated woman in her new dual role, a role still much under discussion these hundred years after.

George Eliot

Because of the magnificent sweep of her vision George Eliot's exploration of woman's role has a greater intrinsic interest than that of any other woman writer. Her freedom from any involvement in narrow class feeling or snobbery gave her an unbiased view of the social scene and her rather invidious position in Victorian society, on account of her association with G. H. Lewes, caused her to achieve a different kind of detachment. Positivist convictions again enabled her to see things differently from either the conservatives or the militant feminists. Many enthusiasts would have liked to enlist her in the ranks of those who fought for 'the cause', but she did not feel she could support the campaign for women's suffrage and she had some doubts about the plans for the higher education of women being evolved by the leaders of that movement, although she certainly believed in the need to improve women's education. From time to time, however, George Eliot did make very careful and guarded statements on these matters. After discussing women's franchise with John Morley, for instance, she sent him a written account of what she had actually meant; it was in this letter that she made her often-quoted statement that 'as a matter of mere zoological evolution, woman seems to me to have the worse share in existence' and she went on to state that the one conviction on the matter which she held with some tenacity was that the goal towards which they were proceeding was

a more clearly discerned distinction of function (allowing always for exceptional cases of individual organization) with as near an approach to equivalence of good for woman and for man as can be secured by the effort of growing moral force to lighten the pressure of hard non-moral outward conditions.[9]

Precisely where this leads is rather difficult to determine, but George Eliot's books are her contribution to discerning more clearly the distinction of function, as she puts it, or to seeking a more clearly-defined role for women, to translate it into the terms of this study, and what she has to say about women in her novels is far easier to understand than any of her guarded direct pronouncements. This she realized better than anyone else; she confessed to Dr Payne that she grew more and more timid, with 'less daring to adopt any formula which does not get itself clothed for me in some human figure and individual experience' and she felt that was perhaps a sign that 'if I help others to see at all it must be through the medium of art'.[10]

In 1853 she declared that it was best that 'enfranchisement of women' was only making 'creeping progress', for 'woman does not yet deserve a much better fate than man gives her'.[11] The wording of 'fate than man gives her' shows the way in which George Eliot looked at women—the recipients of a fate, instead of the masters of it—and the position of women, or rather their 'lot' as she almost invariably calls it, is potentially a tragic because a powerless one. 'She was a woman and could not make her own lot'; 'a woman can hardly ever choose—she is dependent on what happens to her'; 'she must take meaner things, because only meaner things are within her reach'; 'her lot is made for her by the love she accepts'; 'we women must stay where we grow, or where the gardeners like to transplant us'—these quotations summarize the author's fundamental assessment of woman's destiny. It is in this position that most of her heroines from Milly Barton to Gwendolen Harleth find themselves. Such a view of human life might bo defined as that of an Evangelical who no longer has Christian hope; although George Eliot's mature faith has been described as a religion of humanity, it retained the strict moral obligations of her former beliefs—dutiful acceptance of one's place in life, filial regard, family affection, self-sacrifice, self-discipline—together with a full recognition of feminine weaknesses, physical, nervous and emotional. But the promise of help from without and within that the Christian religion could offer, which had been accepted by Jane Austen and by Marian Evans's own contemporaries, even by the fiery spirit of Charlotte Brontë and the Socinian Mrs Gaskell, was no longer there to give strength and comfort in hours of need. In the world of George Eliot's women, the healthy influences of country life, of family affections, of wise moral training, or, in some cases, of the love and devotion of a good man, could all help, but if these did not form part of a woman's given lot, her way was hard indeed. Any efforts she might make to shape or master her own destiny were made at her peril; any expectations she might cherish of the possibility of mastery were folly; any failure to perform the duties demanded by her lot brought inevitable suffering. The individual destinies of the women in the novels show the great variety of ways in which George Eliot perceived this law to be working. Her women characters exhibit a considerable range of spiritual greatness or moral littleness. Many are portraits of women whose potentialities of mind and spirit are not fully realized, either owing to the limitations of their environment or to the inadequacy of their training or again to certain weaknesses, follies or inadequacies in themselves; a few are portraits of women who fulfil themselves in loving others, wishing for nothing else, and their creator's blessing seems to rest with these.

George Eliot's treatment of some of her young women at the outset of their adult lives repays analysis. The central figure of each of the tales making up the *Scenes of Clerical Life* is a woman, in spite of the masculine title, and Caterina Sarti, in 'Mr Gilfil's Love-Story', is a girl whose capacity to love runs to waste because of her misplaced trust in the philandering heir of her benefactor. With one exception, 'her only talent lay in loving; and there, it is probable, the most astronomical of women could not have surpassed her'. The exception mentioned is Caterina's talent for singing which gives her at once a compensation for her lack of physical and mental distinction and a safety channel, although not a fully adequate one, for her powerful emotions. In the blindness of her fury at Captain Wybrow's baseness 'she who used to cry to have the fish put back into the water—who never willingly killed the smallest living thing—dreams now, in the madness of her passion, that she can kill the man whose very voice unnerves her'. Her penitence when she finds him already dead and realizes what she herself had intended to do cures this temporary warping of her nature. But the strain has been too much. Soon after her marriage to Maynard Gilfil she dies. She dies because her nature has been unable to overcome the frustrations of her lot. Caterina has something in common with Mrs Gaskell's Cousin Phillis: both these creations have a great power of loving, unsullied by coquetry or calculation or by any real knowledge of the world, and they suffer for it. If we concentrate on this aspect of the story, as George Eliot herself seems to have done—the story of the sufferings of a sensitive young woman in an indifferent world—we cannot so easily agree with Henry James's view that 'Mr Gilfil's Love-Story' is thin, flat and trivial'.[12]

Most of the women who live among 'the breath of cows and the scent of hay' in *Adam Bede* (1859) are busy countrywomen, preoccupied with normal household duties, with their eye or mind constantly on the butter and the cheeses, but the two main portraits are of feminine beauty—Hetty Sorrel with the rounded, playful beauty of a kitten, and Dinah Morris with the pure and unselfish beauty of a loving spirit.

Although Hetty is plunged into tragedy, it is her selfishness, vanity, folly and ignorance and her childish trust in the easygoing Arthur Donnithorne that lead her astray, not any major and deliberate sin. When Dinah is worried about her, 'that sweet young thing, with life and all its trials before her', it is because her mind seems so unprepared for all the 'solemn daily duties of wife and mother', since she is bent merely on 'little foolish, selfish pleasures, like a child hugging its toys in the beginning of a long toilsome journey, in which it will have to bear hunger and cold and unsheltered darkness'. Hetty's prettiness is the only means by which she has judged her contact with others and its effect has misled her as to what she may expect in life. Dinah has noted the 'absence of any warm, self-devoting love in Hetty's nature'; she has no affection for anyone but Arthur Donnithorne and her feeling for him is only a mixture of passion and girlish vanity, fed by the flattery of the attentions of a gentleman and the daydreams it induces of a fine future with a carriage and rich clothes. She is not blamed by her creator for her shortcomings (except, by implication, for her lack of love) since the equipment with which she has to face the world is so inadequate: she is described by Mrs Poyser as 'no better nor a cherry with a hard stone inside it', but George Eliot's comment, as we watch Hetty fasten Arthur's earrings in her pretty ears, is:

it is too painful to think that she is a woman, with a woman's destiny before her—a woman spinning in young ignorance a light web of folly and vain hopes which may one day close round her and press upon her, a rancorous, poisoned garment, changing all at once her fluttering, trivial butterfly sensations into a life of deep human anguish. (Ch. 22)

The differences between Hetty and Dinah are summarized in the chapter called 'The Two Bed-chambers' in which George Eliot describes the little secret parade of vanity that Hetty enacts when she dresses up in her earrings and black lace scarf, while Dinah, in the adjoining room, is occupied with meditation and with unselfish concern for Hetty's future welfare. George Eliot's use of clothes as symbols of the inward state of the wearer is very evident here. Dinah's simple Methodist dress and unbecoming cap are set against Hetty's pathetic finery. Indeed, the only speech of Adam's that really seems to have meaning for Hetty is that in which he contrasts her dress with Dinah's, and the only *positive* part she plays in any of the family scenes is when she dresses up in clothes to resemble Dinah's and gives as her reason that Adam had said he liked Dinah's gown and cap better than hers and that he felt 'folks looked better in ugly clothes'. This preoccupation with clothes—the pink dress for the party, the fine white stockings, the earrings that Arthur gave her—is a symptom of her fatal vanity. But such vanity and fondness for gewgaws is not confined to pretty Hetty: the blowsy Bessy Cranage is also fond of earrings and small finery:

anyone who could have looked into poor Bessy's heart would have seen a striking resemblance between her little hopes and anxieties and Hetty's. The advantage, perhaps, would have been on Bessy's side in the matter of feeling. But, then, you see, they were so very different outside! You would have been inclined to box Bessy's ear, and you would have longed to kiss Hetty. (Ch. 25)

Dinah has no vanity. She is a gentle, mild woman, who has a 'very tender way with her'; she is patient and kind and delicately sympathetic with the perpetually complaining Lisbeth Bede, with spoilt Totty and with the Poyser boys. She prefers to live and work in a cotton mill in Snowfield, in Stonyshire, among people who are struggling and suffering and whom she loves to help, rather than stay in the comfort of Hall Farm with her aunt. She has a softening and ennobling influence on all she meets: even when she refuses to marry him, Seth Bede, 'instead of bursting out into wild accusing apostrophes to God and destiny . . . is resolving as he now walks homeward under the solemn starlight, to repress his sadness, to be less bent on having his own will, and to live more for others as Dinah does'.

The ending of the novel is generally considered unsatisfactory. It seems to consist of 'rewards' for virtue that are not at all appropriate. Adam marries Dinah but the marriage is difficult to believe in. With Henry James, we should have preferred Dinah to be left 'to the enjoyment of that distinguished celibacy for which she was so well suited'[13] and we should then have had the major novel about a whole-hearted spinster that we have not yet had from a great writer. But we are presumably intended to look on the ending of *Adam Bede* as the final balancing of two entirely different fates—the culmination in happiness of a life of unselfish devotion and love balanced against the tragic consequences of vanity and selfish folly. The scales seem too heavily weighted against the 'sly puss' Hetty and our affections are not sufficiently engaged by the pale Dinah, especially when she becomes Mrs Bede, to accept precisely this ending, but their creator's aim is what concerns us here and she felt it fitting.

Women Awaiting Marriage (2)

The power of physical beauty in a world which longs to kiss the Hettys while it boxes the ears of the Bessy Cranages is analysed in some detail in *Adam Bede*. George Eliot meditates on the problem on several occasions. In Chapter 7 she characterizes Hetty's beauty as one with which 'you can never be angry, but that you feel ready to crush for inability to comprehend the state of mind into which it throws you', and she mentions that even Mrs Poyser 'continually gazed at Hetty's charms by the sly, fascinated in spite of herself'. Later in the book (Ch. 33) occurs her well-known defence of Adam's blindness to everything except Hetty's beauty. In an effort of understanding that went beyond Charlotte Brontë's one-sided consideration of the power of Ginevra's beauty over Dr John, George Eliot says that she respects Adam Bede in spite of his infatuation, since she believes 'the deep love he had for that sweet, rounded, blossom-like dark-eyed Hetty, of whose inward self he was really very ignorant, came out of the very strength of his nature, and not out of any inconsistent weakness' and she proceeds to raise the whole matter to a different level by stating that

Beauty has an expression beyond and far above the one woman's soul that it clothes, as the words of genius have a wider meaning than the thought that prompted them: It is more than a woman's love that moves us in a woman's eyes—it seems to be a far-off mighty love that has come near to us, and made speech for itself there. . . . The noblest nature sees the most of this impersonal expression in beauty . . . and for this reason, the noblest nature is often the most blinded to the character of the one woman's soul that the beauty clothes.

Her breadth of vision leads her further to plead for the recognition of another kind of beauty, the beauty of everyday people and commonplace things, in the famous passage where she says:

In this world there are so many of these common, coarse people, who have no picturesque, sentimental wretchedness. . . . Therefore let Art always remind us of them: therefore let us always have men ready to give the loving pains of a life to the faithful representing of commonplace things. (Ch. 17)

The ability to perceive such beauty demands a deeper human

103

sympathy than the appreciation of obvious or fashionable loveliness; in the world as it is, however, this deeper insight is rare and in *Adam Bede* a rather silly but basically harmless village coquette is loved by a good man, almost to his own destruction. She herself, ill-equipped with any knowledge of reality, is led astray by her own vanity. The judgment of the author is obvious: the better way for women to tread is the path of loving-kindness and unselfishness, the path of Dinah: this is the only way by which women can really transform their inner lives, powerless as they are to mould their outward circumstances.

The Mill on the Floss (1860) is the tragedy of another beautiful young woman, albeit one whose beauty did not flower until years of maturity, one who has a man's mind and a woman's heart and who yearns for a wider life and for deeper intellectual interests than her own environment offers her. The other side of her nature, her sexual susceptibility and her hidden hunger for love, betrays her moral judgment for a brief period, at a time when she needs most to be alert and strong: when she comes to her senses again and sees things in a clearer moral light she has the strength to take the hard way back. The path of repentance is difficult and the sustained suffering almost breaks her but, before the end-by-drowning, life at least brings to her the two things she then needs most, the forgiveness and continued love of the friend she has betrayed and of the beloved brother who has condemned her. Her full potentialities, however, are never realized, the tragedy is one of wasted powers for which the lot of the possessor has provided no outlet.

George Eliot analyses the progress of Maggie's mental, emotional and moral life in great detail but only a few of the indications of growth and of difficulty can be picked out for this study. Maggie does not have the opportunity to mould her own life by positive and constructive action as, for example, her brother Tom does; this is partly because of her lack of training and the limited field of opportunity open to her as a woman and partly because of her own moral and psychological weaknesses, the weaknesses of the kind of woman she is. Henry James points out the restricting aspects of her life, vis-à-vis Tom: 'Poor erratic Maggie is worth a hundred of her positive brother, and yet on the very threshold of her life she is compelled to accept him as her master. He falls naturally into the man's privilege of being always in the right'.[14] And he goes on to refer to the scene with the jam-puff, ending in Maggie's bewildered sense of quite unjustified guilt.

Those who surround the youthful Maggie point out on various occasions that her cleverness is undesirable in a woman. Although very proud of her, her father says: 'she's twice as 'cute as Tom. Too 'cute for a woman, I'm afraid . . . It's no mischief much while she's a little un, but an over-'cute woman's no better nor a long-tailed sheep—she'll fetch none the better price for that' (Bk. 1, Ch. 2), and he also confides in Mr Riley, that 'a woman's no business wi' being so clever; it'll turn to trouble, I doubt'. In addition to this rather dangerous intellectual power Maggie has a crippling psychological need for love and affection, 'the strongest need in poor Maggie's nature', and a 'passionate sensibility'. She takes various steps to escape from the unbearable pressures of her mental and emotional life. Even as a child, when Tom goes off in the holidays with Bob and will never let her go with them, she sits down by the hollow, or wanders by the hedgerow and fancies it all different, 'refashioning her little world into just what she would like it to be. Maggie's was a troublous life, and this was the form in which she took her opium' (Bk. 1, Ch. 6). It was a habit which gave her a tendency to live a kind of dream-life of her own, a life which later could include the intense joy she found in music and in intellectual expansion of all kinds.

At the time of the family disasters when her beloved father is lying stricken in bed, we are given this picture of Maggie's soul:

Maggie, in her brown frock, with her eyes reddened and her heavy hair pushed back, looking from the bed where her father lay to the dull walls of this sad chamber which was the centre of her world, was a creature full of eager, passionate longings for all that was beautiful and glad; thirsty for all knowledge; with an ear straining after dreamy music that died away and would not come near to her; with a blind unconscious yearning for something that would link together the wonderful impressions of this mysterious life, and give her soul a sense of home in it.

No wonder, when there is this contrast between the outward and the inward, that painful collisions come of it. (Bk. 3, Ch. 5)

In her descriptions of 'the old-fashioned family life on the banks of the Floss' George Eliot pauses to explain its importance in the lives of Tom and Maggie:

I share with you this sense of oppressive narrowness; but it is necessary that we should feel it, if we care to understand how it acted on the lives of Tom and Maggie—how it acted on young natures in many generations, that in the onward tendency of human things have risen above the mental level of the generation before them, to which they have been nevertheless tied by the strongest fibres of their hearts. (Bk. 4, Ch. 1)

The gloss may legitimately be added that the pain of outgrowing their background goes deeper in most women than in men, by the very nature of their stronger attachment to the home. When Mr Tulliver partially recovers, the sad, monotonous routine of life is even harder for Maggie to bear, especially as both her father and Tom are too absorbed by their own troubles to give her the old tokens of affection, and at the age of thirteen she is, on account of her eager life in 'the triple world of Reality, Books and Waking Dreams', 'strangely old for her years in everything except in her entire want of that prudence and self-command which were the qualities which made Tom manly in the midst of his intellectual boyishness'.

The mental sustenance that her smattering of formal education and her own eager but limited reading have given her is not sufficient for her needs; she seeks out Tom's old school books and begins to 'nibble at this thick-rinded fruit of the tree of knowledge, filling her vacant hours with Latin, geometry, and the forms of the syllogism, and feeling a gleam of triumph now and then that her understanding was quite equal to these peculiarly masculine studies'. But she is discouraged; she feels it a burden that she is filled with larger wants than others seem to feel:

she was as lonely in her trouble as if she had been the only girl in the civilized world of that day who had come out of her school-life with a soul untrained for inevitable struggles—with no other part of her inherited share in the hard-won treasures of thought, which generations of painful toil have laid up for the race of men, than shreds and patches of feeble literature and false history—with much futile information about Saxon and other kings of doubtful example—but unhappily quite without that knowledge of the irreversible laws within and without her, which, governing the habits, becomes morality, and, developing the feelings of submission and dependence, becomes religion;—as lonely in her trouble as if every other girl beside herself had been cherished and watched over by elder minds, not forgetful of their own early time, when need was keen and impulse strong. (Bk. 4, Ch. 3)

This is George Eliot's most outspoken indictment of the inadequate education, both intellectual, moral and emotional, given to young women in Victorian England.

Then, among some books that Bob has brought along for her, Maggie finds a copy of the *Imitatio Christi* of Thomas à Kempis, and it seems to her a spring in the desert. As she reads, a strange thrill of awe passes through her; she feels that here is insight, strength and conquest, and a teacher to help her; in her youth and inexperience she does not realize that she has missed the true significance of à Kempis's message, that she is in fact looking for a more refined and exalted kind of escape than she had before. When she meets Philip Wakem in the Red Deeps, he points out to her that she is shutting herself up in a self-delusive fanaticism, that she is not resigned, only trying to stupefy herself, and he warns her that she is storing up trouble for the future. He is, of course, right. When Maggie returns from the dreary teaching post she takes after her father's death and stays with her cousin Lucy, she has, after her years of renunciation, slipped back into desire and longing. She is attracted by Stephen Guest, Lucy's fiancé, but before the story moves on to Maggie's tragedy, George Eliot turns aside to point out another truth about the human lot which is relevant; she says:

the tragedy of our lives is not created entirely from within. 'Character', says Novalis, in one of his questionable aphorisms, 'character is destiny.' But not the whole of our destiny. Hamlet, Prince of Denmark, was speculative and irresolute, and we have a great tragedy in consequence. But if his father had lived to a good old age, and his uncle had died an early death, we can conceive Hamlet's having married Ophelia and got through life with a reputation of sanity, notwithstanding many soliloquies, and some moody sarcasms towards the fair daughter of Polonius, to say nothing of the frankest incivility to his father-in-law. (Bk. 6, Ch. 6)

As the attraction between Stephen and Maggie grows stronger and is avowed, her struggle is analysed in detail; the worst aspect of the situation to her is the horror of causing pain to Lucy and to Philip. Stephen appeals to her pity for him and she appeals to him to help her to do what she feels to be right. But, eventually, yielding to the tide of her feelings, she does not notice that the boat in which Stephen is taking her down the river has gone so far that there is no turning back. Only the night's meditation on the deck of the Dutch boat going to Mudport, when Stephen is not by her side to distract her, brings her back to reality again: she realizes that

she had let go the clue of life—that clue which once in the far-off years her young need had clutched so strongly. She had renounced all delights then, before she knew them, before they had come within her reach. Philip had been right when he told her that she knew nothing of renunciation: she had thought it was quiet ecstasy; she saw it face to face now—that sad, patient, loving strength which holds the clues of life—and saw that the thorns were for ever pressing on its brow. The yesterday, which could never be revoked—if she could have changed it now for any length of inward silent endurance, she would have bowed beneath that cross with a sense of rest. (Bk. 6, Ch. 14)

She decides to go back, a way to take that is harder than going forward and marrying Stephen. To his pleas that nothing in the past can annul their right to each other, she replies in terms that show her moral insight and courage, after a brief lapse, to be much more worthy of admiration than Stephen's rather cheap appeal; she tells him that she has never loved him with her whole heart and soul:

I have never consented to it with my whole mind. . . . If I could wake back again into the time before yesterday, I would choose to be true to my calmer affections, and live without the joy of love. . . . We can't choose happiness either for ourselves or for one another: we can't tell where that will lie. We can only choose whether we will indulge ourselves in the present moment, or whether we will renounce that, for the sake of obeying the divine voice within us—for the sake of being true to all the motives that sanctify our lives. (Bk. 6, Ch. 14)

In *The Mill on the Floss* the female figure that is set alongside Maggie's, and to a certain extent contrasted with it, is, of course, that of the small, delicate, pretty Lucy, saved from being too doll-like by her surprising liveliness and skill in ordinary social conversation. Lucy may be compared physically with Rosamond Vincy but she is loving as well as refined and it is the unselfish and affectionate aspect of her character which is stressed and which makes Maggie's betrayal all the more reprehensible. We are to admire Lucy first of all with just the faintest indulgent smile as the model of what a pretty little woman should be, and even Stephen does not fully appreciate her rarest quality: the unwonted irony in George Eliot's description of his obtuseness about his fiancée reinforces the author's own high valuation of Lucy:

Was not Stephen Guest right in his decided opinion that this slim maiden of eighteen was quite the sort of wife a man would not be likely to repent of marrying?—a woman who was loving and thoughtful for other women, not giving them Judas-kisses with eyes askance on their welcome defects, but with real care and vision for their half-hidden pains and mortifications, with long ruminating enjoyment of little pleasures prepared for them? Perhaps the emphasis of his admiration did not fall precisely on this rarest quality in her— perhaps he approved his own choice of her chiefly because she did not strike him as a remarkable rarity. A man likes his wife to be pretty: but not to a maddening extent. A man likes his wife to be accomplished, gentle, affectionate, and not stupid; and Lucy had all these qualifications. (Bk. 6, Ch. 1)

Maggie, with greater insight, sees better the loving spirit in the pretty exterior: ' "You dear, tiny thing", said Maggie, in one of her bursts of loving admiration, "you enjoy other people's happiness so much, I believe you would do without any of your own. I wish I were like you" ' (Bk. 6, Ch. 2). The last words are prophetic. And, of course, with this superior insight Maggie's weakness in half consenting to Stephen's pleas is even more blameable than his selfishness and lack of discrimination in his appreciation of Lucy. Lucy's last action in the book, when she steals away from her family to visit Maggie and comfort her, becomes her even better than all that went before, and is proof of the truth of Maggie's high opinion of her.

Both Lucy and Maggie are powerless to carve out their own happiness on the ordinary level, powerless to shape the outward circumstances of their lives. Maggie, with great potentialities and a great power of loving, is placed in a position where she is subjected to a temptation too strong for the weaknesses of her nature, unstrengthened by education or wise guidance. She has no one who can really help her, although Philip comes the nearest to meeting her need. She yields, against her better judgment, 'to the present moment', and she repents. Once having seen the situation as it really is, she has the inner strength to redeem herself by going back to a life of remorse, loneliness and ostracism. Lucy, with a seemingly happy lot, with beauty, comfort, loving protection around her, still has her life darkened by the unprovoked cruelty of two people who profess to love her, and one of whom is capable of seeing her sterling qualities. She forgives them, with no reproaches, and her only reference to the tragedy, which is hers as much, if not more, than theirs, is as 'the trouble that has come upon us all'.

George Eliot, replying to John Blackwood when he remarked he had found *Silas Marner* (1861) rather gloomy, said that it set, or was intended to set, in 'a strong light, the remedial influences of pure, natural, human relations'.[15] The remedial agents in the story are all women. For Silas it is the influence of the child Eppie that brings him back from his far country of alienation, it is the care of Eppie that forces him out of his isolation. Whereas 'the gold had kept his thoughts in an ever-repeated circle', leading to nothing beyond itself, Eppie carries them away to 'the new things that would come with the coming years' and makes him form ties with his neighbours. Eppie is the living treasure that has come to replace the inanimate one. She has an independence of her own and, like George Eliot's other children, she reveals her author's absolute fidelity in the depiction of childhood—of which the often-quoted incident in the coalhole is but one example. As a young woman she develops the qualities that we have learnt to recognize as those George Eliot admired in women, and these brought a happiness richer than gold to the life of the weaver. Eppie is the gentle, innocent, happy, loving young woman who is a treasure in any household. The ideal relationship between her and Silas is the result of perfect love and this has a refining and elevating effect on both their characters, Eppie's no less than Silas's. Silas has his final reward when Godfrey and Nancy Cass come to the cottage to ask Eppie to go back with them to the Red House as their daughter and she refuses, because Silas would be left alone.

The women in *Silas Marner* have a strength and integrity not to be found in the men around them. It is the rather effeminate weaver who most nearly attains their level, and in his way he becomes almost one of them, living for the same ends of domestic happiness and service. The waste of any greater potentialities in the women is, in this simple story, no more than hinted at; they have found a fair measure of happiness by loving and serving within their own narrow but not frustrating lots.

Romola (1862–3) alone amongst George Eliot's novels has a woman's name as its title and, although critics have frequently praised Tito Melema, as an artistic creation, more than Romola herself, there is no doubt that Romola's character is held up for our admiration. There is an atmosphere of moral amplitude about her such as surrounds none of the other heroines, not even Dorothea. Romola is a woman who knows nothing of pettiness or vanity, she is the exact opposite of a 'narrow souled woman', and her tall, fair, majestic beauty is symbolic of the soul within. Although this outward beauty is of advantage to her in that it brings her the homage and trust of the simple people, it has the disadvantage of attracting Tito Melema to marry her, for it is inconceivable that he could have married a plain woman. Thus, as with Maggie and with Gwendolen Harleth and, on a different level, with Hetty Sorrel, a woman's beauty can in some senses be a curse to her. Romola's majestic type of beauty also makes her a lonely figure among her fellow women: some of them revere her and lean upon her, as do Tessa and Brigida, but she finds with them no real companionship such as she might have enjoyed if the physical differences as well as the mental differences between them had been less great.

Romola's learning also separates her from her fellow women,

111

in spite of the fact that she is the antithesis of all that George
Eliot and her age (the preceding one too) disliked in the conventional figure of the bluestocking, who could not resist showing off her little learning on every occasion. Romola is a scholar
who makes no parade of learning but, within its limits, that
learning has been completely assimilated to make her mind
nobler and her outlook wider. It may be remembered that when
Emily Davies tried to enlist George Eliot's support for the new
women's college that was to become Girton College, at Cambridge, the latter was anxious that the women who were first to
receive higher education should be those who had natures large
and rich enough not to be used up in the pursuit of knowledge;
the gift she later sent to Girton was 'from the author of Romola',
the noblest of her women. Certainly Romola is in no danger of
forgetting the masculine scorn which surrounds her for even her
blind father, to whom she is a devoted amanuensis, underrates
her power of application and openly sighs for the son who has
left him for the Church. He does, however, admit that 'thou hast
a man's nobility of soul: thou hast never fretted me with thy
petty desires as thy mother did' (Bk. 1, Ch. 5), although he
attributes this to his having kept her 'aloof from the debasing
influence of thy own sex, with their sparrow-like frivolities
and their enslaving superstition'.

Romola's filial tenderness towards her father is very beautiful.
Even to Tito, before he realizes that he has sold himself to evil,
'Romola's life seemed an image of that loving, pitying devoted-
ness, that patient endurance of irksome tasks, from which he
had shrunk and excused himself'. But her sheltered life has left
her blind to the characters of men and, ignoring her brother's
warning, she marries Tito. There seems to be something arche-
typal about Romola—Tito at first felt in her presence 'that
loving awe . . . which is perhaps something like the worship paid
of old to a great nature goddess, who was not all-knowing, but
whose life and power were something deeper and more prim-
ordial than knowledge'. It is tempting to think that, although
Romola is usually believed to possess some of the features of
Barbara Bodichon or other friends of the author, George Eliot
possibly created her out of her own need that such a figure
should have existed; certainly, in reply to Sara Hennell's

complaint that Romola is ideal, George Eliot admits she is right and goes on: 'I feel it acutely in the reproof my own soul is constantly getting from the image it has made'.[16]

In *Felix Holt, the Radical* (1866) no author-identification is discernible in the two main female characters: the one (Mrs Transome) is an ageing beauty who has cared only for the power that beauty brought her and who deeply regrets its passing; the other (Esther Lyon) is a young, vain, fastidious girl with shallow views of life, who attains a deeper insight into its true values through the influence and love of the Radical Felix Holt. The fates of these two are sharply contrasted, but the happiness of both is dependent upon the kind of men they love: Mrs Transome commits adultery with a self-seeking and vulgar country lawyer and Esther Lyon has the great good fortune to marry a young idealist, a better human being than herself.

Mrs Transome is already married when we meet her but there is sufficient retrospective description of her as a girl for that part of her life to qualify for inclusion in this chapter. The circumstances of the young Arabella Lingon's lot in life are promising: she is of gentle birth, great beauty and bold spirit. George Eliot's description of her education under a 'superior governess who held that a woman should be able to write a good letter, and to express herself with propriety on general subjects', with some detail given of those general subjects, is scathing, but there are hints at deeper failings, or possibilities of deeper faults in the future, so that Arabella's later liaison with the showy Matthew Jermyn is not so surprising as it might otherwise have been.

By George Eliot's standards the lot of Esther Lyon is more fortunate than that of the lady of Transome Court. Esther is redeemed by the kind of man she loves and the path of redemption is described in detail. Although Esther is—or rather, appears to be—the daughter of Rufus Lyon, a learned, eccentric, lovable minister of the Dissenting Chapel in Malthouse Yard, she has been educated in France and gives French lessons in the Treby neighbourhood. She is pretty, with the long neck of George Eliot's beauties, is graceful in movement and holds her head very high in Treby. In a way more frivolous than Maggie's, she is vaguely discontented with her life: 'she seemed to herself to be surrounded with ignoble, uninteresting conditions, from which there was no issue'. Felix Holt points out to her what 'shallow stuff' her ideas are made of, saying roundly:

You don't care to be better than a bird trimming its feathers, and pecking about after what pleases it. You are discontented with the world because you can't get just the small things that suit your pleasure, not because it's a world where myriads of men and women are ground by wrong and misery, and tainted with pollution . . . (Ch. 10)

He tells her how he sees the kind of influence foolish women exert over the men they meet:

Men can't help loving them, and so they make themselves slaves to the petty desires of petty creatures. That's the way those who might do better spend their lives for nought—get checked in every effort—toil with brain and limb for things that have no more to do with a manly life than tarts and confectionery. That's what makes women a curse; all life is stunted to suit their littleness. (Ch. 10)

The wielding of influence of this kind was later worked out in the character of Rosamond Lydgate in *Middlemarch*, but in *Felix Holt* the heroine has the chance of growth and change. Although Esther is greatly mortified by these words, she begins to wonder, after her indignation has subsided, whether Felix is not right after all. Soon she finds herself falling in love with him. His views on the good life constitute a challenge to her; when he tells her that he weds poverty because it enables him to do what he wants to do most, to 'try to make life less bitter for a few', she replies, in a passage revealing the author's view of the differences of the destinies of men and women:

'That seems a hard lot; yet it is a great one . . .'
'Then you don't think I'm a fool,' said Felix . . .
'Of course, you suspected me of that stupidity.'
'Well—women, unless they are Saint Theresas or Elizabeth Frys, generally think this sort of thing madness, unless they read of it in the Bible.'

Esther's reply is more profound than might have been expected: 'A woman can hardly ever choose in that way; she is dependent on what happens to her. She must take meaner things, because

114

only meaner things are within her reach' (Ch. 27). Esther does derive some pleasure from the few signs she sees of her power over Felix, but the seeming inevitability of his renunciation of ordinary happiness is made all the more bitter; and at this time the hidden qualities of her nature are revealed:

Esther, like a woman as she was—a woman waiting for love, never able to ask for it—had her joy in these signs of her power, but they made her generous, not chary, as they might have done if she had had a pettier disposition. She said, with deep yet timid earnestness—
'What you have chosen to do has only convinced me that your love would be the better worth having.'
All the finest part of Esther's nature trembled in those words. To be right in great memorable moments, is perhaps the thing we need most desire for ourselves. (Ch. 32)

She wants to be worthy of what she admires in Felix, but she is miserable. 'If she might have married Felix Holt, she could have been a good woman. She felt no trust that she could ever be good without him.'

The deepening of her character continues while Felix is in prison, and she has the courage to give evidence on his behalf at his trial. She comes to realize the hollowness of the life offered her at Transome Court as Harold Transome's wife, but she is faced with a difficult choice because, if she chooses to renounce her claims to the Transome estates and goes back to her old life, there is no certainty that Felix will be by her side to share it with her: 'a supreme love, a motive that gives a sublime rhythm to a woman's life, and exalts habit into partnership with the soul's highest needs, is not to be had where and how she wills'. But the night of her decision is the night she hears Mrs Transome pacing up and down in her agony of emptiness. Esther catches a glimpse of 'the dreary waste of years empty of sweet trust and affection' and it afflicts her even to horror. Although Felix may never be her husband, her father still needs her care and love, and when Felix comes out of prison he finds her back with her father. After they are married, George Eliot comments that 'in the ages since Adam's marriage, it has been good for some men to be alone, and for some women also', but Esther was not one of these women: she was intensely of the feminine type, verging neither towards the saint nor the angel. Hers was 'a fair divided excellence, whose fulness of perfection must be in marriage'. With Felix she found happiness and improvement, if not perfection, and this was for her creator the highest happiness woman could expect: 'In this, at least, her woman's lot was perfect: that the man she loved was her hero; that her woman's passion and her reverence for rarest goodness rushed together in an undivided current' (Ch. 46).

In the contrast between the fates of Arabella Transome and Esther Lyon, the one yielding to pride, unwilling to be taught by life, the other setting her vanity aside and allowing herself to be changed by the influence of a man better than herself, one of the most subtle touches is the renunciation by Esther of her rightful claim to the Transome Estate, a claim which, if persisted in, would have reduced Mrs Transome to an even more humiliating position. Esther freely renounces power, while Arabella seeks after it and loses it.

Although *Middlemarch* (1871–2) is, according to its sub-title, a novel of provincial life, a study set against the Loamshire background, it is more particularly a novel about the 'social lot of women' and George Eliot stresses this when she reminds her readers that Herodotus also 'in telling what had been, thought it as well to take a woman's lot for his starting point'. In the very significant Prelude, which in itself is a summary of the author's conception of the lot of nineteenth-century women, the basic tragedy of Dorothea's life is illumined by the likening of her to a St Theresa of Avila, born in an age which forced her to be 'foundress of nothing', 'for these later-born Theresas were helped by no coherent social faith and order which could perform the function of knowledge for the ardent willing soul'. *Middlemarch* contains two tragedies of accomplishment falling far short of potential achievement—the cases of Lydgate and Dorothea: but whereas Lydgate has a clear idea of the field of medicine to which his contribution may be made, Dorothea's circumstances prevent her from attaining any distinct vision of what for her would involve the 'constant unfolding of far-resonant action'; her unattained goodness is dispersed among hindrances. Although its richness offers many other layers, the novel's greatest power is invested in the figure of Dorothea and George Eliot's sympathy with her is obvious from the first; she

has the kind of qualities which the novelist considered important in women. She is noble-minded, with no traces of pettiness
or vanity, and she yearns for a wider view of life than her
education or her environment have provided for her; she also
has a loving heart. She longs to be able to attain 'some lofty
conception of the world which might frankly include the parish
of Tipton and her own rule of conduct there', that is, to see a
role for a woman in her social circumstances which might enable
her to make some contribution to the larger good, as St Theresa
had been able to see *her* role in the Catholic church of her day.
She is interested in practical works of social betterment: she
sets an infant school going in the village and she hopes to
induce her uncle (and is indeed successful in inducing Sir James
Chettam) to build better cottages for his tenants, even drawing
some of the plans herself. Had she been a less 'deep souled
woman' she might have found enough outlet for her energies in
village charities, patronage of the humbler clergy, the care of
her own soul over her embroidery and praying for her husband,
but she wishes very sincerely 'to make her life greatly effective'.
Her ideas about marriage take their colour entirely from an
exalted enthusiasm about the ends of life, an enthusiasm more
suited to great, impersonal dedication than to domestic, everyday living in Victorian England. Unlike her sister, Celia, she
does not look merely for comfort and fashion, but hopes to be
of help to someone greater than herself, to 'have a husband . . .
above me in judgment and in all knowledge'. She is, therefore,
humbly grateful when the middle-aged clergyman, Edward
Casaubon, who has been busy for thirty years collecting material
for a 'Key to all Mythologies' proposes to her. She feels

There would be nothing trivial about our lives. Everyday things
with us would mean the greatest things. It would be like marrying
Pascal. I should learn to see the truth by the same light as great men
have seen it by. And then I should know what to do, when I got
older: I should see how it was possible to lead a grand life here—
now—in England. (Ch. 3)

It all depends, of course, on how deep are the mind and spirit
that she compares with Pascal, how free from triviality the
life and work of the man to whom she is devoting herself, but

117

the aim has nothing small about it; her lack of judgment in mistaking a dried-up pedant for a sage is the fault of her youth and inexperience. That her motives were misunderstood by the lesser people around her is a condemnation of them rather than of Dorothea, and the lack of sympathy and understanding of her nearest and dearest is part of the second-rate quality of her environment.

The depth of Dorothea's nature is contrasted with the narrowness of Rosamond Vincy's. George Eliot's view of Rosamond is obvious, although she expresses no harsh condemnations and makes all allowances for the inadequate training which, in her case as well as Dorothea's, helps to make her what she is. Rosamond's beauty is that of the Eliot siren, with long neck and 'wondrous plaits of fair hair'. She has been the flower of Mrs Lemon's school, the chief school in the county, 'where the teaching included all that was demanded in the accomplished female—even to extras, such as getting in and out of a carriage', and, inevitably, with such training a small-natured girl would spend the rest of her life trying to get into ever grander carriages. Rosamond's aim is to behave like a perfect lady rather than to be one, and she has 'that controlled self-consciousness of manner which is the expensive substitute for simplicity'. She always *seems* rather than *is*. Dorothea, on the other hand, has true simplicity of manner and *is* rather than *seems*. The attitude of George Eliot's characters to music is always significant, and it is worthy of mention that Rosamond's admirable piano-playing is merely cleverly imitated from an outstanding master. She had 'seized his manner of playing and gave forth his large rendering of noble music with the precision of an echo'.

In another way Dorothea is contrasted with her sister, a young woman ideally suited to be happy in the comfortable environment which her lot has provided for her since she is decorative, socially adaptable, and scornful of her sister's uncomfortable 'notions'. She serves to throw Dorothea yet further into relief and to add a depth to the loneliness in which the elder sister really finds herself, with no one in her circle approaching her own level. The woman nearest to her in worth is possibly Mary Garth, a young woman of integrity, whose lot, although by material standards far less enviable than Dorothea's, does bring her the satisfaction of family understanding and affection and the love of a young man who needs her guidance and whose life she can redeem into something worthier than it would be without her.

The importance of 'lot' in *Middlemarch* is even greater than in the other novels—the word itself appears with insistent frequency, almost like a knell, throughout, and there is a special, pervading note of regret about the lot of distinguished women to whom fate offers only the second-rate in opportunities of work or of marriage, but George Eliot offers no solution and prescribes no remedies for these inequalities.

Again in *Daniel Deronda* (1876) George Eliot traces the moral law working in the lives of two widely different women, Gwendolen Harleth and Mirah. Punishment in the form of a loveless marriage comes to a girl who has sought what she wants at the expense of others, while the one man she does love is occupied in Zionist activities and chooses a Jewess to reign in his heart. George Eliot was not personally identified with Gwendolen Harleth as she was with Maggie Tulliver and Dorothea, and the portrait is therefore differently focused. Gwendolen is a young beauty, fond of homage, and 'fed with flattery which makes a lovely girl believe in her divine right to rule'. She feels 'well equipped for the mastery of life' and she decides to master it. The only way of 'mastery' open to Gwendolen, with the pitiful equipment she really possesses, apart from her beauty, is the way of what the world calls a 'brilliant marriage'. Although she is warned that, if she makes the particular brilliant marriage her lot offers her, it will be at the expense of someone else's moral, if not legal, rights, she nevertheless goes ahead and marries Grandcourt, and afterwards pays the inevitable price of misery.

The first description we have of Gwendolen is of a long-necked, serpent-like enchantress. In the casino at Leubronn she appears in an 'ensemble du serpent' of green and silver and is said to have a sort of Lamia beauty; later she walks up the Obere Strasse 'with her usual floating movement, every line in her figure and drapery falling in gentle curves attractive to all eyes except those which discerned in them too close a resemblance to the serpent, and objected to the revival of serpent worship' (Ch. 1). The determination to dominate and the sub-conscious realization that domination is difficult for a woman is already present in her mind when she is said to have visions of being worshipped as a goddess of luck, with her play being watched as a directing augury—'such things had been known of male gamblers; why should not a woman have a like supremacy?'

George Eliot called the first book of *Daniel Deronda* 'The Spoiled Child' and in it Gwendolen's upbringing is described in some detail. The girl has led a rootless existence as the beautiful eldest daughter of a widowed mother, living amidst a bevy of plain younger sisters and being taught by an 'elderly, neutral governess'. It will be noted that this is an all-female household. In the Meyrick family, on the other hand, the girls 'knew what it was to have a brother and to be generally regarded as of minor importance in the world', just as Maggie Tulliver had known. It is tantalizing to speculate how different Gwendolen's story might have been had she had a brother. Her formal education has consisted of two years at a showy school where on all occasions of display she has been put forward, as was Rosa-mond Vincy at Mrs Lemon's. This has only deepened Gwen-dolen's 'sense that so exceptional a person as herself could hardly remain in ordinary circumstances or in a social position less than advantageous', and since the 'unexplained rules and disconnected facts' she has learnt in the schoolroom, and a certain facility in French and music, together with knowledge gained through novels, plays, poems, give her a sense of her own power of forming correct judgment on everything, Gwendolen 'feels ready to manage her own destiny'.

When the apparently eligible Henleigh Mallinger Grand-court appears in her life, her dominant thought is to subdue and later to refuse him, and she deliberately fascinates him with all the skill at her disposal. But the difference between the kind of man that Grandcourt actually is and the way Gwen-dolen thinks of him is ominous. Grandcourt is a dark enigma with a 'withered heart', and this young girl, pitifully ignorant of the characters of men, sets out to use him for her own ends. Her exploitation of him for the sake of her pride and later of her position is, in its way, as reprehensible as his entering into relationship with her as a different kind of 'object'. Grandcourt, from long experience, is extremely skilful in his courtship, although he curses under his breath from time to time. In one of their conversations Gwendolen expresses a point of view about the static lives of women that may provide an additional explanation of her deliberate use of her fascination to subdue and then to scorn; she says:

We women can't go in search of adventure—to find out the North-West passage or the source of the Nile, or to hunt tigers in the East. We must stay where we grow, or where the gardeners like to transplant us. We are brought up like the flowers, to look as pretty as we can, and be dull without complaining. That is my notion about the plants: they are often bored, and that is the reason why some of them have got poisonous. (Ch. 13)

Although Gwendolen is scarcely a St Theresa, foundress of nothing, she does possess greater abilities than can be used in her flimsy environment, so she has become a beautiful but harmful plant, misusing its power of attraction.

As she realizes more clearly what dignities and luxuries she would enjoy as Grandcourt's wife, Gwendolen gradually finds the prospect of marrying him more attractive and she believes that after marriage she will most probably be able to manage him very well. When she meets Lydia Glasher, Grandcourt's mistress, with two of Grandcourt's children and Lydia tells her story, Gwendolen, watching her face while she spoke, 'felt a sort of terror: it was as if some ghastly vision had come to her in a dream and said, "I am a woman's life" '. She flees to Leubronn to think the matter over but, recalled by a letter from her mother on the family's financial crisis, she is faced with the prospect of having to earn her own living. She is forced to contemplate the possibility of taking a post as a governess, either in a bishop's house, or in 'quite a high class of school', but, of course, she has neither the education and training nor the temperament that could be successful in such work. She turns to the possibility of becoming a professional singer but Herr Klessmer points out in no uncertain terms what her true prospects are in that field. Then she begins to think of Grandcourt again, or rather of the comfortable and luxurious life she would lead as his wife, and she realizes that, had it not been for that day in Cardell Chase, she would see no obstacle to marrying him. The next step is to persuade herself that, in marrying Grandcourt, another woman would not really be doing Lydia Glasher and her boy any real injury. When she has actually accepted Grandcourt, she is on one occasion appalled by the realization that she is 'going to do what she had once started away from with repugnance', but, because she has never learnt to consider others

with all her debating she was never troubled by the question whether the indefensibleness of her marriage did not include the fact that she had accepted Grandcourt solely as the man whom it was convenient for her to marry, not in the least as one to whom she would be binding herself in duty. (Ch. 29)

Such an indefensible 'union' is obviously doomed.

As an artistic creation Mirah, compared with Gwendolen, is a sawdust doll; the virtues she possesses are not fully realized and integrated into the portrait but they are interesting in themselves. In the years before *Daniel Deronda* was published George Eliot's mind had obviously been much occupied with Jewish matters: in a letter she wrote to Rabbi Deutsch in 1871[17] she mentions the fact that when Mary Wollstonecraft attempted suicide she had soaked her garments well in the rain, hoping to sink the better when she plunged into the water. It will be remembered that it is just this method Mirah is using when, on her first appearance in the novel, she is wetting her cloak in the Thames so that it may make a heavy drowning shroud. The tragic lot of Mary Wollstonecraft may have had a special interest for George Eliot, although Lewes was mercifully no Imlay, and this pitiful episode was evidently in her mind at the same time as she was studying the Jewish question. The coalescence of the two topics and the use of the cloak-wetting incident in the novel is a tiny but specific example of the transmutation of an artist's current interests into her art.

Mirah's contrast to Gwendolen is worked out in several ways. Gwendolen is a rather indifferent singer with an unjustified over-valuation of her own performance. Mirah is a professional singer who has attained such high standards that she can receive the words of ultimate praise from Herr Klessmer: 'Let us shake hands: you are a musician'. But it is difficult to bring musical excellence alive on the silent page: could we hear Mirah sing she would be a far more vivid figure. Again in contrast with Gwendolen, Mirah's musical training has been in a hard school and she has had to make her own refuge from the damaging influences of life on the stage. Gwendolen had wished to exploit her small musical talent, but Mirah's voice is exploited by her own father. Mirah's submission to others (unless they wish to make her do wrong) is stressed: Mrs Meyrick says to Deronda in reply to his question whether Mirah would be content to wait while a search is being made for her mother: 'No trouble there. It is not her nature to run into planning and devising: only to submit.' This submission may be partly due to her position as a Jewess, but it sits rather irritatingly on the surface of her character, as Henry James noticed. Certainly the submissiveness and absence of planning and devising is in direct contrast with Gwendolen's determination to master, just as there could scarcely be a greater difference between Mirah's early life, which trained her in submission, and the 'spoiled child' girlhood of Gwendolen. Again, Gwendolen has a pseudo-sophistication, although she really knows very little of the world, whereas Mirah has retained, through all the sordidness of her surroundings, a true simplicity and truthfulness: 'Mirah was not childlike from ignorance: her experience of evil and trouble was deeper and stranger' than Deronda's own. Confronted with the real pain of the possibility, or rather certainty, as it seems at one point, that Deronda loves Gwendolen, Mirah faces the prospect with fortitude and resolute acceptance, in contrast with Gwendolen who has snatched at what seems able to provide happiness for herself, no matter who else suffers. These contrasts are more important for the light they throw upon Gwendolen's character than upon Mirah's own.

Catherine Arrowpoint is also contrasted with Gwendolen, both in looks, position, character and musical accomplishment. Expecting to feel superior to the rather plain Miss Arrowpoint, Gwendolen finds her reaction in fact quite different, for Catherine had 'a certain mental superiority which could not be explained away—an exasperating thoroughness in her musical accomplishment, a fastidious discrimination in her general tastes, which made it impossible to force her admiration and kept you in awe of her standard' (Ch. 6). Catherine is not one of George Eliot's major characters but in her case her creator was not intimidated as she was by Mirah's Jewishness and the qualities with which she endows her are the familiar admired ones. Instead of beauty Catherine has wealth. She also has musicianship and taste and the indispensable warmth of character, together with advanced social views. In marrying Klessmer, Miss Arrowpoint, as an heiress, takes a step diametrically opposed to the expectations of her social class, an act of independence which Gwendolen finds quite impossible in her different circumstances. Mr and Mrs Arrowpoint have already felt some anxiety at their daughter's clear head and strong will, because 'she would not accept the view of her social duty which required her to marry a needy nobleman or a commoner on the ladder towards nobility', and when they attempt to dissuade her from the marriage, appealing to her sense of duty to her parents and to society, she replies: 'I am sorry to hurt you . . . But I will not give up the happiness of my life to ideas that I don't believe in and customs I have no respect for . . . I can't see any public good concerned here.' Gwendolen has not, of course, in her own case, been guided by consideration of any public good, however mistaken, but has chosen comfort and the usurpation of the rights of others.

If we regard George Eliot's longer poems as short stories in verse, we can find in them more examples of the kind of women in whom she was obviously most interested. There is again the beautiful, intelligent woman whose lot presents a conflict between love and duty, and the lowly, modest woman who finds her happiness in self-effacing love and tenderness for others. Fedalma, in *The Spanish Gypsy* (1868), one of George Eliot's noble women, is faced with an order to give up her love and to follow her father and lead the gypsy people back to a homeland; she accepts her destiny with a brave but breaking heart. The heroine of *Agatha* (1869) is an elderly old maid who lives her secluded life guided by love and duty, caring for her feeble, aged cousins, helping the neighbours and praying for all. Agatha obviously obeys the same law of love and service to others that was followed by a series of women from Mrs Amos Barton to

Mrs Meyrick, women without any great powers of intellect and with no urge to seek an artificial intensity of life or unusual achievement, who yet find their happiness in love and care for others, and in exerting what George Eliot calls, in contemporary language, 'the soothing charm of gentle womanhood'.

The greatest of George Eliot's feminine portraits are drawn from the inside, from the actual experience of a woman's awareness of life. The rich texture of the novels and their fully detailed background of provincial activities obscure the more profound depth of the realization in the case of the women characters. Men are not 'the others' as they are in Jane Austen, but there is still a difference between this all-embracing consideration of the human condition and the immediacy of the emotional truth of the one sex's experience. The feelings that rose in Mr Brooke's befuddled mind during his disastrous speech to the Electors of Middlemarch or the aspirations of Lydgate in his medical work represent an achievement of imaginative insight, whereas the frustrations that conquered Maggie Tulliver and Dorothea have been lived through.

These heroines did not pass away without issue—Isabel Archer is their direct descendant and Henry James acknowledges his indebtedness in his Preface to *The Portrait of a Lady*. Mr Ehrman Syme Nagel, second secretary at the American Legation in London in James's day, said of him that 'he seemed to look at women rather as women looked at them. Women look at women as persons; men look at them as women'.[18] It was a penetrating and relevant comment.

6

Women as Wives

NOT ONLY did both the convention of the novel and contemporary taste cause our writers to concentrate upon their unmarried heroines but most of them, in considering women as wives, faced the difficulty of examining a role of which they had no first-hand knowledge. Only one of the group was married and did most of her writing during her years as a wife—Mrs Gaskell. Fanny Burney and Charlotte Brontë were married late in life, after their best literary work was done, and Jane Austen, Maria Edgeworth, Anne and Emily Brontë never married at all. George Eliot did not legally marry until she was over sixty, although for this study her years with George Henry Lewes may be considered as years of marriage, albeit marriage with a social difference which caused her to have more detachment than women living in conventional unions. The exploration of the role of wives in most of the great women novelists is, therefore, less thorough than their exploration of the role of the single girl, but this does not mean that they had no views of their own about marriage. The Brontës held very strong views indeed and, in their case, the fact that these views were those of onlookers caused the sisters to express them more forcibly, believing that the view of marriage from the outside has its own contribution to make to the understanding of all concerned. One effect that the lack of any inside experience had upon the treatment of marriage in many of the novels was that the writers saw their married women only as women on whom matrimony had bestowed a higher social status and to whom it offered a wider field of activity than before; they analysed their matrons' behaviour as hostesses and as mistresses of households and in the more public aspects of their relationship with their husbands, not so much in the psychological adjustments involved in the relationship and certainly not with any more than hints about the physical side of marriage.

Fanny Burney

Fanny Burney's first novel was by a young woman about young women and the only married lady of any significance in it is Madame Duval, who is a figure of fun, coming to life only in some of the ridiculous situations in which she finds herself. In *Cecilia*, Mrs Delvile, a woman of taste and cultivation in her own right, is introduced mainly so that, as Delvile's mother, she may use all her efforts to keep the lovers apart.

Miss Burney did, in *Camilla*, create the young wives Mrs Arlbery, Mrs Berlinton, and Lady Isabella Irby. Of little interest in themselves they serve as warnings to any young reader who might be tempted to imitate their behaviour. Mrs Arlbery is beautiful, spirited, and unconventional and her conversation approaches more closely than that of any of Fanny Burney's characters to the fascination of an Austen heroine's. She treats her visitors in a way that surprises Camilla, ordering them all away, but saying that they may come again in the evening, though not too early: she replies to Camilla's unspoken astonishment

'You are not used to my way, I perceive . . . yet I can nevertheless assure you, you can do nothing so much for your happiness as to adopt it. You are made a slave in a moment by the world, if you don't begin life by defying it. Take your own way, follow your own humour, and you and the world will both go on just as well, as if you ask its will and pleasure for every thing you do, and want, and think.' (Vol. 2, Ch. 11)

These are dangerous words to enter the ear of the heroine of a courtesy novel and it is not surprising that Edgar Mandlebert, Camilla's very priggish lover, whose ideas on female behaviour are extremely strict, does not approve of Mrs Arlbery as a friend for her. As he says, although Mrs Arlbery's character is wholly unimpeached, 'she had offended or frightened almost all the county around, by a wilful strangeness of behaviour, resulting from an undaunted determination to follow in everything the bent of her own humour'. Mrs Arlbery, married but unencumbered by her husband's presence, is, of course, free to choose how she shall behave in a manner completely denied to a young, unmarried girl.

Mrs Berlinton, beautiful and clever but far too impulsive and romantic—given for instance, to reading poetry aloud during the night in the open countryside—receives Edgar's more open censure. He contrasts her character with that of Lady Isabella Irby, the model of a female of rank. Mrs Berlinton allows her avowed admirers to approach her without active discouragement, whereas

Lady Isabella, addressed only where known, followed only because loved, sees no adulators encircling her; no admirers paying her homage, for such homage would offend her. She knows she has not only her own innocence to guard, but the honour of her husband. Whether she is happy with him or not, this deposit is equally sacred. (Vol. 3, Ch. 11)

This long-inherited concern for a husband's 'honour' is something the good wife always keeps in mind; his honour must not only be in no danger, it must be seen to be in no danger at all times and under all provocations. Since the attraction that the indiscreet conduct of such women as Mrs Berlinton had for young women might be considerable, Fanny Burney analyses the weaknesses of her character so as to leave no doubt in the reader's mind that Mrs Berlinton's example is not to be followed. The lady had been early left an orphan and was brought up by a 'fanatical' maiden aunt who had taught her her faith and her prayers but had given her no instruction in good works or the practical applications of piety. Then her brother, on his first university vacation, had introduced her to 'the Poets', and the picturesque, tender, noble and enthusiastic in what she read went to her romantic head, unsteadied by anything rational. She had entered the world by a 'sudden and most unequal marriage, in which her choice had no part', with only two self-formed maxims for her guidance:

The first of these was, that from her early notions of religion, no vestal should be more personally chaste; the second, that, from her more recently imbibed ones of tenderness, her heart, since she was married without its concurrence, was still wholly at liberty to be disposed of by its own propensities, without reproach and without scruple. (Vol. 3, Ch. 12)

With such dangerous notions, Mrs Berlinton's downfall is

inevitable, and she soon takes to flirtation and coquetry, misled by 'Faro and Fashion'.

In accordance with their vows in the marriage service, wives must, of course, obey their husbands. Fanny Burney makes an occasion to introduce this point rather contrivedly, when she says of Camilla's mother that

had this lady been united to a man whom she despised, she would yet have obeyed him, and as scrupulously, though not as happily, as she obeyed her honoured partner. She considered the vow taken at the altar to her husband, as a voluntary vestal would have held one taken to her Maker: and no dissent in opinion exculpated, in her mind, the least deviation from his will. (Vol. 1, Ch. 1)

Miss Burney herself never suggests the possibility of any deviation from such standards. When the marriage relationship is regarded in this light it is not surprising that it was considered improper to discuss its problems with any degree of frankness.

Maria Edgeworth

Maria Edgeworth's father was so frequently given to matrimony that his daughter had unrivalled opportunities for surveying the relationship from close at hand. She certainly peoples her novels with a large number of married women, but their married state serves mainly to provide them with wider opportunities for benevolent activities than their single condition would have allowed. Miss Edgeworth uses them, too, as embodiments of certain stock domestic faults or virtues. Griselda Bolingbroke in *The Modern Griselda* (1805) is an example of a wife whose temper is not sufficiently disciplined: she is prone to touchiness, over-sensibility and the desire to show her power over her initially adoring husband, and she eventually loses him. The use of the description 'modern Griselda' is obviously intended to satirize the deterioration in contemporary manners in comparison with older, stricter standards. Griselda is contrasted with her former friend, Emma Cooke, now Mrs Granby, who, although not possessing Griselda's beauty and talents, is yet able to acquire power over her husband 'by not desiring it'. Maria Edgeworth had already mentioned the intoxication that power

129

exercised over the female mind in her earlier *Letters for Literary Ladies*; in Griselda the weakness is considered to denote a lack of self-discipline, there is no sign that it might be regarded as an indication that a vigorous spirit, given no other outlet for its energy, is apt to over-exert itself in the only ways that are open to it. The dangers of novel-reading to such minds is, however, mentioned in Miss Edgeworth's anti-sensibility novel, *Leonora* (1806), in which the villainess, Lady Olivia, is full of the 'delusion of passion and sensibility', fed first by metaphysics and then by German novels. These 'women of feeling', Leonora's mother, a Duchess, explains to her, 'want excitation for their morbid sensibility' and they care not at what expense it is produced: 'the mental intemperance that they indulge in promiscuous novel reading destroys all vigour and clearness of judgment; everything dances in the varying medium of their imagination' (Letter VI). Excessive sensibility does not usually lead to anything worse than mild folly, causing pain to the woman-of-feeling herself, but in Lady Olivia its results are more serious, leading her to steal the heroine's husband. Fortunately Leonora, by her uncomplaining attitude to the whole affair, wins him back again. The Duchess fears that women will, by their foolishness, lose the advantages they have recently gained: she says that of late years, due in certain measure to French influence, 'we have heard more of the rights of woman than of her duties'; she predicts that this will end in the ultimate law of force, and 'if men find that the virtue of women diminishes in proportion as intellectual cultivation increases, they will connect, fatally for the freedom and happiness of our sex, the ideas of female ignorance and female innocence'. The double standard of morals is accepted in *Leonora* without question: that Lady Olivia should endeavour to captivate Leonora's husband is condemned, but not the fact that he yielded to the temptation; and Mr L's letters to the General about Olivia, basically disloyal to her, are condoned, whereas those from Olivia to Madame de P., in a similar vein, are condemned and, indeed, bring about her downfall.

Although Maria Edgeworth made no attempt to investigate in any depth the effect the accepted standards had upon the adjustment of the individual to her deepest problems, she is skilful and amusing when less adult passions are involved, as in *Manoeuvring* (1809), which sets out to show how reprehensible are the methods of domestic scheming used by an arch-practitioner, Mrs Beaumont. The methods do not, of course, meet with any lasting success. Miss Edgeworth is also resourceful in suggesting some practical ways of helping other people that are open to married women of goodwill. The heroine of *Madame de Fleury* (1809), one of the Tales of Fashionable Life, opens a kind of nursery school for poor children in Paris, after she has been touched by the plight of a family whose mother has to leave her children while she goes out to work. Madame de Fleury later reaps the reward of her good works through the devotion and help of her pupils when she herself has to flee the country during the revolutionary upheavals. The description that Miss Edgeworth gives of Madame de Fleury may serve as an indication of her creator's ideal of a lady, with its characteristic stress on the useful rather than the ornamental in such a character:

with all the natural sensibility and graceful delicacy of her sex, she had none of that weakness or affectation, which incapacitates from being useful in real distress. In most sudden accidents, and in all domestic misfortunes, female resolution and presence of mind are indispensably requisite: safety, health, and life, often depend upon the fortitude of women. Happy they who, like Mad. de Fleury, possess strength of mind united with the utmost gentleness of manner and tenderness of disposition!

In the same novel Miss Edgeworth advocates the use of the 'influence' of women of which the conforming Victorian ladies later made so much. The ways in which she suggests it should be exercised reveal her own attitude to society, particularly when it is remembered that the novel is about revolutionary France:

Without meddling with politics, in which no amiable or sensible woman can wish to interfere, the influence of ladies in the higher ranks of life may always be exerted with perfect propriety, and with essential advantage to the public, in conciliating the inferior classes of society, explaining to them their duties and their interests, and impressing upon the minds of the children of the poor sentiments of just subordination and honest independence.

Her analysis of domestic happiness at an everyday level is more subtle. In *Émilie de Coulanges* (1812) she introduces two contrasted female characters, Mrs Somers and Lady Littleton. Mrs Somers is full of ambitiously generous plans for others but if she does not meet with instant response and gratitude from those she assists she takes offence, is often consumed with jealousy, and reacts violently to petty irritations. This leads to domestic unhappiness. Lady Littleton, on the other hand, creates a calm atmosphere around her. The lesson is made more explicit by pointing out that Lady Littleton employs her excellent understanding in studying the minute circumstances which tend to make people of different characters and tempers live happily together; she practises the *honest* arts of pleasing (Miss Edgeworth never goes so far as to recommend the dishonest arts) and she accomplishes everything without any violent effort but with that 'calm, gentle, persevering kindness of temper, which, when united to good sense, forms the real happiness of domestic life, and the true perfection of the female character'. It was to help her readers attain this true perfection of the female character, as she saw it, that so many of Maria Edgeworth's novels were written.

Jane Austen

The marriages which Jane Austen's heroines are about to contract when they leave us are all likely to prove happy ones, so suitably are the couples matched in every respect. Jane Austen's belief that marriage to an unprincipled man was one of the greatest evils that could befall a woman is expressed in *Sense and Sensibility* through Elinor's feelings of relief after Marianne has received Willoughby's cruel letter, and she considers the escape 'a deliverance the most real, a blessing the most important'. None of her heroines is allowed to suffer the fate of marrying a man without principles. The characters of her hero and heroine, however, are not always equal in strength and one feels in this same novel that Edward Ferrars is a weaker character than Elinor, although he does possess the indispensable good principles. Elinor will bring more resources of personality to the marriage than Edward does, and she will need them in order to keep it on the requisite high level of 'spirits'.

In spite of the good auguries for the future happiness of the heroines, an examination of the novels does not reveal comparable happiness amongst those who are married already: the quality of the marital life of Mr and Mrs John Dashwood, Sir Thomas and Lady Bertram and Mr and Mrs Charles Musgrove scarcely measures up to the highest standards. Greater happiness seems to have been the lot of the less socially ambitious couples like the Gardiners and the Crofts, simple, comfortable people living good-tempered domestic lives on an uneventful level.

Although there is nothing for very high praise, there is something for blame in many of the marriages, and Miss Austen does not hesitate to uncover the responsibility of the wife where this is justified, as in the tragi-comedy of the marriage of Mr and Mrs Bennet. Mrs Bennet is 'a woman of mean understanding, little information and uncertain temper' and the effect of such a character on her husband and children is worked out with the infallible strokes of the delicate but deadly brush. The picture is too well known to need anything save a reminder here but it is enlightening to contrast Mrs Bennet with Lady Littleton of Maria Edgeworth's *Émilie de Coulanges*. The qualities which enable Lady Littleton to create domestic happiness around her are entirely lacking in Mrs Bennet. Another failure to reach the author's high standards is detectable in her slightly amused contempt for the marriage of the John Knightleys and the self-absorbed and smug satisfaction of Isabella with her family. But although the shortcomings of wives may be blamed for some of their husbands' faults, Miss Austen has considerable faith in the power of a good wife to redeem the unsatisfactory character of her husband. In the first chapter of *Sense and Sensibility* she says of John Dashwood that 'had he married a more amiable woman, he might have been made still more respectable than he was; he might even have been made amiable himself', but, since his wife was 'a strong caricature of himself; more narrow-minded and selfish', she is able, in the famous conversation in Chapter 2, to persuade her husband to disobey his promise to his dying father and, in place of the three thousand pounds he had intended to settle on his sisters, to feel at ease with giving them occasional presents of fish and game. And in her last novel, she says of Charles Musgrove, who in sense and temper was 'undoubtedly superior to his wife': 'a more equal match might have greatly improved him; and a woman of real understanding might have given more consequence to his character, and more usefulness, rationality, and elegance to his habits and pursuits' (Ch. 6).

A wife superior in character to her husband could do much; such an one was Lady Elliot, who

had been an excellent woman, sensible and amiable, whose judgment and conduct, if they might be pardoned the youthful infatuation which made her Lady Elliot, had never required indulgence afterwards. She had humoured, or softened, or concealed his failings, and promoted his real respectability for seventeen years; and though not the very happiest being in the world herself, had found enough in her duties, her friends, and her children, to attach her to life, and make it no matter of indifference to her when she was called upon to quit them. (Ch. 1)

And where credit is due in different unfavourable circumstances it is justly given, as when Elizabeth Bennet acknowledges Charlotte's success as the wife of the Rev. Mr Collins.

This is marriage seen from the outside, and to this view the marital relationship does not excuse any woman from responsibility both for her own character and the moulding of her husband's. Marriage is a religious and social institution, closely linked with family alliances and the transfer of land and fortunes, and, because it is irrevocable for all ordinary people, the more equally matched the couples are, the better. Yet even if the match is unequal in any sense, a sensible woman can still make something of her own life, and her duty is to help her husband make the best of his by her quiet and intelligent influence.

Most of the existing marriages in the Austen novels are only there, however, to form a necessary social background for the heroine and, individual as the characterization is, the focus is not upon the wife as a marriage partner, but as providing a hostess or a friend or a foil for the heroine.

Women as Wives

In contrast with Jane Austen, the Brontë sisters subjected the whole marriage relationship as their contemporaries saw it to criticism, and expressed their views with more frankness than was acceptable in their age. Anne and Charlotte, with a passionate lack of detachment, considered marriage from the standpoint of the wife with the emotional and intellectual restrictions which Victorian marriage placed upon her, and they spoke out against those restrictions with vehemence. Having witnessed a seamier side of life than Jane Austen knew, they introduced into their novels the problems confronting wives of drunkards and profligates. They accepted the duties involved in Christian marriage but they re-examined their implications in the changed circumstances of their own times. In *Wuthering Heights* the marriage relationship is unconnected with ordinary social experience and the women who marry are in no way changed from what they were before, but even Emily Brontë retained the conviction that a wife's duty was to return to the bedside of a sick husband.

Anne Brontë

Helen Huntingdon is a married woman during most of *The Tenant of Wildfell Hall* and there is ample opportunity for her to express her views on marriage. She confides to her diary that Arthur is not a bad husband but his notions of matrimonial duties and comforts are not hers:

Judging from appearances, his idea of a wife, is a thing to love one devotedly, and stay at home—to wait upon her husband, and amuse him and minister to his comfort in every possible way, while he chooses to stay with her; and, when he is absent, to attend to his interests, domestic or otherwise, and patiently wait his return; no matter how he may be occupied in the meantime. (Ch. 29)

'A thing to love one devotedly' is the most telling phrase. When Helen upbraids Arthur for his behaviour to Lord Lowborough's wife and asks him whether the marriage vows are a jest, he retorts by reminding her of *her* marriage vows and says he 'won't be dictated to by a woman, though she be my wife'. Such a confrontation makes explicit their different views, frankly shown. More disturbing than the revolting drunken scenes in the novel is the feeling of Helen's intimate union with, and dependence upon, such a man as Arthur; the physical sordidness of the situation, as seen from the wife's point of view, is hinted at. The more brazen women in the Huntingdon circle are at home in this milieu, or at least accept it without question, but Helen seems surrounded by a waste of shame from which she is separate in her inner self but which all her efforts are vain to improve. These descriptions of a good and sensitive woman's inability to arrest the deterioration of her husband's character are a deeper exploration of some of the difficulties of marriage than is made by any of our previous authors; Jane Austen's wives, except in the case of Fanny's mother, are not involved in anything more degrading than vanity or lack of judgment in their husbands, they face no sottishness or brutish behaviour— Mr Bennet, provoked as he was, never took to drink, his escape was into emotional detachment and irony. In *The Tenant of Wildfell Hall*, a woman, tenderly nurtured, has stepped outside the confines of her usual sheltered experience and faces a chaos from which there appears no protection and no escape. Helen's full realization comes by gradual and painful stages. She tells Arthur she wishes to leave him but he refuses to agree to a separation on any terms. For her son's sake, she finally takes the child and flees to become the mysterious Mrs Graham, tenant of Wildfell Hall. At that time, when divorce laws worked one way only, and the wife's property, except for any 'settlements', was under the control of the husband, to take such a step was brave indeed. As well as safeguarding her own freedom and her son's future, Helen also makes a gesture of independence of her husband's maintenance, and proves her capacity to earn her living in the unusual role of a painter selling her own canvasses to dealers.

In spite of her humiliating experiences, Helen still remains the wife of Arthur Huntingdon and, by contemporary standards, she is still required to go to him when he really needs her, as she does in his last illness. She must also try, as a Christian, to bring him to repentance, but she does not succeed in bringing him to seek real forgiveness. Only by his death is she free to marry Gilbert Markham.

Gilbert Markham's views of marriage are quite different from those of Arthur. He and his mother discuss the matter together, thus showing the difference between the old-fashioned notions of a wife's duties held by Mrs Markham and Gilbert's own advanced views. In reply to his mother's statement that he would only know what he owed to her when he married some 'trifling, self-conceited girl' or 'some misguided obstinate woman like Mrs Graham, ignorant of her principal duties, and clever only in what concerns her least to know', he says:

'It will do me good, Mother; I was not sent into the world merely to exercise the good capacities and good feelings of others—was I?—but to exert my own towards them; and when I marry, I shall expect to find more pleasure in making my wife happy and comfortable, than in being made so by her: I would rather give than receive.' (Ch. 6)

Gilbert Markham is not a very vividly realized character, and these opinions seem to be spoken by him as a mouthpiece of the writer rather than from his own inner conviction. Mrs Markham's reply to her son's statement is:

'Oh! that is all nonsense, my dear—it's mere boy's talk that! You'll soon tire of petting and humouring your wife, be she ever so charming, and *then* comes the trial.'

'Well, then, we must bear one another's burdens.'

'Then, you must fall each into your proper place. You'll do your business, and she, if she's worthy of you, will do hers; but it's your business to please yourself, and hers to please you.' (Ch. 6)

The fact that Gilbert is claiming the necessity for a husband to abide by the tenets of the Gospels generally accepted as binding for *both* sexes is totally ignored by his mother; she sees women as endowed with a brief period of power until their sexual novelty wanes and then forced to spend the rest of their lives pleasing their husbands. Her praise of her own husband is enlightening:

'as good a husband as ever lived, and after the first six months or so were over, I should have as soon have expected him to fly, as to put himself out of the way to pleasure me ... he was steady and punctual, seldom found fault without a reason, always did justice to my good dinners, and hardly ever spoiled my cookery by delay—and that's as much as any woman can expect of any man.' (Ch. 6)

These are not great expectations.

A slightly different but still conventional view of marriage is held by Helen's aunt, who thinks the principal thing is not love, nor intellectual companionship, but respect. The qualities she praises in Mr Boarham, Helen's middle-aged suitor, are of such a kind as to merit respect:

'*But*, Helen! How many such men do you expect to meet with in the world? Upright, honourable, sensible, sober, respectable!—Is *this* such an every day character, that you should reject the possessor of such noble qualities, without a moment's hesitation?—Yes, *noble*, I may call them; for think of the full meaning of each, and how many inestimable virtues they include (and I might add many more to the list), and consider that all this is laid at your feet: it is in your power to secure this inestimable blessing for life—a worthy and excellent husband, who loves you tenderly, but not too fondly so as to blind him to your faults, and will be your guide throughout life's pilgrimage, and your partner in eternal bliss! . . .' (Ch. 16)

The emotionally charged, flattering phrases could only help to obscure any clear thinking about marriage. There is a greater clarity of vision in Helen's advice to Esther Hargrave to

keep both heart and hand in your own possession till you see good reason to part with them; and if such an occasion should never present itself, comfort your mind with this reflection—that, though in single life your joys may not be very many, your sorrows, at least, will not be more than you can bear. Marriage may change your circumstances for the better, but, in my private opinion, it is far more likely to produce a contrary result. (Ch. 51)

Anne Brontë thus has the unusual courage, not only as a woman writer but also as a Victorian clergyman's daughter, to examine marriage afresh. She considers all the accepted views: the pleasure principle of the profligate (Arthur), the romantic view of the young girl who hopes to reform the fascinating profligate (the young Helen), the good-cook-who-knows-her-place view (Gilbert's mother), the respectable, semi-religious view (Helen's aunt) and the licentious view of increase of opportunity under the cover of the name of matron (Lady Lowborough), and she traces the consequences of these views in daily life after the marriage ceremony is over. But she gives her approval to the view, held by Gilbert Markham and the mature Helen, of marriage as a partnership of two human beings who neither lose their identities, sacrifice their intellectual interests, nor arrest their own personal development, that is, a marriage of two dignified human personalities. Such an equalitarian view of marriage has no axe to grind in the cause of the theoretical rights of either party but is deeply concerned with the necessity for both men and women to confront their problems as they arise with as much honesty and goodwill as they possess, and to help each other in their solution, a marriage of two equal human beings who do not need to keep insisting on 'their equality'. Anne Brontë realizes, subconsciously perhaps, that such a marriage depends upon that being the view of it taken by the husband—his is the accepted position of dominance in marriage and unless he, as the acknowledged holder of power, is willing to abrogate it, there will be a gradual slipping back to the accepted view; it is, therefore, essential that Gilbert Markham hold progressive views. Because she did not carry on the novel after the marriage of Helen and Gilbert, the author did not work out what effect the social attitudes and pressures surrounding the couple would have upon their relationship on a new plane. That would have been an interesting investigation.

Charlotte Brontë

In *The Professor*, Crimsworth's conversations with Frances give us the opportunity to deduce some of Charlotte Brontë's views on marriage. Frances states that 'though the only road to freedom' from union with an incurable profligate, prodigal, drunkard or tyrant 'lie through the gates of death, the gates must be passed; for freedom is indispensable': this is going even further than Helen in *The Tenant of Wildfell Hall*. Charlotte introduces the idea of a woman working with her husband in a joint undertaking, as Frances and Crimsworth work together in their school, an arrangement which gives the woman financial independence. She believed that a marriage of two equal beings —and she insisted on their equality before God—must be accompanied by financial and even emotional independence. Jane Eyre does not want to be 'crushed by crowded obligations' and wishes to continue to act as Adèle's governess even after her marriage, earning her board and lodging and thirty pounds a year besides, out of which she would furnish her own wardrobe; Rochester should give her nothing but his regard and she would give hers in return, which would make them 'quits', that is, still equals. This is a complete reversal of the common ambition of young women to make good matches, that is, to be provided with an establishment even better than ordinary social expectations might consider satisfactory, for, instead of reaping the social and financial advantages of marrying the master of Thornfield Hall, Jane Eyre wishes to continue working for him as before. Jane also wishes to maintain between herself and Rochester an emotional distance and detachment which will be to their mutual advantage, and she tells him quite plainly that this is her intention. There is, indeed, perfect honesty and ease between them, so that they are able to live in each other's presence. She does not have to prostitute her genuine feeling to a doubtful sense of duty; their love has no element but its own truth.

In contrast to this freely expanding feeling between two happily married people, in *Shirley* Charlotte Brontë describes, although not at great length, an unhappily married woman in Mrs Pryor. When Caroline asks her whether the young are wrong in looking forward to marriage as 'the brightest, the only bright destiny that can await them' she replies with the warning that love is bitter and strong, 'most of the *cheats* of existence are strong' (the italics are mine) and its sweetness is transitory.

Elizabeth Gaskell

As the wife of a well-known Unitarian minister, writing under her married name, Mrs Gaskell was not as free as Acton and Currer Bell to express unorthodox views on marriage, even if she held them. At first glance she seems to accept in its entirety the contemporary conservative view of the place of the wife, but a closer scrutiny does reveal incidental statements which suggest she sometimes questions its unchanging validity.

In *Mary Barton* Mrs Gaskell hints at some undesirable consequences of married women working outside their homes, a new problem. Jane Wilson tells Mary that she is very sure that women ought not to work in factories after they are married: she can count nine men she knows who have been driven to the public-house by having wives who worked in factories and who thought 'there was no harm in putting their little ones out at nurse, and letting their house go all dirty, and their fires all out', with the result that the husbands soon frequented the clean and cheerful gin-shops. The duty of the wife in such cases is obvious.

Most of Mrs Gaskell's attention is given to the position of the wife within the home itself. The relationship between Lizzie's mother and father in *Lizzie Leigh* is the one we have come to accept as the usual contemporary model:

They had been two-and-twenty years man and wife; for nineteen of those their life had been as calm and happy as the most perfect uprightness on the one side, and the most complete confidence and loving submission on the other could make it. Milton's famous line might have been framed and hung up as the rule of their married life, for he was truly the interpreter, who stood between God and her; she would have considered herself wicked if she had ever dared even to think him austere, though as certainly as he was an upright man, so surely was he hard, stern and inflexible.

Her husband's refusal to help Lizzie in her trouble does fill Mrs Leigh's heart 'with a hidden, sullen rebellion, which tore up all the old landmarks of wifely duty and affection, and poisoned the fountains whence gentlest love and reverence had once been for ever springing', but his dying words of forgiveness to Lizzie 'replaced him on the throne in her heart' and she felt that 'if she had only been more gentle and less angrily reserved he might have relented earlier—and in time?' Mrs Gaskell makes no comment on such a husband-wife relationship.

Wives of the older generation in *Ruth* are also conservative. Mrs Bradshaw is 'sweet and gentle-looking, but as if she was thoroughly broken into submission'. 'Castle-building, after the manner of the Minerva Press, was the outlet by which she escaped from the pressure of her prosaic life, as Mr Bradshaw's wife.' But the implied sympathy with her is not developed, she has little personality and her mind is commonplace.

Women as Wives

Amongst the older women in *North and South*, John Thornton's mother, strong-minded, proud, unbending, dependable in any crisis, is contrasted with Mrs Hale, who has no resources in herself and can never really adjust to a way of life less easy than the one to which she was brought up. In these women the contrast between 'north' and 'south' is marked and permanent; Mrs Hale, with her consciousness of class, can never make the necessary accommodation to the north, whose vigour is more enduring than her own ill-health and backward-looking thoughts.

Sylvia's mother in *Sylvia's Lovers* is again the old-fashioned wife who looks up to her husband in everything, but there is a slight questioning of the fairness of this in the description of Daniel, the husband:

Although Daniel himself was unreasoning, hasty, impulsive—in a word, often thinking and acting very foolishly—yet somehow, either from some quality in his character, or from the loyalty of nature in those with whom he had to deal in his every-day life, he had made his place and position clear as the arbiter and law-giver of his household. On his decision, as that of husband, father, master, perhaps superior natures waited. (Vol. 2, Ch. 11)

The 'perhaps superior' may be thought to have a little significance. In such a patriarchal system there is little real companionship amongst men and women, and 'once the first blush and hurry of youth is over' there is no great pleasure in the conversation of the other sex. Farmers would have 'contemptuously considered it as a loss of time to talk to women' and they were often more communicative to the sheep-dog that accompanied them on their work than they were to their womenfolk. Bell Robson 'really believed her husband to have the serious and important occupation for his mind that she had been taught to consider befitting the superior intellect of the masculine gender; she would have taxed herself severely if, even in thought, she had blamed him'(Vol. 1, Ch. 11). She takes no pleasure in the attention which her daughter's beauty attracts, because her own opinion is 'that it was creditable to a woman to go through life in the shadow of obscurity—never named except in connection with good housewifery, husband or children', and Sylvia's attitude to her fiancé, Philip, is based upon what her mother has taught her to be right: once or twice Philip finds that Sylvia is doing what he wishes out of a 'spirit of obedience, which, as her mother's daughter, she believed to be her duty towards her affianced husband'. Later, Sylvia's behaviour after her marriage obviously worries her mother a great deal, especially her habit of taking rambles on her own. As Mrs Robson lies ill and delirious these fears are expressed in her half-conscious speech: 'Sylvie, if thou're not a good wife to him, it'll just break my heart outright. A woman should obey her husband, and not go her own gait. I never leave the house wi'out telling father, and getting his leave' (Vol. 3, Ch. 4). Even when Sylvia discovers the deception that Philip has practised with regard to Kinraid's supposed death, her sense of duty to her marriage vows, her baby and her own soul forbids her running away with Kinraid as she is tempted to do. The emotional intensity of the passage in which Sylvia makes her decision creates a powerful effect in Mrs Gaskell's usually placid pages.

Wives and Daughters again contains two contrasted portraits of women of the older generation, Mrs Gibson (formerly Mrs Kirkpatrick) and Mrs Hamley, the Squire's wife, and again one of them receives the author's implied approval and the other her censure, a little more strongly brought out in this last novel than had been Mrs Gaskell's practice up to then. Mrs Gibson is a completely convincing portrait of a pretty, shallow, middle-aged woman with a pseudo-romantic outlook on life which conceals her very careful attention to her own comfort. To all who can see beyond her surface refinement, or rather, distaste for what she calls 'coarseness', and her strict adherence to all the outward proprieties, she is vain and vulgar and stupid. The fact that Mr Gibson lacks the penetration to see this and that he marries her, goes along with his lack of appreciation of the sterling qualities of his own daughter and his wish to keep her ignorant and uneducated even when she herself is thirsting for education. Mrs Gibson accepts his proposal of marriage merely because she feels 'how pleasant it would be to have a husband once more;—some one who would work while she sate at her elegant ease in a prettily-furnished drawing-room'. Her selfish archness is part of her daily expression, as in the characteristic speech she makes to Molly when her illness has kept the girl from attending a party:

'I am so sorry to be the cause of detaining you from this little party, but dear papa is so over-anxious about me. I have always been a kind of pet with gentlemen, and poor Mr Kirkpatrick never knew how to make enough of me. But I think Mr Gibson is even more foolishly fond: his last words were, "Take care of yourself, Hyacinth", and then he came back again, to say, "If you don't attend to my directions I won't answer for the consequences". I shook my forefinger at him, and said, "Don't be so anxious, you silly man".' (Ch. 48)

The complete lack of realization that her husband is trying to make sure that his unreliable and stupid wife will not do something rash and foolish about the directions he has given her adds an unusually astringent touch to the portrait.

The contrast between the home atmosphere created by Mrs Gibson and that created by Mrs Hamley, the Squire's semi-invalid wife, is striking. Mrs Hamley supervises her household from her sofa, and her husband, who is often restless and angry from one cause or another: 'always came to her to be smoothed down and put right. He was conscious of her pleasant influence over him, and became at peace with himself in her presence; just as a child is at ease with someone who is both firm and gentle' (Ch. 22). These wives are examples of two different varieties of women's influence inside the home: the one kind is that of a selfish and self-seeking woman, and the other takes the form of unselfish concern for the comfort and peace of mind of others; the latter is Mrs Gaskell's attractive portrayal of that domestic happiness that has been described in so many of our novels in different forms. She was not anxious to disrupt that harmony with uncomfortable new theories about marriage.

George Eliot

The same appreciation of quiet domestic happiness created by an affectionate woman is found in George Eliot. Her description of Milly Barton in *The Sad Fortunes of the Rev. Amos Barton* analyses the feminine qualities that are able to create such an atmosphere:

Soothing, unspeakable charm of gentle womanhood; which supersedes all acquisitions, all accomplishments. You would never have asked, at any period of Mrs Amos Barton's life, if she sketched or played the piano. You would even perhaps have been rather scandalised if she had descended from the serene dignity of *being* to the assiduous unrest of *doing*. Happy the man, you would have thought, whose eye will rest on her in the pauses of his fireside reading— whose hot aching forehead will be soothed by the contact of her cool soft hand—who will recover himself from dejection at his mistakes and failures in the loving light of her unreproaching eyes! (Ch. 2)

The impatience with the 'accomplishments' that formed the content of Victorian female education, often to be decried in George Eliot's novels, begins here, as does the almost nostalgic description of a domestic fireside. She once wrote that 'the only ardent hope I have for my future life is to have given me some woman's duty—some possibility of devoting myself where I may see a daily result of pure calm blessedness in the life of another',[1] and this wish is granted, temporarily at least, to the first of her heroines. Milly Barton lives a life of sweet, unselfish devotion to her husband and children. She is powerless to better the economic conditions of her life, made difficult by her husband's small stipend, her six children, her own delicate health, and, as a final straw, the extra drain on all these resources of the stay of the Countess Caroline Czerlaski in the house as a guest. Milly shields her husband from as many difficulties as she can and she makes up for the rest of his problems by extra care and love; in living for him and for others in this way she is happy and she sheds a radiance around her while she lives, even though her environment is limited. The regret of the reader when she dies young is at the preventable waste of such a loving nature but, although she is in effect killed by the overwork and worry of her narrow environment, she transcends it in her life and her memory and influence remain powerful after her death.

Janet Dempster, of *Janet's Repentance*, is another loving woman, but one whose love is not appreciated and who seeks oblivion from her unhappy lot in drink. The chief strength in Janet's nature lies in 'her affection, which coloured all the rest of her mind', 'kindness is her religion'. But she has no children, her mother does not need her tendance, and her husband's indifference and, at times, brutality, are more than she can bear. At the climax of the story when, drunk and furious, he turns her out of the house in the middle of the night, George Eliot uses the occasion of her sitting shivering on the doorstep to express the sense of waste in this woman's life, the waste she felt to be part of many women's destinies:

with the door shut upon her past life, and the future black and unshapen before her as the night, the scenes of her childhood, her youth, and her painful womanhood, rushed back upon her consciousness, and made one picture with her present desolation. . . . All her early gladness, all her bright hopes and illusions, all her fits of beauty and affection, served only to darken the riddle of her life; they were the betraying promises of a cruel destiny which had brought out those sweet blossoms only that the winds and storms might have a greater work of desolation, which had nursed her like a pet fawn into tenderness and fond expectations, only that she might feel a keener terror in the clutch of the panther. (Ch. 15)

Although Janet's husband has failed her, the kindness of Mrs Pettifer, who takes her into her house, and later, the convincing personal faith and humility of an Evangelical clergyman, Mr Tryan, open to her the necessary sources of strength to overcome her weakness. She never knows happiness with her husband, but she does return to him when he is dying, carrying out the inescapable duty of every wife in the novels within the scope of this study.

The kindness of Mrs Pettifer to Janet and of Janet to old Mrs Crewe shine in contrast to the dark cruelty in Janet's life, while the atmosphere of snug domesticity and homely peace in the description of the White House and the preparations that Janet, her mother and Mrs Pettifer make for Mr Tryan's comfort at Holly Mount express the joy in a well-run household which George Eliot shared with Charlotte Brontë, Mrs Gaskell and Harriet Martineau. This is a special feminine satisfaction and, indeed, compensation for some special feminine trials.

The married women in *Adam Bede* and *The Mill on the Floss* belong to the famous 'characters' of the Eliot novels, some are good housewives and shrewd observers, like Mrs Poyser, and some are colourless worriers, like Lisbeth Bede. With Aunt

Tulliver, they tend to accept the traditions into which they have been born, and to preserve family solidarity; they are preservers of old standards rather than innovators, and they do not stand in the first rank of George Eliot's women.

Between *The Mill on the Floss* and *Silas Marner* George Eliot wrote two short stories. In the first, contrary to her almost invariable practice, she creates a woman who is a symbol of feminine evil. Bertha Latimer is slender, thin-lipped, and, like Rosamond Lydgate, she has a head crowned with massive blonde hair, arranged in cunning braids and folds that look almost too heavy for her slight figure. Her eyes are like those of the cruel-eyed woman in Giorgione's picture of Lucretia Borgia. She wears a white ball-dress with green leaves and an emerald brooch in the shape of a serpent, and she is obviously the first of George Eliot's Lamia women, and the most pernicious. But the mysterious power her beauty wields over Latimer passes with 'the blessed possibility of mystery, doubt, and expectation', and he is able, one evening after his father's death, to see her as she really is:

The terrible moment of complete illumination had come to me, but I saw that the darkness had hidden no landscape from me, but only a blank prosaic wall: from that evening forth, through the sickening years which followed, I saw all round the narrow room of this woman's soul—saw petty artifice and mere negation where I had delighted to believe in coy sensibilities and in wit at war with latent feeling—saw the light floating vanities of the girl defining themselves into the systematic coquetry, the scheming selfishness of the woman —saw repulsion and antipathy harden into cruel hatred, giving pain only for the sake of wreaking itself. (*The Lifted Veil,* Ch 2)

This analysis of one whom George Eliot saw as an evil woman is interesting for the characteristics she condemns in Bertha – most of all the narrowness of a soul given up to scheming selfishness.

In the second short story, *Brother Jacob*, the foolish house-wife, Mrs Steene, is a veterinary surgeon's wife who yields to the temptation of buying her mince-pies at the confectioner's instead of baking them herself, as all good housewives naturally should. George Eliot is unusually ironic on the subject and conveys one of her indirect criticisms of women's education when she says of Mrs Steene:

I fear she had been rather over-educated for her station in life, for she knew by heart many passages in *Lalla Rookh*, the *Corsair* and the *Siege of Corinth*, which had given her a distaste for domestic occupations, and caused her a withering disappointment at the discovery that Mr Steene, since his marriage, had lost all interest in the 'bulbul', openly preferred discussing the nature of spavin with a coarse neighbour, and was angry if the pudding turned out watery.

Not only does Mrs Steene buy her mince-pies ready baked, but she also falsifies her household accounts in order to conceal this fact from her husband: 'This was the second step in a downward course, all owing to a young woman's being out of harmony with her circumstances, yearning after renegades and bulbuls, and being subject to claims from a veterinary surgeon fond of mince-pies.'

For a woman to be out of harmony with her circumstances is another paraphrase for a woman's inability to accept and adjust herself to her lot in life. Silas Marner's village of Raveloe does not harbour married women who are out of harmony with their circumstances in this way, but most of them have characters of greater strength than those around them. If Dolly Winthrop had not been at hand to help and advise the lonely weaver, he would have found it very difficult to bring up Eppie, and Dolly is indeed generous in her assistance with the dressing, the washing, the nursing, and the attempts at discipline and guidance. Her all embracing charity includes anyone in the village who needs nursing at any time. One incident that reveals her character in all its unselfishness occurs on the night of the dance, when Silas breaks into the festivities to say a woman lies ill at his cottage. It is Dolly Winthrop that Godfrey Cass immediately thinks of to go to the stricken woman, and Dolly has no thought that it is a hardship for *her* to walk through the snow to a stranger, only being anxious lest Godfrey spoil *his* dancing pumps, and spoil them, to add a further resonance to the contrast, to go to a woman who is actually his own wife. Dolly is one of the 'good livers' of Raveloe, one of the strongest of the remedial influences that George Eliot mentioned to John Blackwood.[2]

The peace and happiness promoted by the background of an ordered household (the work of women) is one of the minor themes in *Silas Marner* and the lack of such a background is deplored at the Red House: 'the Squire's wife had died long ago, and the Red House was without that presence of the wife and mother which is the fountain of wholesome love and fear in parlour and kitchen' (Ch. 3). The effect of this lack on Godfrey has been greater than upon the more vicious Dunstan, for 'Godfrey's was an essentially domestic nature, bred up in a home where the hearth had no smiles and where the daily habits were not chastised by the presence of household order.' When Godfrey finally marries Nancy Lammeter, the expected transformation of the Red House duly takes place and is described in loving detail, 'all is purity and order in this once dreary room, for, fifteen years ago, it was entered by a new presiding spirit'.[3]

There are unused depths in Nancy, not realized by her husband until he sees how mistaken he was to keep Eppie's identity a secret from her; had he had enough understanding and faith to acknowledge Eppie their household need not have remained childless. He at last comes to know that 'he had not measured this wife with whom he had lived so long'. Nancy herself had to live with her powers unused. We are shown her sitting one Sunday afternoon with the Bible open before her; 'the spirit of rectitude and the sense of responsibility for others, had made it a habit with her to scrutinize her past feelings and actions with self-questioning solicitude'. She is evidently undertaking the self-examination which Jane Austen's heroines felt they needed in order to bring their emotions and thoughts under control, but the nineteenth century was inclined to regard such practices as morbid and George Eliot feels called upon to explain Nancy's Sunday occupation in the following terms: 'This excessive rumination and self questioning is perhaps a morbid habit inevitable to a mind of such moral sensibility when shut out from its due share of outward activity and of practical claims on its affections—inevitable to a noble-hearted, childless woman, when her lot is narrow' (Ch. 17).

The ends to be attained by self-examination both by the Austen and the Eliot heroines are the same—peace of mind and adjustment to outward circumstances—and the means are

149

basically the same; only the ways in which contemporary opinion regards the means are different, the eighteenth century seeing it as a method of controlling unruly wills and affections, the nineteenth as a rather reprehensible passive substitute for more practical activity within a narrow and inescapable environment.

There are even deeper unused qualities in Romola as a wife but George Eliot does not permit them in her case to run to waste; they are used to serve more desperate human needs. When Romola discovers Tito's baseness she leaves him, but it is Savonarola himself who sends her back to her duty in Florence with his stinging words, and from this path of duty, renunciation and love, she never subsequently departs, even at the time when Savonarola's own weaknesses and narrow views seem to be worthy of her condemnation. The two years she devotes to the tending of the sick in the Florentine pestilence take the place in her life of devotion to family:

All that ardour of her nature which could no longer spend itself in the woman's tenderness for father and husband, had transformed itself into an enthusiasm of sympathy with the general life. She had ceased to think that her own lot could be happy—had ceased to think of happiness at all: the one end of her life seemed to her to be the diminishing of sorrow. (Bk. 3, Ch. 44)

This sympathy for the general life is given another outlet when, after her godfather is betrayed by Tito, the boat in which she lies down carries her not to death but to a village where the pestilence is raging. And even when she returns to Florence after Savonarola's arrest and Tito's death, she finds her clearest duty is to seek out Tessa and the children and to take care of them. Again she does this partly to fulfil certain needs of her own nature:

She never for a moment told herself that it was heroism or exalted charity in her to seek these beings; she needed something that she was bound specially to care for; she yearned to clasp the children and to make them love her. This at least would be some sweet result, for others as well as herself for all her past sorrow. (Bk. 3, Ch. 70)

Tessa is contrasted with Romola as Hetty Sorrel is with Dinah but, unlike Hetty, Tessa is a loving little thing, 'a sweet, adoring creature', one of George Eliot's rounded, appealing women, and life in the shape first of Tito and then of Romola takes care of her. Tessa looks up to Romola as to a saint and Romola does not disappoint her. It is doubly fitting that Romola should take the last step of noble conduct and look after this innocent victim of her own husband's deception. Tito had had no plans to take his wife with him into his future but it is that wife who looks after Tessa when his plans are cancelled by death. Romola thus fulfils her last obligation even to him as well as to Tessa, her accepted obligation balancing his neglect of his duty as a husband.

Romola is essentially a lonely, noble figure, lonely in her learning, her beauty, and her integrity, nobler than all who surround her. The man she trusted has failed her. She is led away by a handsome face, as Maggie was, but there is nothing sordid in her marriage to Tito and there is no betrayal of others. Had Tito not chosen the path he did, their marriage would have been happy, but this was not to be her woman's lot. In spite of her suffering, however, she follows the path of tenderness and love for others that her nature needs and she turns her lot into something most noble. The wisdom by which she lives is not for women only, such integrity is for all mankind at its highest, but only women—in most cases—can make this special contribution of tenderness and love.

It will be recalled that Mrs Transome in *Felix Holt* has received, with the due differences of class, as insufficient and foolish an education as Mrs Steene in *Brother Jacob*, but, given the environment and personality, the effect is more serious than surreptitious purchases at the pastrycook's. As a young, imperious beauty, Arabella marries the weak-minded Mr Transome of Transome Court; the marriage, in accordance with the aims that have been set before her, is one for place and prestige. Her husband's weakness enables her to be master ('she had come of a high family and had a spirit') and also makes it easy for her to deceive him. She falls in love with the family lawyer, Matthew Jermyn, handsome, showy and morally vulgar and has a son by him, brought up as her legitimate son Jermyn uses his position to milk the estate for his own purposes and through the years Arabella comes to realize the kind of man for whom she has sinned against her husband and the only standards in which she believes—those of family and property. She seeks the 'opiate for her discontent in the exertion of her will about smaller things' on the estate, and she looks forward, when her son returns, to having a greater share in its management. But, ironically, when Harold returns from the East after the death of the eldest son, he returns with oriental ideas about the position of women and the belief that all women want is luxury. His mother's hopes for a future share in the management of the estate are destroyed. The inevitable discovery comes when Jermyn tells Harold of his paternity in an effort to stop proceedings against his mishandling of the Transome affairs. Baulked of her hopes, Arabella's obsession is still with power, but she realizes that the power she did possess lay in her beauty and has faded with it. In a memorable scene Denner, the lady's-maid, finds her mistress seated before a mirror regarding her ageing face, 'to see what an old hag I am'. She says with bitterness, 'A woman never has seen the worst till she is old, Denner', and they proceed to discuss the lot of women in general; Mrs Transome bursts out:

'A woman's love is always freezing into fear. She wants everything, she is secure of nothing. This girl [Esther] has a fine spirit—plenty of fire and pride and wit. Men like such captives, as they like horses that champ the bit and paw the ground; they feel more triumph in their mastery. What is the use of woman's will?—if she tries, she doesn't get it, and she ceases to be loved. God was cruel when he made women.'

Denner is used to such outbursts and replies by listing what she considers to be the compensations for women, unsatisfying though they may be:

'It mayn't be good luck to be a woman,' she said. 'But one begins with it from a baby: one gets used to it. And I shouldn't like to be a man—to cough so loud, and stand straddling about on a wet day, and be so wasteful with meat and drink. They're a coarse lot, I think.' (Ch. 39)

Mrs Transome is left in her loneliness with a son who knows her guilty secret. She has been damned by the man whose love she accepted and for whom she betrayed her deepest beliefs in family allegiances. She had 'no ultimate analysis of things that went beyond blood and family—she had never seen behind the canvas with which her life was hung; her potentialities of energy and spirit had been devoted to sterile and selfish ends, which went beyond selfishness in their inevitable consequences. She had no other resources left.'

The aims of the heroine of the next novel, *Middlemarch*, are far from selfish: when Dorothea marries Edward Casaubon she plans to be the devoted helpmeet of a great scholar. She does make an effort to help him with his book but her own education has been so inadequate that she is really of little use and the attempt has to be abandoned. There is disappointment in this for Casaubon, who has expected a more disciplined and educated amanuensis than his wife proves to be. He has also expected the emotional support of an adoring wife, which Dorothea's gradual disillusion with her marriage prevents her from providing. When Ladislaw tells Dorothea that the work Casaubon has been so laboriously preparing is of little worth and she realizes that, far from being a sage, he is only a dried-up pedant, she sees this to be the truth but, when she thinks of the waste of her husband's life and hopes, there does awaken in her 'the first stirring of pitying tenderness fed by the realities of his lot and not by her own dreams'. Yet, when Casaubon dies with his labours unfinished, she does not feel she can shoulder the task of completing his sterile work as he had hoped. Her duties as a landowner and mistress of Lowick Manor, with the patronage of a living attached to it, do, however, interest her. The prospect of a life of motiveless ease—'motiveless, if her own energy could not seek out reasons for ardent action'—does not attract her, but she finds it more difficult than she has imagined to know how best to apply herself and her possessions. She says to Ladislaw 'I used to despise women a little for not shaping their lives more, and doing better things. I was very fond of doing as I liked, but I have almost given it up' (Ch. 54). She does try to make plans for useful activity, and she gains the approval of Mr Garth by telling him: 'I should like to feel, if I lived to be old, that I had improved a great piece of land and built a great many good cottages, because the work is of a healthy kind while

it is being done, and after it is done, men are the better for it'
(Ch. 56). This scheme, however, comes to nothing, partly because
of the lack of positive support by her nearest and dearest.
The difficulties are not really insurmountable, the truth is that
Dorothea lacks the driving will to overcome the lethargy around
her. Nor are her emotions sufficiently strongly engaged with
rural housing to give her the energy to consider that work
absorbing enough to 'make her life greatly effective'. Although
such a large and comprehensive plan fails, Dorothea does do
positive good in other ways that present themselves to her, for
instance, in granting the Lowick living to Mr Farebrother. Her
greatest opportunity reaches her in the person of Lydgate,
whom she helps not only with money but by her sympathetic
understanding of what he aims to do; Lydgate says of her, 'she
seems to have what I never saw in any woman before—a
fountain of friendship towards men—a man can make a friend
of her'. Her visit to Rosamond to reconcile her with her husband
is made out of pure goodwill, and, through its own complete
disinterestedness, finally redounds to her own good.

But, baulked of any great and adequate outlet for her energies in a field of her own choice, Dorothea finally renounces the
possessions Casaubon left her and marries Ladislaw. Many of
those who knew and valued her could not consider this as a
completely happy arrangement and George Eliot herself is not
wholly satisfied:

No life would have been possible to Dorothea which was not filled
with emotion, and she had now a life filled also with a beneficent
activity which she had not the doubtful pains of discovering and
marking out for herself. Will became an ardent public man, working
well in those times when reforms were begun with a young hopeful-
ness of immediate good which has been much checked in our days,
and getting at last returned to Parliament by a constituency who
paid his expenses. Dorothea could have liked nothing better, since
wrongs existed, than that her husband should be in the thick of the
struggle against them, and that she should give him wifely help.
Many who knew her, thought it a pity that so substantive and rare
a creature should have been absorbed into the life of another, and be
only known in a certain circle as a wife and mother. But no one
stated exactly what else that was in her power she ought rather to
have done—not even Sir James Chettam, who went no further than

the negative prescription that she ought not to have married Will Ladislaw. (Finale)

Esther Lyons renounces possessions in order to marry a man better than herself: Dorothea, whose lot is less happy, renounces possessions to marry a lesser man. With those possessions she also renounces the possibility of carrying out the housing plans that had formerly meant so much to her. The position of a wife, able only to give 'wifely help' and exert 'influence' in any schemes for the betterment of wrongs is a definite sacrifice of some of her own best endeavours. That there will be little opportunity for those endeavours as Ladislaw's wife is foreshadowed by the way in which that aspect of her character affected Will long before, when she was pouring out her feelings about conditions in the village to him and to her uncle:

For the moment, Will's admiration was accompanied with a chilling sense of remoteness. A man is seldom ashamed of feeling that he cannot love a woman so well when he sees a certain greatness in her: nature having intended greatness for men. But nature sometimes made sad oversights in carrying out her intentions. (Ch. 30)

That 'certain greatness' in her will not fulfil itself, for Dorothea's lot is to marry Ladislaw. There is no other suitable husband free to present himself; a marriage with Lydgate, which has appealed to some readers, is, of course, impossible in the circumstances of the novel. Many have felt, as Sir James Chettam did, that if Dorothea had chosen 'to espouse her solitude' the resolution would have 'well become her', but her nature is one that needs the support of close ties of love and affection to sustain it, so that she could not have remained unmarried. George Eliot's own judgment on Dorothea's marriage is given in the two last paragraphs of the book. As Professor Barbara Hardy has pointed out,[4] the first and second edition versions of this differ. The edition-in-parts of 1871-2 includes the following passage in its penultimate paragraph, after the statement that Sir James never ceased to regard Dorothea's second marriage as a mistake and that the Middlemarch view was that, had Dorothea been 'a nice woman' she would not have married a sickly clergyman old enough to be her father, and, little more than a

155

year after his death, have given up her estate to marry his cousin, young enough to have been his son:

Among the many remarks passed on her mistakes, it was never said in the neighbourhood of Middlemarch that such mistakes could not have happened if the society into which she was born had not smiled on propositions of marriage to a girl less than half his own age—on modes of education which make a woman's knowledge another name for motley ignorance—on rules of conduct which are in flat contradiction with its own loudly-asserted beliefs.

George Eliot, therefore, transfers the blame for marrying an elderly man from Dorothea to a society that smiled upon propositions of marriage to a girl less than half a man's age (although she had just said that the Middlemarch view was *against* the marriage). Significantly she adds another of her condemnations of women's faulty education. In the edition of 1874 the above paragraph was omitted and the blame dispersed into wider and vaguer terms, with more emphasis placed upon Dorothea's good 'influence' than upon her frustrated personal possibilities:

Certainly those determining acts of her life were not ideally beautiful. They were the mixed result of young and noble impulse struggling amidst the conditions of an imperfect social state, in which great feelings will often take the aspect of error, and great faith the aspect of illusion. For there is no creature whose inward being is so strong that it is not greatly determined by what lies outside it. A new Theresa will hardly have the opportunity of reforming a conventual life, any more than a new Antigone will spend her heroic piety in daring all for the sake of a brother's burial: the medium in which their ardent deeds took shape is for ever gone. But we insignificant people with our daily words and acts are preparing the lives of many Dorotheas, some of which may present a far sadder sacrifice than that of the Dorothea whose story we know.

Her finely touched spirit had still its fine issues, though they were not widely visible. Her full nature, like that river of which Cyrus broke the strength, spent itself in channels which had no great name on earth. But the effect of her being on those around her was incalculably diffusive: for the growing good of the world is partly dependent on un-historic acts; and that things are not so ill with you and me as they might have been, is half owing to the number who lived faithfully a hidden life, and rest in unvisited tombs.

The marriage of Rosamond to Lydgate is definitely one which receives contemporary social approval. With an even less adequate educational equipment for life than Dorothea's, she marries Tertius because he carries 'a certain air of distinction congruous with good family' and possesses 'connections which offered vistas of that middle-class heaven, rank'; and she feels that, as a man of talent, it would be 'especially delightful to enslave him'. The enslavement, instead of being transformed into a partnership, becomes ever more irksome to Lydgate. Rosamond's attitude to his work, to his fervent wish to add something to fundamental medical knowledge, a wish parallel to Dorothea's idea of doing some active good, which 'haunted her like a passion', is confined to a certain pride in a husband who could 'make discoveries'. In Lydgate's case he is completely frustrated by his wife's narrowness and selfishness and obstinacy; it is not long after their marriage that he begins to realize that his work is being seriously neglected and that Rosamond cares nothing for his profession. In spite of her seeming mildness she has a terrible tenacity:

There was gathering within him an amazed sense of his powerlessness over Rosamond. His superior knowledge and mental force, instead of being, as he imagined, a shrine to consult on all occasions, was simply set aside on every practical question. He had regarded Rosamond's cleverness as precisely of the receptive kind that became a woman. He was now beginning to find out what that cleverness was. (Ch. 58)

Rosamond, on the other hand, has been taught by society to look on marriage as a romantic means to social advancement and, for her, too, disillusion comes:

the terribly inflexible relation of marriage had lost its charm of encouraging delightful dreams. It had freed her from the disagreeableness of her father's house, but it had not given her everything that she had wished and hoped. The Lydgate with whom she had been in love had been a group of airy conditions for her, most of which had disappeared, while their place had been taken by everyday details which must be lived through slowly from hour to hour, not floated through with a rapid selection of favourable aspects. The habits of Lydgate's profession, his home preoccupation with scientific subjects, which seemed to her almost like a morbid vampire's taste, his peculiar view of things which never entered into the dialogue of

157

courtship—all these continually-alienating influences, even without the fact of his having placed himself at a disadvantage in the town, and without that first shock of revelation about Dover's debt, would have made his presence dull to her. (Ch. 64)

In her husband's hour of greatest need, when he is suspected of complicity with Bulstrode in the death of Raffles, 'even this trouble, like the rest, she seemed to regard as if it were hers alone. He was always to her a being apart, doing what she objected to.' Small-souled, and with only dreams of conquest to seek comfort in, Rosamond turns to Ladislaw for the consolation of a new romance—some other man should put her again on a pedestal. When this proves vain, and she at least makes the gesture to Dorothea of an honest explanation, she turns back to Lydgate. In the fashionable practice which he takes on after his dream of adding to medical knowledge has finally faded, his acquaintances envy him so charming a wife, but to him she is his 'basil plant', the plant that flourished wonderfully on a murdered man's brains.

The greatest change that befalls any young woman in George Eliot's novels comes in *Daniel Deronda* to Gwendolen Harcourt after her marriage. Disillusionment soon overtakes her, though she considers it her part to bear herself with dignity and to appear happy: Mrs Grandcourt 'run away' would be a more pitiable creature than Gwendolen Harleth condemned to teach the bishop's daughters. When she turns desperately to Deronda for advice on the way she should conduct herself, the advice he gives is vague, although it may be taken to approximate to George Eliot's own view of the best course for unhappy women to pursue and the worthwhile things for which frustrated women might live:

Look on other lives beside your own. See what their troubles are, and how they are borne. Try to care about something in this vast world besides the gratification of small selfish desires. Try to care for what is best in thought and action—something that is good apart from the accidents of your own lot. (Ch. 36)

In order to obtain 'some real knowledge which would give . . . an interest in the world beyond the small drama of personal desires', Gwendolen, like Maggie and Dorothea, turns to books, but her unguided efforts to read Descartes, Bacon, Locke, Butler, Burke, and Guizot, do not, understandably, help her very much. She still leans upon Deronda, and it is a dreadful shock to her when he tells her of his impending marriage to Mirah. Henry James, through the lips of Constantius, has said of the ending of the novel:

George Eliot always gives us something that is strikingly and ironically characteristic of human life; and what savours more of the essential crookedness of our fate than the sad cross purposes of these two young people? Poor Gwendolen's falling in love with Deronda is part of her own luckless history, not of his.[5]

This young woman whose beauty had promised so much by the standards of her world, passes out of our knowledge with no further indication of her future than the declaration in her letter to Deronda on his wedding morning that, 'It is better— it shall be better with me because I have known you.'

7

Women as Mothers

IT MIGHT have been expected that women writing in the late eighteenth century and the Victorian era would have a great deal to say about women as mothers and that the later writers, at least, would join in a chorus of mother worship. This is not so. Mothers appear in the novels in numbers but their role is quietly accepted without emotional over-valuation of its status. The power and concentration devoted to the delineation of the young unmarried women in the novels is nowhere matched by any comparably deep examination of women as mothers. Absence of sentimentality on this subject is not surprising in authors of such distinction but that they should exhibit little positive interest in the topic itself does cause the reader to pause. Any interpretation offered must change with changes in the novel and its background of contemporary thought. In the earlier works where the conduct-book tradition of moral education is stronger, the stress is always on leading the young reader along the path she should go before marriage. After marriage and motherhood, responsibility will lie with the head of the family, the husband and the father, and our novels were not planned for his reading. One of the sidelights the novels throw upon the eighteenth-century family is the tacit assumption of the father's unquestioned responsibility for his daughters' moral welfare and the pains good fathers took to provide moral guidance.

In the later novels the emphasis changes. While the role of women was being fundamentally re-examined in the light of the claims of the radical thinkers that women should have the opportunity for improved education and independent work, and some women were trying to visualize the implications of this expansion of opportunity, others were finding the prospect a daunting one and were seeking compensation in the insistence on the importance of 'woman's influence', a term with a high emotional charge. As has been mentioned above (p. 19) Aimé-Martin's treatise *De l'éducation des mères de famille, ou la civilisation du genre humain par les femmes* was widely read in the abridged English translation entitled *Woman's Mission* published in 1839, and its high valuation of the influence of mothers upon their sons would obviously evoke considerable support. But, in progressive circles, even this book was used as a basis for the discussion of more controversial views. The radical *Westminster Review*, in an article on the thirteenth edition of the book in 1849, pleaded for more opportunities for women to work in occupations previously considered unsuitable, and a few years before this article appeared Mrs Hugo Reid's forward-looking *Plea for Women* (1843) had pointed out, with refreshing common sense, that it was absurd to speak as though female influence were the only influence, ignoring the possibility of a more powerful male influence counteracting and circumventing it. The harmful influence that could be exerted by a father on his children is indeed referred to in some of the later novels, notably those of the Brontës and Mrs Gaskell.

Since the emotional concentration on the role of women as mothers in both the early and the late novels is scant, this chapter is only able to produce a few scattered examples of the way in which the great women novelists regarded mothers—not so much as 'women of no importance' but as figures standing in the wings of their stage where the spotlight was on the woman struggling for personal identity.

Fanny Burney, Maria Edgeworth, Jane Austen

Fanny Burney expends most of her energy in describing the attitude of daughters to their natural guardians rather than the attitude of mothers to their children. The unquestioning obedience to parents that was considered axiomatic in so many eighteenth-century novels, where the position of a child embracing the knees of mother or father seems to be taken up quite naturally and frequently, distances the possibility of any criticism of the parents' role. The compensations of a relationship in which absolute obedience was expected on the one side are to be found in the very detailed care and guidance of their children that was required of parents. In Miss Burney's novels this is more apparent in the father and daughter (or ward) relationship than in the relationship between mother and child. It is Evelina's guardian, the Rev. Mr Villars, who gives her thoughtful advice on the smallest difficulties that confront her; in *Camilla*, even though both Mr and Mrs Tyrold neglect none of their duties to their daughters, it is the father who seeks to shield the heroine from pain by setting out minutely the necessity for delicacy of behaviour towards Edgar, and it is *his* kindness and wisdom that try to fortify Eugenia in her sufferings over her own plain looks. By contrast, in *Cecilia*, Mrs Delvile, the mother of the hero, is the embodiment of family pride and prejudice and therefore a negative influence.

Maria Edgeworth devotes little attention to the role of the mother outside the schoolroom, but she omits no opportunity of drawing a useful lesson from a mother's conduct; for example, in *Helen* the fact that Lady Davenant neglects her daughter is mentioned as one reason to censure the mother's interest in politics and her absorption in the conduct of a political salon, but the more important point seems to be the condemnation of Lady Davenant's pursuit of political influence, unseemly for any woman, whether she be a mother or not.

Jane Austen's view of mothers is hardly flattering and she has absolutely no trace of sentimentality about children and motherhood. In *Sense and Sensibility* Mrs Dashwood is only an older Marianne, unable to see clearly because of her own romantic notions, and not even satisfactory when directly appealed to by Elinor to help reinforce sense and good judgment. Her mother's close attachment to Marianne also leaves Elinor in greater isolation, in spite of the affection of the two sisters for each other. In the same novel, when Mrs John Dashwood is able to persuade her husband to break his promise to his dying father, it is (ironically) by playing on his own emotions as a father, using such loaded phrases as 'how could he answer it to himself to rob his child, his only child', 'to ruin himself and their poor little Harry', 'it could never be restored to our poor little boy', and so on that she renders John duly receptive to her views and can proceed to wield franker arguments to gain her end. The Austenian irony is evident again in the description of Lady Middleton as a mother who humoured her children, this being her only resource; she had the advantage over her husband, however, who since he had another resource, sport, could only indulge in humouring his children half the time. Lady Middleton's

foolish fondness makes her swallow all the insincerity of the Miss Steeles: a fond mother, though in pursuit of praise for her children, the most rapacious of human beings, is likewise the most credulous; her demands are exorbitant; but she will swallow anything; and the excessive affection and endurance of the Miss Steeles were viewed therefore by Lady Middleton without the smallest surprise or distrust. (Ch. 21)

Lydia Bennet is her foolish mother's daughter, with the addition of 'high animal spirits' and 'a sort of natural self-consequence'. She is left without the guidance that parents ought to give to their children, and particularly to empty-headed and flirtatious young daughters; her downfall, therefore, is largely to be laid at the door of Mr and Mrs Bennet. She is saved from final disaster not by her father but by Mr Darcy, who wishes to be of service to her sister Elizabeth, and, even before that, it is Elizabeth who is the only member of the family to bestir herself to warn Mr Bennet of the disgrace which Lydia may bring upon the family, and to urge him to take action: 'If you, my dear father, will not take the trouble of checking her exuberant spirits, and of teaching her that her present pursuits are not to be the business of her life, she will soon be beyond the reach of amendment' (Ch. 41). Mrs Bennet's inadequacies as a mother have rendered her husband's care for his children all the more imperative and must not be shrugged off with amused indifference; he, the responsible head of the family, has to have his duty pointed out to him by his own daughter, a reversal of the accepted roles. Lydia's self-important flaunting of her wedding-ring after her enforced marriage has ended the incident in outward respectability and her mother's subsequent condonement of the whole affair underline the unsatisfactory family position. As Lydia is the sister to fall, the situation receives a slight but subtle resonance from the fact that it was she who yawned and interrupted Mr Collins when he, with monotonous solemnity, began reading Fordyce's sermons to women aloud to the ladies.

The young people in *Northanger Abbey* are again without wise guidance. Mrs Morland, although kind, is too busy to give any real understanding to her daughter; Mrs Thorpe is shallow, worldly and stupid, and Mrs Allen can think of nothing but dress. The mothers in *Mansfield Park* are even worse. Fanny's mother is without personality, bowed down by poverty and child-bearing, while her comfortably circumstanced sister, Lady Bertram, neglects her duty of training Maria and Julia—'to the education of her daughters Lady Bertram paid not the slightest attention. She had not time for such cares'—a strong indictment indeed. The shortcomings in the education of the Bertram daughters are, however, realized belatedly by their father when he looks back upon the reasons for Maria's elope- ment with Henry Crawford (who himself was 'ruined by early independence and bad domestic example'). Sir Thomas feels that the excessive indulgence and flattery of the girls' aunt have been continually contrasted with his own severity, but this has not been the most direful mistake:

Something must have been wanting *within*, or time would have worn away much of its ill effect. He feared that principle, active principle, had been wanting; that they had never been properly taught to govern their inclinations and tempers by that sense of duty which alone can suffice. They had been instructed theoretically in their religion, but never required to bring it into daily practice. To be distinguished for elegance and accomplishments, the authorized object of their youth, could have had no useful influence that way, no moral effect on the mind. He had meant them to be good, but his cares had been directed to the understanding and manners, not the disposition: and of the necessity of self-denial and humility, he feared they had never heard from any lips that could profit them. (Ch. 58)

Jane Austen's unusually outspoken comment upon the girls' aunt is given after Mrs Norris has discussed Fanny's so-called ignorance and stupidity with her two cousins: 'Such were the counsels by which Mrs Norris assisted to form her nieces' minds; and it is not very wonderful that, with all their promising talents and early information, they should be entirely deficient in the less common acquirements of self-knowledge, generosity and humility.' These three Christian qualities Mrs Norris, as a clergyman's wife, should have possessed herself and should have helped her nieces to acquire; they were all three, of course, to be found in the character of the despised Fanny.

For Emma Woodhouse, it is her governess who supplies the place of the mother, and she has the advantage of being taught by a woman whose distinction of mind and soundness of judgment have laid excellent foundations for the future. The relationship between the two is completely satisfactory, the more so, perhaps, because the absence of a closer family bond removes certain emotional dangers. In *Persuasion* this influence of an older woman on a motherless girl is used in a mistaken, if well-intentioned direction. The moral insight and sensitivity of the girl are superior to the worldly standards and lack of insight of the woman she reveres enough to listen to, and near-tragedy is the result.

Jane Austen considered the widespread self-indulgence of parents through their children to be just as reprehensible as more personal manifestations of the same fault. Her children, it is noticeable, have little personality of their own, but are introduced to add another dimension to the pictures of their parents or of the other adults around them.

The Brontës

In the novels of the Brontës, mothers are viewed through the eyes of humiliated governesses. The children of Mrs Bloomfield in *Agnes Grey*, 'though superior to most children of their years in abilities' (as their mother believes) are behind them in attainments, while their manners are uncultivated and their tempers unruly. Mrs Bloomfield attributes this to a 'want of sufficient firmness, and diligent, persevering care' on the part of their governess, whereas it is obviously the result of the lack of such qualities in herself; she has abdicated the moral responsibilities of motherhood, hoping another will undertake them on her behalf. Agnes Grey's perseverance with Master Tom and Mary Ann Bloomfield as the months pass by is described in detail, but she lacks all support from their parents, and just when she has 'instilled something into their heads' she is dismissed by a mother incapable of seeing her children as they really are.

In the second household in *Agnes Grey*, Mrs Murray, a 'handsome dashing lady of forty' is quite incapable of giving wise care and guidance to her children nor is she interested in doing so. Anne Brontë's treatment of children in this novel has certain affinities with that of Jane Austen in so far as the children are used to reveal, in the shortcomings of their behaviour and character, the lack of wisdom or the weak indulgence of their parents, particularly the mother, but the effect of these errors of upbringing on the children themselves is worked out in a detail with which Jane Austen was not concerned. The children's general behaviour in *Agnes Grey* is horrifying and they have the power to make their governess's life a misery, while she lacks the requisite authority to discipline them. Jane Austen's view of children may be characterized as that of an aunt, Anne Brontë's that of a despised governess.

Some of the weaknesses of Arthur Huntingdon's character in *The Tenant of Wildfell Hall* are blamed on his upbringing. Soon after marriage Helen discovers that 'he has no more idea of exerting himself to overcome obstacles than he has of restraining his natural appetites' and she lays this to the charge of his 'harsh yet careless father and his madly indulgent mother'. She resolves that, 'if ever I am a mother I will zealously strive against this *crime* of over-indulgence—I can hardly give it a milder name when I think of the evil it brings'. When her son is born she does become a new kind of mother: caring deeply for her child, she is yet without sentimentality and self-indulgence in her relationship with him and she uses her intelligence and clear moral judgment to decide what is best for him, instead of accepting the standards of those around her. She sees her husband's deterioration and his bad influence on their son and yet she has to watch the boy's growing affection for the permissive father who is fast ruining him, the father in whom contemporary opinion vested the greater responsibility for the child's welfare. It is for little Arthur's sake that she finally flees, taking the boy with her.

The difference in the moral education of boys and girls is also a subject on which Helen Huntingdon holds views strongly in opposition to contemporary opinion; during a call on Mrs Markham she says:

'You would have us encourage our sons to prove all things by their own experience, while our daughters must not even profit by the experience of others. Now *I* would have both so benefit by the experience of others, and the precepts of a higher authority, that they should know beforehand to refuse the evil and choose the good, and require no experimental proofs to teach them the evil of transgression. I would not send a poor girl in to the world, unarmed against her foes, and ignorant of the snares that beset her path; nor would I watch and guard her, till, deprived of self-respect and self-reliance, she lost the power, or the will to watch and guard herself.' (Ch. 3)

And she goes on to plead for an attitude to the training of young men widely different from that generally accepted; the strength of her language shows how strong is her conviction:

'as for my son—if I thought he would grow up to be what you call a man of the world—one that has "seen life"! and glories in his experience, even though he should so far profit by it, as to sober down, at length, into a useful and respected member of society I would rather that he died tomorrow!—rather a thousand times.' (Ch. 3)

Charlotte Brontë's views of children are cool and detached. Adèle in *Jane Eyre* is described in totally unsentimental terms, an attitude which her creator feels called upon to explain:

This *par parenthese*, will be thought cool language by persons who entertain solemn doctrines about the angelic nature of children, and the duty of those charged with their education to conceive for them an idolatrous devotion; but I am not writing to flatter paternal egotism, to echo cant, or prop up humbug; I am merely telling the truth. I felt a conscientious solicitude for Adèle's welfare and progress, and a quiet liking to her little self. (Ch. 12)

This detachment is indeed the coolest exhibited by all our women writers; as Swinburne said, 'the fiery-hearted Vestal of Haworth had no room reserved in the palace of her passionate and high-minded imagination as a nursery for inmates of such divine and delicious quality'[1] as George Eliot's Totty and Eppie.

Elizabeth Gaskell

Mrs Gaskell, the only one of the group of authors who was herself a mother during her period of literary activity, comes nearest to sharing the Victorian uncritical reverence for motherhood, but, as in her attitude to the accepted position of a wife, doubts do appear to creep in from time to time. Even in *Mary Barton*, when describing Mary's mourning for the loss of her mother and her wish for her mother's aid in her perplexities, Mrs Gaskell comments that she was 'unconscious of the fact that she was far superior in sense and spirit to the mother she mourned'.

Lizzie Leigh's mother adopts the accepted view of the fallen girl and the treatment to be meted out to her. She acquiesces in the father's treatment of Lizzie, and although Mrs Leigh's heart is filled with a hidden and sullen rebellion against such harshness, she does not rebel. After her husband's death, however, she takes the positive action of moving to Manchester with her sons to find Lizzie and they finally make a home together.

Of the influences that bring about the return of Ruth's self-respect, the redemptive power of motherhood, that is, her own love for her illegitimate son, may be said to be the mightiest. In Mrs Gaskell's phrasing 'the angel of her son drew her nearer and nearer to God'. In this novel, in which the delicacy of the main theme makes her anxious not to offend contemporary susceptibilities more than she need, Mrs Gaskell echoes conventional views more frequently than elsewhere. For instance, when Mr Benson, unable to rise from his couch, is anxious to prevent Ruth from going out again to make some desperate effort at suicide, he commands her to stay where she is 'in your mother's name, whether she be dead or alive', and she stays. When Ruth first goes to the Benson household, she finds the 'same unconsciousness of individual merit, the same absence of introspection and analysis of motive, as there had been in her mother'. This implied praise of an absence of introspection and analysis is strengthened by the fact that Mrs Gaskell does not analyse the 'influence' of the mother, nor question its value; for her there is no use for the intellect in these matters. She does, however, give an example of failure in the duty of a mother to train her son in good basic principles when she describes with some subtlety the relationship between Mr Bellingham, Ruth's seducer, and his mother. It had given Mrs Bellingham great happiness to extort from her son's 'indifference or his affection, the concessions which she never sought by force of reason or by appeals to principle'; thus Mrs Gaskell acknowledges the moral error of a mother's emotional and personal appeal to her child in order to attain her own ends and satisfy her own vanity, instead of considering impersonally the best training she can give her son. Bellingham has obviously used with Ruth methods similar to his mother's, but Ruth, with a greater love for her own son, takes a surprisingly strong and brave line for the sake of the boy. Indeed the sense of responsibility for her child's welfare is the main factor in Ruth's refusing to marry her seducer when he finally offers her marriage; her last words to him are:

You shall have nothing to do with my boy by my consent, much less by my agency. I would rather see him working on the roadside than leading such a life—being such a one as you are . . . If there were no other reason to prevent our marriage but the one fact that it would bring Leonard into contact with you, that would be enough. (Vol 2, Ch. 11)

Ruth's refusal to marry Bellingham is a brave action in two ways: by it she not only declines the offer of restored social respectability and economic security for herself and Leonard but she also takes the bold step of judging the fitness of a child's father to perform his most solemn parental responsibilities. Her regard for Leonard's moral welfare holds first place in her mind, taking second place to his material welfare and the restoration of a legitimate name and father to him in a society where these were of supreme importance.

George Eliot

George Eliot's appreciation of the essence of childhood is un- matched and of her child portraits the description of the little orphan, Job Tudge, in *Felix Holt*, is possibly the most endearing, if less often quoted than the description of Eppie in the coal-hole. There is, however, a degree of detachment in George Eliot's depiction of the mothers in her novels, except in the case of some of the minor figures like Dolly Winthrop and Mrs Garth. The father-daughter relationship is a much stronger bond, most powerfully expressed in Maggie Tulliver's close ties with her father and Silas Marner's devotion to the child who replaces his lost treasure. George Eliot also touches upon one aspect of maternal behaviour not often mentioned, that is, the harshness of some mothers to their daughters in contrast to the indulgence they frequently show to their sons. Such a mother is the handsome Mrs Irwine in *Adam Bede*; vanity and love of fine dressing are characteristics of this 'beautifully aged brunette, whose rich-toned complexion is well set off by the complex wrappings of pure white cambric and lace about her head and neck . . . it must take a long time to dress that old lady in the morning'. She is very fond of her son, the Rector of Broxton, but she has slight sympathy with her more commonplace daughters, though they are unselfish and show much kindness to the poor people in the village. Because of George Eliot's concentration on the importance of woman's 'fate', it is relevant to point out here the difference in the lot of the two vain women in this book—Hetty and Mrs Irwine. The latter's lot has fallen in pleasant places, she is admired by everyone and has a devoted son; her vanity, therefore, unlike Hetty's, is visited with no tragic consequences to herself, however much unhappiness it may cause her daughters.

Some impatience with the contemporary sentimentality surrounding motherhood is also detectable in George Eliot: she chooses the unusual relationship between Mrs Transome and Harold to remark:

It is in fact a little too much in the background, that mothers have a self larger than their maternity, and when their sons have become taller than themselves, and are gone from them to college or into the world, there are wide spaces in their time which are not filled with praying for their boys, reading old letters, and envying yet blessing those who are attending to their shirt-buttons. Mrs Transome was certainly not one of those bland, adoring, and gently tearful women. After sharing the common dream that when a beautiful manchild was born to her, her cup of happiness would be full, she had travelled through long years apart from that child to find herself at last in the presence of a son of whom she was afraid, who was utterly unmanageable by her, and to whose sentiments in any case she possessed no key. (Ch. 8)

The unwonted asperity of the language adds to the impact of this unusual moment of Victorian truth with its reminder of the needs of mothers as individuals with 'a self larger than their maternity'. There is, however, no sharpness in George Eliot's description of Celia's attitude to her baby in *Middlemarch*, the accepted attitude of the wealthy Victorian, surrounded by the comfort of a tastefully furnished nursery, over-anxious for her baby's health, self-absorbed through her child and expecting the rest of the world to have the same absorption. Yet the built-up detail of the description accentuates the increasing isolation of Dorothea, further removed than ever from her commonplace and conforming sister.

Closest attention to the role of mother is paid in *Daniel Deronda*: Deronda's mother is a true artist but neither gentle nor feminine, indeed rather tense and masculine. When her son finally meets her she is suffering physical pain and 'her worn beauty had a strangeness in it as if she were not quite a human mother, but a melusina, who had ties with some world which is independent of ours'. The fish-tail connotation of the name Melusina is interesting in the general context of George Eliot's Lamia women. In spite of the imaginative power in the depiction of the motives that governed Alcharisi, the underlying judgment of Deronda and of George Eliot also is one of regret for her failure as a mother, and for her fundamental lack of womanliness as both understood it. To Deronda the meeting with his mother is a deep disappointment, 'it made the filial yearning of his life a disappointed pilgrimage to a shrine where there were no longer the symbols of sacredness' (Ch. 53), and as they say farewell 'it seemed that all the woman lacking in her was present in him'. It is indeed the woman in Daniel Deronda which makes him such an ideal sympathizer with the women who come into his life. Even in his relationship with Sir Hugo he is 'moved by an affectionateness such as we are apt to call feminine, disposing him to yield in ordinary details'; in this he is the antithesis of Henleigh Grandcourt who never yields in anything but wishes to bend all, particularly women, to his smallest wishes. When Deronda first meets Mirah preparing to drown herself, 'the agitating impression this girl was making on him stirred a fibre that lay close to his deepest interest in the fates of women'; it is because of the unknown fate of his own mother that he is, from the beginning, particularly concerned in the fates of all women, watching them with an understanding attention, and Mirah's search for her own lost mother is a parallel to his own search, engaging his deepest personal sympathy. He makes up in himself by his feminine sympathy and affection for that lack in his mother which so disappointed him. Indeed, it is not an untenable view that the best parents, or substitute parents in George Eliot's novels are not women, but men—from Silas Marner through Felix Holt, to Daniel Deronda.

8

Women Standing Alone

IT WAS inevitable that the new claims for women to have both the right and the opportunity to engage in satisfying work outside the home should direct attention to the woman standing alone. In the social structure of the time the protection afforded by a stable family and home background was of paramount importance and any step outside the home, whether taken voluntarily or enforced by stern economic necessity, was a step into a strange and unsympathetic world in which women were especially vulnerable. Unless the driving force was purely economic it was only the unusual woman who would take such a bold step, but both those who were forced to stand alone and those who chose to do so had to progress along an unknown way inch by inch; having no tradition behind it, the role of the woman on her own had to be explored from the beginning. In the early years only a few women were affected by the need for such a fundamental rethinking of their place in society, but gradually their numbers increased and their occupations became more varied. Women might be regarded as standing alone negatively, as spinsters or solitaries with independent means, however slender, or positively, as teachers, writers, artists, shop-assistants and factory-workers, pursuing their way outside the haven of a fully understood social environment. The anomaly of a distinguished spinster's social standing was recognized even in the eighteenth century to the extent that unmarried ladies of a certain age and respectability were granted the courtesy title of 'Mrs', the most revered holder of the distinction being Mrs Hannah More; this title, the customary mark of a woman having made the transition from a minor to a more adult role, and automatically acquired by marriage, was in such cases conferred as a recognition of the woman's own achievement as an individual.

173

Women Standing Alone

It is obvious that a wide variety of adjustments had to be made both by society in accepting the 'new women' and by the women themselves under the stresses of such fundamental changes. Serious discussion of some of the implications had only begun at the opening of our period and they had not advanced very far by the end of it, since pertinent reflection had to wait upon actual experience. Nor was the novel the place for theoretical consideration of such problems. It was the place, however, where such problems could be placed in their individual human settings, could be viewed as 'experiments in life', and it was natural that our authors, artists themselves, should be interested in pioneer women of any kind, even if the tradition of the novel as the story of a young woman awaiting marriage remained the dominant influence in their writing. The early novels include both spinsters with conservative views as well as revolutionary young women given to declaiming the new doctrines (or travesties of them). In the novels of the middle period it is the plight of the governess and the teacher that attracts most interest, whereas later novels examine the difficulties facing the woman artist and writer. Any expansion of professional opportunities for women depended upon an improvement in their education and this topic is touched upon with increasing frequency; the earlier novels deride the bluestocking and her vanity, but the later turn to more serious consideration of the value of a sound foundation of knowledge and training of the mind. Also, out of the experience of writers themselves there emerges the additional problem of woman's duality: how can she both fulfil her biological and emotional function as a woman and also exercise her talents as writer and artist; is renunciation of one or the other inevitable, or can she really perform a dual role? Except in so far as the emphasis in the novels changes from derision of the revolutionary woman to sympathy with the no longer ridiculous but still extraordinary woman, there is no over-all pattern discernible during so brief a span; but the attitudes and insights of the individual novelists have a special interest in this field of pioneer thinking and unexamined popular reactions. Under their surface variations is to be found a common realization of the deep problems involved in these far-reaching changes.

174

Fanny Burney

Although she cannot be numbered amongst advanced thinkers on the rights of women, Fanny Burney was aware of the views of the revolutionaries. She also showed interest in women's education. Her own studies of Latin under the guidance of Dr Johnson were stopped in deference to Dr Burney's opinion that women should not learn the dead languages, which, in an age when education was based upon the classics, amounted to believing that women should receive no education at all, or none worthy the name by contemporary standards. A fashionable eighteenth-century amusement was to deride the spinster and the bluestocking, and in *Camilla* it is the unpleasant and ignorant governess, Miss Maryland, who conforms to this viewpoint, when she tells Sir Hugh Tyrold that Indiana 'could never cope with so great a disadvantage as the knowledge of Latin' when she came to be of a proper age for thinking of an establishment. Indeed, Eugenia's learning causes her to be stared at even more than her ugliness. But Miss Burney, although not wishing to offend the conventions of society, does admit that something deeper and more lasting may be achieved by a woman who has received an unusual education, worthwhile in itself for what it can add to her stature as a human being. Eugenia's two sisters turn to her in time of crisis for comfort and strength; her youth (she is fifteen) does not prevent them from revering her superior wisdom:

Her species of education had early prepossessed them with respect for her knowledge, and her unaffected fondness for study, had fixed their opinion of her extraordinary understanding. The goodness of her heart, the evenness of her temper, and her natural turn to contemplation, had established her character alike for sanctity and for philosophy throughout the family. (Vol. 4, Ch. 2)

Surprisingly enough, the only female revolutionary in the popular tradition to be encountered in our novels is Elinor Joddrell in Fanny Burney's *The Wanderer*. The author uses heavy-footed irony in her treatment of Elinor but the views expressed through this character are interesting. She is a believer in the rights of women who has absorbed her ideas from revolutionary France. She abhors all falsehood and hypocrisy and her exposition of her point of view has a certain feeling of 'mental enlargement' reminding the reader of the young Wordsworth's reaction to revolutionary thought. At one meeting with Harleigh she says:

You think me, I know, tarnished by those very revolutionary ideas through which, in my own estimation, I am ennobled. I owe to them that I dare hold myself intellectually, as well as personally, an equal member of the community; not a poor degraded however necessary appendant to it: I owe to them my enfranchisement from the mental slavery of subscribing to unexamined opinions, and being governed by prejudices that I despise. I owe to them the precious privilege, so shamefully new to mankind, of daring to think for myself. But for them—should I not at this moment be pining away my lingering existence, in silent consumption? They have rescued me from that slow poison! (Vol. 1, Ch. 18)

She expresses her views on the attitude of men to women in the following words:

By the oppression of their own states and institutions, they render us insignificant; and then speak of us as though we were so born! But what have we tried, in which we have been foiled? They dare not trust us with their own education, and their own opportunities for distinction;—I except the article of fighting; against that, there may perhaps be some obstacles: but to be condemned, as weaker vessels in intellect, because inferiour in bodily strength and stature, we cannot cope with them as boxers and wrestlers!

This Woman, whom they estimate thus below, they elevate above themselves. They require from her, in defiance of their examples—and in defiance of their lures!—angelical perfection. She must be mistress of her passions; she must never listen to her inclinations; she must not take a step of which the purport is not visible; she must not pursue a measure of which she cannot publish the motive; she must always be guided by reason, though they deny her understanding! Frankness, the noblest of our qualities, is her disgrace—sympathy, the most exquisite of our feelings, is her bane! (Vol. 3, Ch. 42)

In spite of the author's obvious ridicule of her speeches, Elinor's views are courageous and her language is always arresting and full of energy. As a human being she is honest and generous: for instance, on one occasion she gives Juliet a fifty-pound note and is thoughtful enough to give it in a sealed envelope to avoid embarrassing the recipient. But her views are proved to be unworkable in society as it is actually organized; in the anguish of her disappointment she realizes that 'she has strayed from the beaten road, only to discover that all the others are path less'. How far Madame d'Arblay's sympathies were engaged with this character whom she depicts as brave but ridiculous is difficult to say, but Albert Harleigh's judgment is probably the novelist's own, it is certainly the conventional conduct-book judgment, when he says:

There is no relying upon the patience, or the fortitude, of one so completely governed by impulse; and who considers her passions as her guides to glory—not as the subtlest enemies of every virtue . . . Ah! how could she imagine such a one calculated to engage my heart? How wide is it from all that, to me, appears attractive! Her spirit I admire; but where is the sweetness I could love? I respect her under-standing; but where is the softness that should make it charm while it enlightens? I am grateful for her partiality; but where is the dignity that might ennoble it, or the delicacy that might make it as refined as it is flattering? Where—where the soul's fascination, that grows out of the mingled excellencies, the blended harmonies, of the understanding with the heart and the manners? (Vol. 1, Ch. 19)

He feels, however, that, when Elinor, with her fine qualities of mind, 'sees the fallacy of her new system' and finds how vain it is to 'tread down the barriers of custom and experience, raised by the wisdom of foresight, and established after trial, for public utility', she will return to the habits of society and common life.

Fortunately for her, Elinor is possessed of private means and is thus not confronted with the problem of earning her own living as Juliet was.

Maria Edgeworth

The Edgeworths were serious about the value of education and, therefore, about the value of the teacher, and they plead for teaching to be considered a real profession for women, with adequate remuneration:

The reward ought to be such as to excite women to cultivate their talents, and their understandings, with a view to this profession. A profession we will call it, for it should be considered as such; as an honourable profession, which a gentlewoman might follow without losing any degree of the estimation in which she is held by what is called the world. There is no employment, at present, by which a gentlewoman can maintain herself without losing something of that respect, something of that rank in society, which neither female fortitude nor male philosophy willingly forgoes. The liberal professions are open to men of small fortunes; by presenting one similar resource to women, we should have a strong motive for their moral and intellectual improvement.[1]

They go on to suggest a salary of three hundred pounds a year, for twelve or fourteen years, the space of time a 'preceptress' must probably employ in the education of a young lady. Such provision would enable a governess, after the pupil's education is completed, either to settle in a family of her own or to be happily independent, 'secure from the temptation of marrying for money'.

Jane Austen

Jane Austen's nearest approach to a bluestocking, Mary Bennet, is different from the usual stock figure although her extremely self-conscious pursuit of knowledge seems an indication that she belongs to that despised company. Her secondhand opinions and 'observations of threadbare morality' are suited to an aged female pedant and therefore the more ridiculous in a young girl. The judgment upon her is a moral rather than a social or intellectual one, however, since it is vanity that has given her application, at the same time giving her 'a pedantic air and conceited manner, which would have injured a higher degree of excellence than she had reached'.

No one could be further from the stock figure of an old maid than Miss Bates. The current opinion that 'a single woman with a narrow income must be a ridiculous old maid' is, on the surface, correct, but even society reverses its own usual strictures in approving of Miss Bates, just as she herself approves of society. She triumphs very successfully over her handicaps, and Mr Weston says of her that 'she is a standing lesson of how to be happy'. The admiration Jane Austen had for female simplicity, cheerfulness and good nature, even if not supported by elegance and cultivated taste, is nowhere so clearly expressed as in her description of this untypical old maid who:

Enjoyed a most uncommon degree of popularity for a woman neither young, handsome, rich nor married. Miss Bates stood in the very worst predicament in the world for having much of the public favour, and she had not the intellectual superiority to make atonement to herself, or frighten those who might hate her into outward respect. (Ch. 3)

Yet the characteristic of Miss Bates that made her popular was not one which Jane Austen could whole-heartedly admire—Miss Bates was not wanted as a counsellor 'but as an approver (a much safer character) she was truly welcome. Her approbation, at once general and minute, warm and incessant, could not but please.' But the more genuine side of her rather simple nature receives praise untouched by any side-glances at the vanity of her easily pleased hearers, for 'the simplicity and cheerfulness of her nature, her contented and grateful spirit, were a recommendation to everybody, and a mine of felicity to herself'.

It is difficult to escape the impression that Miss Austen lacked either a basic sympathy with Jane Fairfax or felt that her own knowledge of the circumstances of a life lived outside a protecting family background was too scanty to afford the depth of penetration which her integrity as an artist demanded. The disadvantages of Jane's social position strike Emma forcibly when she hears that Miss Fairfax is shortly to leave for a post as governess to a friend of Mrs Elton's and that Frank Churchill has obeyed the summons to Mrs Churchill's bedside: 'the contrast between Mrs Churchill's importance in the world and Jane Fairfax's struck her; one was everything, the other nothing— and she sat musing on the difference of woman's destiny' (Ch. 44). The direct statement concerning woman's destiny is an unusual one, but no more is openly made of it.

Her creator's full approval and understanding are, however, accorded to the other Austenian governess, Miss Taylor, later Mrs Weston. Emma, unlike her father, realizes the advantages that marriage to Mr Weston and an establishment of her own, bring to the former Miss Taylor, even although she had received respect and much affection at Highbury. Mrs Weston's excellence is set off by the 'self-important, presuming, familiar, ignorant and illbred' Mrs Elton, who is astonished to find the governess 'quite the gentlewoman'. The possibility of social humiliation is thus admitted to lurk in the background of the life of a governess, even if Miss Taylor was spared its rigours in the gentle environment of the Woodhouse household.

Harriet Martineau

Although Harriet Martineau can claim no place amongst the greater women novelists, one novel, *Deerbrook*, which she wrote in 1839, is of sufficient interest to justify including her in this chapter. Miss Martineau, who resembled Maria Edgeworth in her strong common sense, and shared with George Eliot an admiration for Comte, was an influential writer for entirely different reasons from those which brought fame to the rest of our novelists. Guizot chose her for the subject of his first biographical sketch in a new periodical, the reason he gave for his choice being that she afforded the only instance on record of a woman's having substantially affected legislation otherwise than through the influence of some man in high position; he presumably judged that legislation was affected by the Leaders Miss Martineau wrote for the *Daily News* between 1853 and 1856, dealing with a wide range of topics, including foreign affairs, education and the position of women. Her chief interest in this section of our study, however, is for the character of Maria Young in *Deerbrook*.

Maria is the lame, ailing and lonely governess to the two chief trading families in the village of Deerbrook; she is a young woman who uses her mind independently and who expresses her views about her work as a teacher in a way that is new. She regrets that she can do little for her pupils and wishes she had them in a house by herself to spend their whole time with her, so that she could 'educate instead of merely teaching them'; she says in conversation: 'teaching has its pleasures,—its great occasional and small daily pleasures, though they are not to be compared to the sublime delights of education' (2nd edn, 1884,

p. 21). When asked whether teaching is an occupation in which anybody can be happy, she replies:

'Why not, as well as in making pins' heads, or in nursing sick people, or in cutting square blocks out of a chalk pit for thirty years together, or in any other occupation which may be ordained to prove to us that happiness lies in the temper and not in the object of the pursuit? Are there not free and happy pin-makers, and sick nurses, and chalk-cutters?' 'Yes! but they know how much to expect. They have no idea of pin-making in itself being great happiness.'

'Just so. Well: let a governess learn what to expect, set her free from a hankering after happiness in her work, and you have a happy governess.'

Maria herself has to face the future 'infirm and suffering in body, poor, solitary, living by toil, without love, without prospect', but she does so with high courage and the belief that 'there can be nothing mortally fatal in a trial which many of the wisest and best have sustained',

Harriet Martineau felt that the best friends of the women's cause were 'the happy wives and the busy, cheerful, satisfied, single women who have no injuries of their own to avenge and no painful vacuity or mortification to relieve'. She also felt that the best advocates for it would be those women who were obtaining access to 'real social business', the women doctors and professors in America, the women of business and the female artists of France, and the hospital administrators, nurses, educators and substantially successful authors of Britain. She believed that, let women be educated and their powers cultivated to the extent for which the means were already provided, the rest would follow. Whatever a woman proved herself able to do, society would be thankful to see her do, just as if she were a man.[2] In her own case this had proved to be true.

The Brontës

In direct contrast with Harriet Martineau's realistic views of the life of a governess were the expectations with which Agnes Grey embarked on her own career. In the early pages of Anne Brontë's novel Agnes muses on how delightful it will be to become a governess; to go out into the world, try her unknown powers, earn her own living, and vindicate herself in the eyes of her mother and Mary. She believes she is competent for the task of training the tender plants and watching their buds unfold day by day (the poetical expression of her dreams is, of course, significant) and she puts a great deal of trust in the memories of her own childhood to guide her in gaining the confidence and affection of her pupils. Such an attitude is almost certain to meet with disappointment, concentrated as it is on the satisfactions that she herself is to derive from the work, with absolutely no idea of the everyday endurance demanded of a governess. It is an approach typical of a 'young lady' who thinks such a post provides an easy and absorbing way of earning a living. Reality, of course, proves quite different when Agnes arrives at Wellwood, and her sufferings at the hands of the unruly children and the social humiliations inflicted by the parents are described with a realism in complete contrast with the day-dreaming of her expectations. The subject is treated seriously, with scarcely a touch of humour: a governess's basic economic and social dependence was not easily accepted and distanced by the Brontës. To add a final touch, there comes Agnes's realization that when Master John Murray is sent to school, in a state of scandalous ignorance, this, 'doubtless would be laid to the account of his education having been entrusted to an ignorant female teacher, who had presumed to take in hand what she was wholly incompetent to perform'. In actual fact, in ways quite different from those that would be implied by the complainants, Agnes is incompetent to perform this particular task in these particular circumstances; someone tougher and more ignorant could have done what was necessary much more adequately and without such a price of suffering. The social humiliation Agnes undergoes is closely connected with her status as a lady: the subtle slights and snubs are inflicted by her employers upon a young woman who, although their inferior in worldly wealth, is their equal, if not their superior, in birth, manners and education, that is, in the acknowledged characteristics of a lady. In *Pride and Prejudice* Elizabeth suffered from ill-bred members of the aristocracy and their sycophants but in *Agnes Grey* the differences in social position have their foundations in money rather than birth and

182

none of the Austen heroines found herself economically dependent upon the Mrs Bloomfields and Mrs Murrays of this world. The narrowness of Agnes Grey's life is further illuminated by the contrast between her lot and that of the young curate. Agnes feels sorry for Mr Weston's lonely and homeless condition, but she reflects that: 'he is not so miserable as I should be under such a deprivation: he leads an active life and a wide field for useful exertion lies before him, he can *make* friends—and he can make a home, too, if he pleases' (Ch. 4).

Anne Brontë's expressed intention in recounting this unfortunate governess's trials was 'to benefit those whom it might concern' and she felt that if any parent had gathered any useful hint from the description of the vexatious propensities of the pupils, she would be well rewarded for her pains. It is interesting to note that Bertrand Russell's mother felt she would like to give a copy of *Agnes Grey* to every family with a governess and resolved to read it through again herself when she had to engage a governess, in order to remind her to be human.

In *The Tenant of Wildfell Hall* Helen Huntingdon, having had the great courage to flee from her husband on account of his evil influence on their child, maintains herself and the boy by working as an artist –a profession admirable in itself as all serious art is admirable, and without the distressing dependence of the life of a governess in other people's houses. The work of women as artists and writers was considered with increasing seriousness by the Brontës, and they felt women's work should be judged by the same standards as men's. In the preface to the second edition of *The Tenant*, Anne says that she makes no effort to satisfy speculations as to her identity because she is satisfied that 'if a book is a good one, it is so whatever the sex of the author may be'. Charlotte Brontë held similar views. She was impatient of being judged by rules deemed to be observable by women writers only, she believed that the only valid criterion for all artists was whether they had been faithful to the view of life presented to them. This belief led her to question the absolute honesty of Mrs Gaskell's depiction of life as given in her books, and in a letter to her of 9 July 1853, she asks whether no luminous cloud ever came between her and the severe truth as 'you know it in your own secret and clear-seeing soul', was she never tempted to make her characters more amiable than life, by the inclination to 'assimilate your thought to the thoughts of those who always *feel* kindly, but sometimes fail to *see* justly?' But she immediately withdraws the question, saying it is not intended to be answered.

Mrs Gaskell relates that Charlotte had a 'corroding dread at her heart' of becoming a 'stern, harsh, selfish woman' in her dreary solitude and we see this dread personified in the outward manners of the two old maids in *Shirley*, who have none of the redeeming pleasantness of disposition that Miss Bates showed. They are old maids with crusty exteriors in the tradition of the typical spinster in a novel. But Charlotte Brontë probes more deeply beneath the asperities of appearance and manner and shows the heroism involved in adjusting to difficult lives by the exercise of will and character rather than by the easy way of pleasing hypocrisy. The active goodness of Miss Ainley, indeed, influences Caroline to try to plan her own life on similar lines, though 'she still felt with pain that the life which made Miss Ainley happy could not make her happy: pure and active as it was, in her heart she deemed it deeply dreary because it was so loveless—to her ideas, so forlorn'.

In the same novel Rose Yorke gives voice to the longing for satisfying work that can really use up the energies she possesses. She says to her mother:

if my Master has given me ten talents, my duty is to trade with them, and make them ten talents more. Not in the dust of household drawers shall the coin be interred. I will *not* deposit it in a broken-spouted tea-pot, and shut it up in a china-closet among tea things. I will *not* commit it to your work-table to be smothered in piles of woollen hose. I will *not* prison it in the linen press to find shrouds among the sheets: and least of all mother . . . least of all will I hide it in a tureen of cold potatoes, to be ranged with bread, butter, pastry and ham on the shelves of the larder. (Ch. 23)

Rose is like the other girls in the neighbourhood whose brothers are engaged in business or professions, while the sisters 'have no earthly employment, but household work and sewing; no earthly pleasure, but an unprofitable visiting'. The men expect their women to sew and cook, 'contentedly, regularly, uncomplainingly all their lives long, as if they had no germs of faculties for anything else: a doctrine as reasonable to hold, as it would be that the fathers have no faculties but for eating what their daughters cook, or for wearing what they sew'. The author breaks off the narrative to apostrophize the 'men of Yorkshire' and the 'men of England', urging them to alter these things, to cultivate their girls' minds instead of keeping them narrow and fettered, to 'give them scope and work'. But in spite of all these protestations, neither Rose nor Shirley nor Caroline accomplishes anything very much in the way of work nor of exercising her talents, each continues to await marriage. Charlotte's friend, Mary Taylor, takes her up on this point, writing from New Zealand to say:

I have seen some extracts from *Shirley* in which you talk of women working. And this first duty, this great necessity, you seem to think that some women may indulge in, if they give up marriage, and don't make themselves too disagreeable to the other sex. You are a coward and a traitor . . . It is very wrong of you to *plead* for toleration of workers on the ground of their being in peculiar circumstances, and few in number or singular in disposition. Work or degradation is the lot of all except the very small number born to wealth.[3]

Charlotte's interest in women as authors is worked into the fabric of *Villette*: in Lucy Snowe, apart from the story of her gradual maturation of character, we have the picture of a girl who is writing her own story, a woman writer who utilizes all her resources of letters and private devoirs, watching herself as she comments for the benefit of the reader. The qualities for which she loves Monsieur Paul include his powers as a creative and descriptive writer; although he never writes for publication, his literary talents open up new vistas on life and literature for Lucy, enriching her mind and personality, and she responds with all the ardour of a fellow-writer. As Jane Eyre turns to her sketching, Lucy finds relief through her pen.

Just as Lucy Snowe is Charlotte's most deeply realized heroine, so the old maid in *Villette* is a more grandly tragic type than the old maids in *Shirley*, and she, like Lucy, has very strong feelings. Lucy admires her: 'she gave me the originality of her character to study: the steadiness of her virtues, I will add the power of her passions, to admire, the truth of her feelings to trust. All these things she had, and for these things I clung to her' (Ch. 4). These virtues are exhibited when, in a reminiscent mood on the night before she dies, she tells Lucy of the tragic love of her life. She doubts whether she has made the best use of her calamities: 'soft, amiable natures they would have refined to saintliness; of strong, evil spirits they would have made demons; as for me, I have only been a woe-struck and selfish woman'.

Elizabeth Gaskell

Mrs Gaskell, in her *Life of Charlotte Brontë*, discusses the special difficulties that a woman author, unlike a man, for whom writing is probably just a change of some other employment, must confront:

But no other can take up the quiet, regular duties of the daughter, the wife, or the mother, as well as she whom God has appointed to fill that particular place: a woman's principal work in life is hardly left to her own choice; nor can she drop the domestic charges devolving on her as an individual, for the exercise of the most splendid talents that were ever bestowed. And yet she must not shrink from the extra responsibility implied by the very fact of her possessing such talents. She must not hide her gift in a napkin; it was meant for the service of others. In an humble and faithful spirit must she labour to do what is not impossible, or God would not have set her to do it. I put into words what Charlotte Brontë put into actions. (Ch. 16)

The modesty of the last sentence conceals the fact that Mrs Gaskell also took seriously the responsibilities of her own dual role. It has sometimes been suggested that she was mistaken in straining to write her industrial novels and should rather have confined herself to a smaller local canvas as in *Wives and Daughters*, but she obviously felt a moral necessity to call attention to the problems of the north in her writings. The setting is in any case a background for a very personal interpretation of the need for women's redeeming influence in social problems, and her belief that reconciliation and right action would follow from understanding and neighbourly concern. In her view the remedial effects follow always from *personal* qualities, and one of the chief embodiments of these virtues is the old spinster, Alice Wilson, in *Mary Barton*. All Alice's

186

relationships are filled with her outgoing sympathy and affection; these extend even to her early association with her master and mistress, for when Mary Barton says she is glad that she (Mary) had not gone into service, Alice replies: 'Eh, lass! thou little knows the pleasures o'helping others; I was as happy there as could be; almost as happy as I was at home.' A sphere of homely influence for servants is not mentioned by other writers, but Mrs Gaskell gives several examples of this. It is Sally, the Benson's maid in *Ruth*, who preaches to the dejected heroine the 'gospel of housework well done' which she herself had learned from her old mistress. Seeing Ruth making beds in a half-hearted way because she is concentrated on her own woes, Sally tells her that this is the duty God has set her:

'I know it's not the work parsons preach about; though I don't think they go so far from the mark when they read, "whatsoever thy hand findeth to do, that do with all thy might". Just try for a day to think of all the odd jobs as to be done well and truly as in God's sight, not just slurred over anyhow, and you'll go through them twice as cheerfully, and have no thought to spare for sighing or crying.' (Vol. 2, Ch. 3)

And Betty, the maid in *Cousin Phillis*, standing far enough outside the drama to see the matter clearly, takes the situation in hand when all the efforts of Phillis's parents are in vain to restore her interest in life. Betty approaches the sofa on which Phillis is lying:

'Now, Phillis!' said she . . . 'we ha' done a' we can for you, and the doctors has done a' they can for you, and I think the Lord has done a' He can for you, and more than you deserve, too, if you don't do something for yourself. If I were you, I'd rise up and snuff the moon, sooner than break your father's and mother's hearts wi' watching and waiting till it pleases you to fight your own way back to cheerfulness. There, I never favoured long preachings, and I've said my say.' (Part 1)

And these bracing words have the intended effect: Phillis fights her own way back to cheerfulness.

Most of Mrs Gaskell's women exercise their influence in the ordinary life of a home, but in *Ruth* some thought and expression is given to views on nursing as a profession for women.

When the parish surgeon finds employment for Ruth as a sick-nurse, she looks upon the opportunities for service that this gives her in a different way from the usual contemporary attitude to such work; her attitude has more in common with that of the religious nursing sisterhoods than with that of Sarah Gamp, whose acquaintance the British reading public had made ten years earlier. Florence Nightingale is reported to have expressed approval of the order in which Ruth proceeds in her new profession, although she does not appear to have met Mrs Gaskell herself until after the publication of the novel. The Crimean War broke out in the following year so the subject of nursing was of topical interest. Mrs Gaskell's discussion of it as a 'calling' to which women might well devote themselves, fits in with her general attitude to works of mercy and kindness for which she considered women to be well fitted.

Such an attitude to nursing was not shared by Elizabeth Barrett Browning who, although she honoured Florence Nightingale from her heart and felt that 'she has fulfilled her woman's duty where many men have failed', believed Miss Nightingale's work to be in some ways retrogressive; she saw in it only a 'revival of old virtues':

Every man is on his knees before ladies carrying lint, calling them 'angelic she's', whereas, if they stir an inch as thinkers or artists from the beaten line (involving more good to general humanity than is involved in lint), the very same men would curse the impudence of the very same women and stop there.[4]

And, of course, *Aurora Leigh* itself is one long plea for recognition of the woman artist, the woman poet. Mrs Browning, like Harriet Martineau and George Eliot, believed that, if women produced really good work, instead of wasting their energies in just talking about it, this work would be recognized as good by ultimate standards and not just half-praised as good work for a woman:

. . . Whoso cures the plague,
Though twice a woman, shall be called a leech.

Cranford appeared in the same year as *Ruth*, and it is difficult to imagine a wider difference of theme in books about the life of women. The sheltered female community of Cranford, so near

188

geographically to Drumber (Manchester) is yet in atmosphere whole worlds away. It is a Community of Amazons, albeit very gentle ones, and feminine standards are the ones that prevail. Their good breeding and their sheltered existences have made the ladies good and kind-hearted; most of them are unsoured spinsters with faults no more blamable than mild snobbery, the concealment of their own comparative poverty, and a few amusing foibles. Any new-fangled ideas about the position of women have not affected them, but the famous views of Miss Jenkyns on this subject are the tacitly accepted law of Cranford: this lady would have despised the modern idea of women being equal to men—'Equal indeed! she knew they were superior!' In such an environment, so exquisitely houseproud, men can cause certain practical inconveniences, but they certainly have their uses, and these are described by Miss Matty:

I don't mean to deny that men are troublesome in a house. I don't judge from my own experience, for my father was neatness itself, and wiped his shoes on coming in as carefully as any woman; but still a man has a sort of knowledge of what should be done in difficulties, that it is very pleasant to have one at hand ready to lean on. (Ch. 13)

When Mary Smith considers the problem of what Miss Matty can do when the Town and County Bank has stopped payment, leaving the old lady with only five shillings a week to live on, she is forced to conclude that, because of the inadequacies of the 'education common to ladies fifty years ago' there was nothing Miss Matty could teach to the rising generation of Cranford, 'unless they had been quick learners and imitators of her patience, her humility, her sweetness, her quiet contentment with all that she could not do'. In the end, of course, in spite of the rallying round of her friends and the gestures of selling tea, it is a man, her brother Peter, home from India, who really comes to Miss Matty's rescue. The ladies of Cranford have no adequate knowledge or resources to enable them to cope with any crises that occur in their sheltered lives, and in their time of real trouble it is masculine help that must rescue them. Yet the quiet, feminine virtues are valuable and they are held up for praise in this nostalgic novel—the little delicate gestures of kindness and affection of the ladies to those around them, and the discipline of their genteel self-control. Final judgment is expressed by Mary's father when he says 'see, Mary, how a good, innocent life makes friends all around'.

George Eliot

The Brontës, Mrs Gaskell and Mrs Browning, in their discussions of the work of women authors were taking part in a debate of considerable interest to their contemporaries. Miss M. A. Stodart's *Female Writers: thoughts on their proper sphere, and on their powers of usefulness* had appeared in 1842, some years before the publication of *Jane Eyre*, and the controversy raged even more fiercely after the shock of the Brontë novels. As there has been a detailed recent study[5] of the Victorian idea of the sphere of the woman novelist as it affected the Brontës, this investigation needs only to touch upon the fact that others were greatly exercised in examining women's role as writers. Indeed this was one of the subjects to which both George Eliot and G. H. Lewes devoted considerable thought. George Eliot seems to have been influenced by the important article Lewes wrote on 'The Lady Novelists' in the *Westminster Review* in 1852, during the period when she herself was its Assistant Editor. At that time she had produced no imaginative writing, but she wonders at women having the courage to write 'the false and feeble representations of life and character that most feminine writers give'. After she joined Lewes she wrote more on the subject; in the *Westminster Review* for October 1854 there appeared her 'Woman in France, Madame de Sablé', which expresses views close to those of Lewes; 'with a few remarkable exceptions our own feminine literature is made up of books which could have been better written by men . . . when not a feeble imitation they are usually an absurd exaggeration of the masculine style'. This imitation is, she feels, the more regrettable because women have a real and distinctive contribution to make in literature:

A certain amount of psychological difference between man and woman necessarily arises out of the difference of sex, and instead of being destined to vanish before a complete development of women's intellectual and moral nature, will be a permanent source of variety and beauty as long as the tender light and dewy freshness of morning affect us differently from the strength and brilliancy of the mid-day sun.

The article closes with a statement of her faith in the value of intellectual co-operation between men and women.

The best-known expression of her opinion of women as authors is given in her article on 'Silly Novels by Lady Novelists' in the *Westminster Review* for October 1856. She divides the genus into four species by 'the particular quality of silliness that predominates in them', namely the mind and millinery, the oracular, the white neck-cloth and the modern-antique species. She apportions more blame to female vanity than Lewes did and she calls for a truly serious and professional attitude on the part of the woman-writer to her work, more patient diligence, a keener sense of the responsibility involved in publication and 'an appreciation of the sacredness of the writer's art', with a greater exercise of self-criticism. Her own novels bear testimony to the faithful following of these precepts.

In *Janet's Repentance* even the description of the bluestocking, Miss Platt, has a dignity about it lacking in the description of any other bluestockings, although it is obvious that George Eliot in no way holds her up as an example to other women. This charity of judgment and understanding, clear sighted and yet womanly, is part of the total view of women that George Eliot alone fully conveys. Her knowledge of contemporary sociological thought also gives her a greater insight into the motives that lead the old maids of Milby to seek a socially approved compensation for their own limited or distasteful opportunities for marriage. Of their ridiculed attachment to the clergy she says with sympathy and penetration:

Poor women's hearts! Heaven forbid that I should laugh at you, and make cheap jests on your susceptibility towards the clerical sex, as if it had nothing deeper or more lovely in it than the mere angling for a husband. Even in these enlightened days, many a curate who, considered abstractly, is nothing more than a sleek bimanous animal in a white neckcloth, with views more or less Anglican, and furtively addicted to the flute, is adored by a girl who has coarse brothers, or by a solitary woman who would like to be a helpmate in good works beyond her own means, simply because he seems to them the model of refinement and of public usefulness. What wonder then, that in Milby society, such as I have told you it was a very long while ago, a zealous evangelical clergyman, aged thirty-three, called forth all the little agitations that belong to the divine necessity of loving implanted in the Miss Linnets, with their seven or eight lustrums and their unfashionable ringlets, no less than in Miss Eliza Pratt, with her youthful bloom and her ample canon curls. (Ch. 10)

She also analyses the moral improvement that their devotion to Mr Tryan achieves. Her description of Miss Rebecca Linnet as she was before and after his arrival looks beyond the outward change of dress into the inward improvement in temper and in depth of character.

George Eliot turns her attention in her later work to women who are themselves artists, a topic near to her own level. The poem *Armgart*, whose heroine is a singer, introduces the situation of a lover being unable to rejoice in a woman's artistic achievement for itself, but only because, if she renounces her art for him, his triumph is then the greater:

> I sang him into love of me: my song
> Was consecration, lifted me apart
> From the crowd chiselled like me, sister forms,
> But empty of divineness. Nay, my charm
> Was half that I could win fame yet renounce!
> A wife with glory possible absorbed
> Into her husband's actual.

When she loses both voice and lover, fate forces her to adopt a way of life of self-forgetfulness and devotion to others which redeems her failure on another plane. This poem touches, although very briefly, upon the neglected and difficult problem of a man's attitude to a woman's superior talent.

Charlotte Brontë had voiced the determination of women to do useful work as teachers, working alongside other teachers, but such teaching was only the extension of the work of the governess on a slightly higher plane. George Eliot goes further and in *Daniel Deronda* she faces the problem confronting women who wish to adopt an artistic and public profession and to become musicians of real distinction. She works out the requirements in the interview between Herr Klessmer and

Gwendolen concerning her prospects of success as a professional singer. Klessmer tells Gwendolen that the life of the artist is an honourable one, 'but the honour comes from the inward vocation and the hard-won achievement; there is no honour in donning the life as a livery'. He warns her that, if she aims at becoming a real artist, if she takes 'music and the drama as a higher vocation' and wishes to 'strive after excellence', she will face hardships and humiliations for a long period and will finally hardly achieve more than mediocrity. Gwendolen has neither the determination nor the real interest to go ahead with her plans for a musical career after that. By contrast, Mirah is a true professional, selfless and dedicated. George Eliot's own joy in artistic excellence, expressed in Deronda's statement that 'excellence encourages one about life generally; it shows the spiritual wealth of the world' illuminates the value she places on supreme competence and artistic integrity, sources of strength for her own great achievement.

9

Conclusion

AFTER so many pages of close scrutiny it is time to step back to view these eighty years of women's work more broadly and to recapitulate in brief the contribution each writer made to a more authentic reflection of women's experience of life in the English novel. These writers were of widely diverse minds and varying backgrounds but they had in common their sex and the fact that they lived in the same epoch of far-reaching change in the role of women in the West. The contribution made by each of them to the novel, although individual, formed part of a pattern that was not very clearly defined but was significant for the advancement of literature.

Fanny Burney, the earliest of the group, in spite of her unquestioning conformity to conduct-book ideals, did make a serious pioneer contribution to the English novel by being the first woman who wrote from the inner viewpoint of a woman, or rather, of a young girl. Her heroines are all pleasant young creatures, equipped with a superficial education and code of manners, but with no knowledge of society outside their own narrow experience; possessed of religious principles but needing help in translating these into the terms of their formalized environment; graceful and charming within the sheltered limits of their social circle, they are totally vulnerable if guidance and protection are withheld. Miss Burney, by the time she wrote *The Wanderer*, realized the inadequacy of the accepted code but she had nothing with which to replace it. She brought her conduct-book young ladies to graceful life against a deftly drawn background of eighteenth-century society, but as they were young ladies living by rules, their characters were dictated by the book and were only superficially realized.

Maria Edgeworth's novels, except for the brief flowering of *Castle Rackrent* and *The Absentee*, were also governed by a code,

194

the code of sanity and common sense that prevails in a well ordered schoolroom. Avowedly designed to point out those errors to which 'the higher classes of society were disposed', her stories are contrived, her characters sticklike, and her heroines, eminently sensible and practical, are fictionalized examples of young women conducting their lives along the paths of domestic order and decorum, avoiding the temptations of fashionable frivolity, high learning or passionate romance. Her books are stories for good children translated into adult terms, retaining the fascination of authentic period detail and a wholesome lack of subtlety. They were as much contributions to the educational reading of good wives and mothers as to literature, although to literature Maria Edgeworth contributed a penetrating eye for the small foibles and flaws of ordinary society, expressed without hypocrisy or concealment.

Jane Austen likewise did not seek to revolutionize the accepted standards of her day, but hers was not a superficial code of behaviour, it was a way of christian life led at the level of the true gentlewoman. She accepted its principles, to which many paid only lip-service and interpreted them in their fullest implications, eschewing all insincerity and compromise. Because of the depth of her insight her characters are fully realized, and because the same principles provided a touchstone by which all members of society could be judged, her attitude is completely consistent. Complete consistency and full mastery dictated an inevitable form. Her art was a quintessential expression of the best in eighteenth-century womanhood complete in itself and for its period.

After Jane Austen there came a breathing space. The ideas about women's rights that had shocked and frightened the conservatives in Revolutionary days seemed less subversive to the minds of a new generation. During the hidden years before new women writers took up their pens, the power of the older codes was breaking and women were left more free to work out their own salvation instead of having salvation thrust upon them.

The early Victorian Brontës wrenched the view of women in the novel to a different level by the power of their own emotional involvement. Anne Brontë, with a courage beyond all

Conclusion
expectations of a daughter of the parsonage, deliberately set herself the task of telling the truth about women, in particular the truth about the hard lot and social humiliation suffered by governesses in contemporary country houses, and the truth about good and intelligent wives bound irrevocably to alcoholic and caddish husbands. She even examined the contemporary view of marriage and found it wanting, and with an outlook astringent but not bitter she concluded that the correct view of marriage must be that of a union between two equal beings each with his or her inviolable personality.

Charlotte Brontë's greater emotional intensity sought even more passionately to change the contemporary view of the relationship between the sexes, and to point out the immorality of regarding marriage as a means of social security and advancement. In her novels she creates a new woman, strong, passionate but demure and controlled, independent and hardworking, bringing to the love relationship the devotion of her whole being but determined at the same time to maintain her intellectual and spiritual autonomy. Seeing women as handicapped by lack of any opportunities for satisfying work, Charlotte Brontë cried out against the waste of women's intellectual and emotional powers in mid-nineteenth-century England. She also made clear the effort demanded of all women if they were to maintain their own integrity in a world of pretence and half truths. By analysing women's passions with a frankness unknown before and by insisting that women face the truth about their own natures and destiny, she added another dimension to the delineation of women in literature.

The Brontëan power in *Wuthering Heights* lifted women to a shared place with men on a plane so beyond ordinary social experience that they become creatures of elemental energy in the one novel that remains out of this world.

Mrs Gaskell was, in contrast with the Brontës, a typical Victorian woman with no frustrations to give emotional incentive to her writings, yet she reveals a quiet progress in her thought about women that must have been shared by many others of her time. She began by accepting woman's place as laid down by contemporary convention, but a few doubts later assailed her belief in the infallibility of husbandly superiority or parental wisdom. Once she had seen the social miseries of the new industrial towns she felt strongly that women should respond to these needs and work side by side with men in the effort to solve the evils of overcrowding, poverty, sickness and industrial discontent; she thought that women could make a special contribution to neighbourly understanding and sympathy in the troubled areas, and she began to see women in contact with greater human problems than those which concerned their immediate families, and to feel that they faced a new challenge to increase their tolerance and to enter wider spheres of involvement, carrying into these their own human values. Her most original contributions to the contemporary understanding of the position of women lay in her positive response and welcome to the exciting challenge of the new and expanding environment of industrial Britain and her acceptance of woman's new dual role, the role of the woman of intelligence who also had ties of family, who would bury a God-given talent at her peril, but who would also be called to give final account for any neglect of family obligations. Women's dilemma in balancing the two claims was one she at least touched upon although she could not resolve it.

George Eliot's view of the role of women was a sombre one: women had no control over their own fate and few fates were happy. It was no solution for women to strive to shape their own lives; if they tried they only courted disaster, handicapped as they were by the physical and emotional disadvantages of their womanhood and their inadequate understanding of the forces of society. Their best course was to accept their lot and use all the opportunities it offered them for loving, self-forgetful service. Happiest were the gentle, loving, simple women who sweetened the lives of others and found in that their own quiet joy. George Eliot turned away from the hope of any easy solution of women's problems by the methods that claimed the interested allegiance of her contemporaries. But she did not turn aside from the contemplation of these problems in their deeper social implications, the implications for men as well as for women. The limitations of this study have forced us to wrest women's problems from the rich texture of her novels in order to bring them into sharper focus, and to draw attention to an important current in her thinking which has been swallowed up in more general considerations of her genius, but it is only right to acknowledge that these problems were always set in the wider context of her outlook on other contemporary social problems and the even wider sweep of her view of the human condition. Yet in her religion of humanity the deepest human values were feminine ones.

It may have some value to compare the two most eminent of our writers, Jane Austen and George Eliot. George Eliot represented the ultimate that the wider-ranging minds of the best Victorian women could achieve, just as Jane Austen gave expression to what was best in the lives of the more limited eighteenth-century women of class and breeding. Their contrasts are inherent in their own times and social circumstances. Jane Austen's was the self-contained eighteenth-century neighbourhood of middle-class families, conscious, but not over conscious, of the importance of rank, exacting a conformity of surface belief and conduct but granting to the individual woman leisure and opportunity to attend to the minutiae of her own reactions and feelings within an environment both sheltered and civilized, and allowing her to live a life out of the public eye, but well adjusted through self-knowledge and self-evaluation. George Eliot's was the wider world of the Victorian intellectual and liberal thinker, classless because cosmopolitan, cultured and travelled, affording wide vistas of science, literature and music, without the firm foundation of an accepted religious faith, but seeking its 'region of liberty' in the things of the mind, a life lived in the public eye yet with the detachment imposed by the unconventionality of her connection with Lewes. Jane Austen's standards were imposed by authority but by an authority fully accepted, understood, and improved upon in practice, the woman, as artist, completely in control of her limited material. George Eliot's was the individual mind questing for meaning, guided by an accepted but impersonal moral law, sustained by such strength as a religion of humanity is able to provide. Her vision was not prescribed and was therefore open-ended to the possibilities of the future, cherishing a forward belief in the power of the mind to bring the inhuman cosmos within the understanding of man, a belief in the value of high endeavour and in the function of human love to mitigate the harshness of reality. Her creative power was such that her characters have almost a fourth dimension of familiar depth afforded by her own human sympathy and understanding, not pared down by the demands of art. Neither of these two authors worked within any straightjacket of training; they produced their masterpieces by observation and insight and complete command of their own experience broken down and recreated in their art. As they had their own artistic graces so they had their own methods of attaining a necessary measure of detachment in their books. Jane Austen accomplished it through her irony and the impersonality conferred by the abstractions of an eighteenth-century vocabulary. George Eliot surmounted her personal vulnerability by constant reference to great and impersonal moral issues.

The pressing need to examine their own role which was present, consciously or subconsciously, in this group of women writers, seems to have worked itself out by the end of the eighty years. With it passed the passionate drive which gave such power to their exploration of new relationships at varying depths of emotional involvement. For this period they had acted as the mouthpieces of other women, expressing an interest which was general and intense, reading and writing themselves and others into comprehension and articulateness concerning their own problems. Constant reinterpretation and readjustment, minute shifts of viewpoint, flashes of new insight, all these provided the elements that gradually built up a more adequate picture of the lives of women from which all who ran and read could derive increased understanding.

These writers also added to the dimensions of the novel as a whole. They had found it a genre in which women were seen only from the viewpoint of men, and they added to it woman's particular experience of life depicted from the inside. Exploration of the changing role of women introduced new kinds of women into the novel. Women in all their variety and drawn in authentic detail took the place of the stock characters of heroine, siren, hoyden, sentimental mother. The novel's background was enriched by their keen eye for local and concrete detail, an eye

199

Conclusion

extremely sensitive to minor gradations of colour in narrow environments, although not yet accustomed to scan wider horizons. To the interpretation of standards laid down by law and precept they brought the redeeming influence of feeling and sympathy, and to constricting loyalties of family, class and neighbourhood, they brought an increasing concern with wider human needs.

If every work of art may be said to have two faces, one for its own time and one for all time, we may regard the historical face of these novels as a valid and interesting picture of the life of women at a formative stage of their social development in England. But their value is incomparably greater as records of the vital experience of powerful and distinguished women's minds transmuted into works of art that transcend the centuries. In this time of turmoil the experience of something so closely affecting themselves went very deep, nourishing the springs of their creative ability, and enriching their books with a vitality powerful for all time. To paraphrase Whitman, 'they were women, they suffered, they were there'.

NOTES

1. INTRODUCTION

1. 'Woman in France, Madame de Sablé', *Westminster Review*, lxii (October, 1854). Reprinted in *Essays of George Eliot*, ed. Thomas Pinney (London, 1963), p. 53.
2. Letter to Eliza Fox, April 1850. *The Letters of Mrs. Gaskell* (Manchester, 1966), p. 109.

2. THE CLIMATE OF OPINION

1. See, for example, Vera Brittain, *Lady into Woman: A History of Women from Victoria to Elizabeth II* (London, 1953); Roger Fulford, *Votes for Women: The Story of a Struggle* (London, 1952); D. L. Hobman, *Go Spin, You Jade! Studies in the Emancipation of Women* (London, 1957); Winifred Holtby, *Women* (London, 1941); John Langdon-Davies, *A Short History of Women* (London, 1948); Marian Ramelson, *The Petticoat Rebellion: A Century of Struggle for Women's Rights* (London, 1967); Doris Mary Stenton, *The English Woman in History* (London, 1957).
2. Joyce Hemlow, 'Fanny Burney and the Courtesy Books', *PMLA*, lxv (1950), pp. 732-61.
3. *Pride and Prejudice*, Chapter 14.
4. Letter dated 30 August 1805. *Letters*, ed. R. W. Chapman (Oxford, 1959), p. 169.
5. *Rambler*, no. 66, 3 November 1750.
6. Quoted in Eleanor Flexner, *Century of Struggle: the Woman's Rights Movement in the United States* (Cambridge, Mass., 1959), p. 14.
7. Article on 'The Equality of the Sexes', *Massachusetts Magazine* (March/April 1790), p. 133. Quoted by Flexner, op. cit., p. 16.
8. *Vindication of the Rights of Woman*, Everyman's Library (London, 1929), p. 103.
9. Ibid., p. 108.
10. Ibid., pp. 194-5.
11. See Mary Wollstonecraft's Prefatory Note to *A Vindication* . . .
12. H. N. Brailsford, *Shelley, Godwin and their Circle*, 2nd edn (London, [1954]), p. 143.
13. See M. G. Jones, *Hannah More* (Cambridge, 1952), p. 116.
14. *Aurora Leigh* . . . *with prefatory note by Algernon Charles Swinburne* (London, 1898), p. ix.
15. S. J. Hale, *Woman's Record: or, Sketches of All Distinguished Women from the Beginning till A.D. 1850* (New York, 1853), General preface, p. xxxvii.
16. S. S. Ellis, *Wives of England* [1843], p. 119.
17. *A Woman's Thoughts about Women* (1859), p. 25.
18. William Lovett, *Life and Struggles of William Lovett . . . with an Introduction by R. H. Tawney*, 2 vols (London, 1920), i, p. 174.
19. *The Subjection of Women*, conclusion of Chapter 3.

Notes, Pages 22–68

3. THE LESSER WOMEN NOVELISTS

1. *The Progress of Romance;* reproduced from the edn of 1785 (New York, 1930), part 2, p. 7.
2. Letter to Sir W. W. Pepys, 13 December 1809. William Roberts, *Memoirs of the Life and Correspondence of Mrs. Hannah More* (London, 1834), iii, p. 313.
3. Letter to Cassandra, 30 January 1809. *Letters*, ed. Chapman (1959), p. 66. Presumably Jane Austen, living in an age of Biblical christian names, expected the hero's name to be Caleb, and she comments 'the name of Caleb . . . has an honest, unpretending sound; but in Coelebs, there is pedantry and affectation. —Is it written only to Classical scholars?'
4. *A Survey of English Literature, 1780–1830* (London, 1912), i, p. 174.
5. See Lawrence M. Price, 'The English domestic novel in German, 1740–1799', *Festschrift für Hermann Tiemann* (Hamburg, 1959), p. 218.
6. They were Susanna Rowson's *Charlotte Temple*, Hannah Foster's *The Coquette* and Regina Maria Roche's *Children of the Abbey.* See Frank Luther Mott, *Golden Multitudes: The Story of Bestsellers in the United States* (London, 1947), Appendix A.
7. Quoted in J. M. S. Tompkins, *The Popular Novel in England, 1770–1800* (London, 1932; re-issued 1962), p. 123.
8. Letter to Cassandra, 11 October 1813. *Letters*, ed. Chapman, p. 344.

4. WOMEN AWAITING MARRIAGE (1)

1. Mr Villars had a feminine namesake in an early book of domestic morality, Maria Susannah Cooper's *The Exemplary Mother, or Letters between Mrs. Villars and her Family* (1769).
2. See Joyce Hemlow, 'Fanny Burney and the Courtesy Books', *PMLA*, lxv (1950), pp. 732–61, particularly p. 758.
3. Lecture VI on the English comic writers.
4. Letter to Mrs Stark, 6 September 1834. *Life and Letters of Maria Edgeworth*, ed. A. J. C. Hare (London, 1894), ii, p. 255.
5. See Isabel C. Clarke, *Maria Edgeworth, her Family and Friends* (London, 1949), p. 82. The temptation to write such a book was, however, yielded to by William Mudford, who wrote *Nubilia in Search of a Husband* (London, 1809); in his Preface he says that 'the title of the book sufficiently proclaims that it has been written from the suggestion of *Coelebs in Search of a Wife*'.
6. Bulwer Lytton, *What will he do with it?* (1848).
7. Quoted in Margaret E. Spence, 'Ruskin's Correspondence with Miss Blanche Atkinson', *Bulletin of the John Rylands Library*, xlii (1959), p. 206.
8. *Minor Works*, ed. R. W. Chapman (Oxford, 1958), p. 453.
9. Thomas Gisborne, *An Enquiry into the Duties of the Female Sex*, 11th edn (London, 1816), pp. 12–13.
10. 'Mansfield Park', *The Opposing Self* (London, 1959), p. 211.
11. R. P. Utter and G. B. Needham, *Pamela's daughters* (London, 1937), p. 372.
12. *Jane Austen, 1775–1817.* Writers and their Work, no. 17 (London, 1957).

5. WOMEN AWAITING MARRIAGE (2)

1. See Winifred Gérin, *Anne Brontë* (London, 1959), p. 230.
2. *Daily News*, 3 February 1853.
3. See *The Brontës; their Lives, Friendships and Correspondence* (Oxford, 1932), iv, p. 42.
4. Quoted in Elizabeth Gaskell, *Life of Charlotte Brontë.* Everyman's Library (London, 1958), p. 136.
5. 'Caroline Helstone's Eyes', *Publications of the Brontë Society* (1961).
6. *Early Victorian Novelists.* Penguin edn (Harmondsworth, 1948), p. 153.
7. Review of *Wives and Daughters* in *The Nation* for 22 February 1866, reprinted in *Notes and Reviews* (Cambridge, Mass., 1921), pp. 154–5.
8. Lord David Cecil, op. cit., p. 153.
9. Letter to John Morley, 14 May 1867. *The George Eliot Letters*, ed. Gordon S. Haight (Yale, 1954–8), iv, pp. 364–5.
10. Letter to Dr Joseph Frank Payne, 25 January 1876. Haight, vi, pp. 216–17.
11. Letter to Mrs Peter Taylor, 1 February 1853. Haight, ii, p. 86.
12. 'The Novels of George Eliot', *Views and Reviews*, ed. Le Roy Phillips (Boston, 1908), p. 7.
13. Ibid., p. 17.
14. Ibid., pp. 29–30.
15. Letter to John Blackwood, 24 February 1861. Haight, iii, p. 382.
16. Letter to Sara Hennell, 23 August 1863. Haight, iv, p. 103.
17. Letter to Rabbi Deutsch, 7 July 1871. Haight, v, pp. 160–1.
18. Quoted in Leon Edel, *Henry James, the Conquest of London, 1870–1883* (London, 1962), p. 360.

6. WOMEN AS WIVES

1. Letter to Mr and Mrs Charles Bray [4 December 1849]. Haight, i, p. 322.
2. See above, Ch. 5 note 15.
3. It is in connection with Nancy that George Eliot gives her definition of a lady:
    'There is hardly a servant-maid in these days who is not better informed than Miss Nancy; yet she had the essential attributes of a lady—high veracity, delicate honour in her dealings, deference to others, and refined personal habits, —and lest these should not suffice to convince grammatical fair ones that her feelings can at all resemble theirs, I will add that she was slightly proud and exacting, and as constant in her affection towards a baseless opinion as towards an erring lover' (Ch. 2). Esther Lyon defines her idea of a *fine* lady when she contrasts such an one with the vulgarity of Miss Jermyn: 'A real fine-lady does not wear clothes that flare in people's eyes, or use importunate scents, or make a noise as she moves: she is something refined, and graceful, and charming, and never obtrusive' (*Felix Holt*, Ch. 5).
4. *The Novels of George Eliot, a Study in Form* (London, 1959), p. 52.
5. *Daniel Deronda, a Conversation.* Appended to F. R. Leavis, *The Great Tradition* (London, 1955), p. 259.

7. WOMEN AS MOTHERS

1. 'A Note on Charlotte Brontë', *Complete Works of Algernon Charles Swinburne* (London, 1926), xiv, p. 22.

8. WOMEN STANDING ALONE

1. *Essays on Practical Education* (1822), i, p. 414.
2. *Autobiography*, 2nd edn (London, 1877), i, p. 401.
3. Letter dated 29 April 1850. Clement Shorter, *The Brontës, Life and Letters* (London, 1908), pp. 131–2.
4. Letter to Mrs Jameson, 24 February 1855. *Letters*, ed. F. G. Kenyon (London, 1897), ii, p. 189.
5. Inga-Stina Ewbank, *Their Proper Sphere* (London, 1966).

INDEX

References to the most important discussions on each main author are printed in heavy type; titles of books are entered under authors' names.

Index

Index